1982

Disadvantaged
Preschool
Children

D1418156

Disadvantaged Preschool Children

A Source Book for Teachers

by

Michael Bender, Ed.D.
Director of Special Education
The John F. Kennedy Institute for Handicapped Children
and
Assistant Professor of Education and Pediatrics
The Johns Hopkins University and The Johns Hopkins School of Medicine

Rosemary King Bender, B.S.Ed.
Special Education Consultant
The John F. Kennedy Institute for Handicapped Children

·P A U L·H·
BROOKES
PUBLISHERS

Baltimore

Paul H. Brookes, Publishers
Post Office Box 10624
Baltimore, Maryland 21204

Typeset by The Composing Room of Michigan, Inc. (Grand Rapids)
Manufactured in the United States of America by Bay Printing, Inc.
(Baltimore)

Library of Congress Cataloging in Publication Data

Bender, Michael, 1943–
Disadvantaged preschool children.

Bibliography: p.
Includes index.
1. Socially handicapped children—Education—
Handbooks, manuals, etc. I. Bender, Rosemary, joint
author. II. Title.
LC4065.B36   371.9'67   79-12001
ISBN 0-933716-00-1

Contents

Preface

Impoverished children are everywhere and constitute major populations in many of the states in this country. More children who may be defined as disadvantaged are created each day than are provided with help. Existing innovative educational programs are unable to provide enough intensive remediation to counter the debilitating effects of poverty on the development of human potential.

No matter what set of statistics is used to identify the numbers of these children, one fact has become painfully clear: disadvantaged children are universal. They are not specific to one race; they are not specific to rural America; they are not peculiar to inner cities; and they are not confined to Indian reservations or to those intolerable areas known as unlivable slums. They are the children of the unemployable, the underemployed, the jobless, the hungry, the migrant, and those people who live with a sense of hopelessness.

This source book has been developed as a practical response to the demanding educational needs of the culturally deprived or socioeconomically restricted child. This book emphasizes a preschool population and contains curricula, activities, and suggestions that are applicable to both nonhandicapped and handicapped children in early education programs. It is especially appropriate for Head Start programs as well as public and private nursery school programs.

Discussions of legal mandates and evaluation strategies are included in the initial sections of this book to help the educator in his or her program planning. A curriculum section includes more than 100 activities in the domains of cognitive development, socialization, motor skills, and language skills. Additionally, activities are provided in the areas of music, art, industrial arts, and preacademic skills.

Models for intervention, which include preschool demonstration projects as well as preschool programs for the handicapped, are discussed, as is the critical importance of parent involvement.

A concluding part of this source book presents the reader with information regarding interviewing, scheduling, and the development of teaching strategies for preschool disadvantaged children. Classroom organization and physical room arrangements, as they relate to this population of children, are also discussed.

As a supplemental resource, over 100 learning aids in reading, arithmetic, language, motor development, music, and art are listed with suggested grade levels and sources for obtaining these materials.

This book is dedicated to the disadvantaged children the authors taught in Wareham, Massachusetts in the 1960s. It was through working with these children that the authors came to realize the unrelenting need for sound educational programming.

Acknowledgments

To Elaine Rosemary, Lorraine Richter, and Marguerite Csar for their typing, editing, and patience in preparing this manuscript.

To Stephen Benjamin Bender for modifying his busy schedule so his parents could develop this source book.

A special acknowledgment is offered to Melissa Behm for her expert and creative work in refining this manuscript. Her ability to clarify and rewrite portions of the contents is greatly appreciated by the authors.

The Authors

Michael Bender has taught handicapped and disadvantaged children since 1966. He was a Title I ESEA Project Coordinator and teacher of the disadvantaged in 1969 and has taught all levels of handicapped children. He is presently the Director of The Kennedy Preschool Program for the Handicapped and the school programs in the Department of Special Education at The John F. Kennedy Institute for Handicapped Children in Baltimore, Maryland. He also is Project Director of two Bureau of Education for the Handicapped grants in the areas of interdisciplinary training and the profoundly retarded. He is co-author, along with Peter J. Valletutti and Rosemary King Bender, of *Teaching the Moderately and Severely Handicapped,* Volumes I, II, and III, and has written numerous published articles and chapters.

Rosemary King Bender taught on the first national Head Start Project in the mid 1960s and has been a curriculum development specialist for the last ten years. She also has taught nursery school classes and classes for primary-age handicapped children. She has been a Title I ESEA Project Coordinator and teacher of the disadvantaged and is presently a special education teacher in the Harford County (Maryland) Public Schools.

A Note on Style

Stylistic devices, used in this source book for clarity and fluency, are called to the reader's attention.

1. The student or child is referred to as male throughout this source book. The decision to use the masculine form has been based upon practical considerations of grammatical simplicity and should not be interpreted to infer preferential or discriminatory treatment.

2. The teacher is referred to as female throughout this source book, indicative of the larger number of women who teach preschool disadvantaged students.

3. The word *student* is used interchangeably with *child* and in all cases refers to the learner.

4. In various parts of the source book, the classroom is referred to as the educational environment. This approach is used to emphasize that teaching and learning can take place anywhere, not just in a classroom, and that the activities are applicable in any setting.

Section I
INTRODUCTION

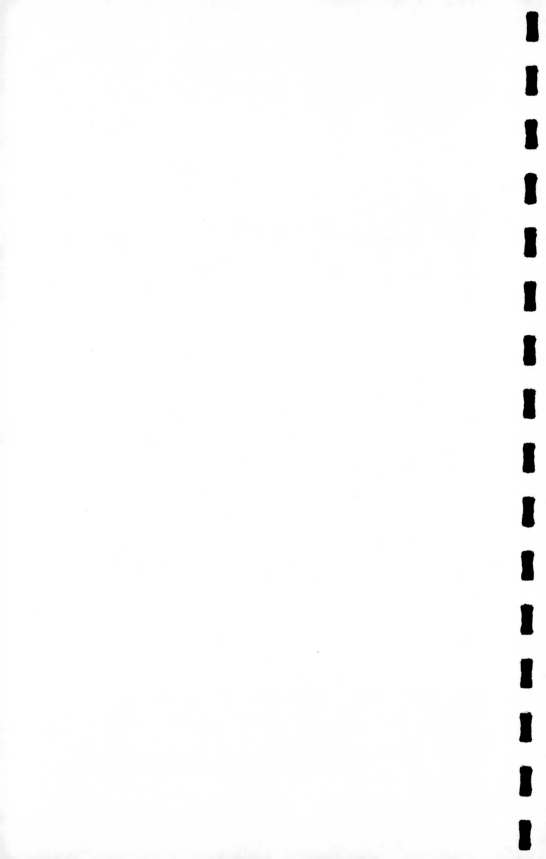

Chapter 1
Educational Needs
of the Disadvantaged
Preschool Child

The number of students attending school in the United States has continued to decline during the 1970s, resulting in a surplus of teachers and physical facilities. According to the statistics compiled by the National Center for Education, part of the Education Division of the U. S. Department of Health, Education, and Welfare (HEW), high school enrollment dropped 1% between 1977 and 1978, with an estimated 15.7 million students attending high school in 1978. Elementary school enrollment, at 33.3 million, is down by approximately 3.7 million when compared to the peak year of 1969. It appears inevitable that secondary schools will begin to feel the pressures of declining enrollment and move toward consolidating school programs and maximizing the use of their resources.

Kindergarten enrollments, like secondary and elementary enrollments, experienced a decline of 8% in 1978, a decline which represents the first significant decrease in this school-age population in more than 30 years. The large drop in birth rate, noticeable 5 years earlier, primarily accounts for the lower enrollments. Attributable in part to the use of more sophisticated birth control procedures, the increasing pressures of a society, which make it exceedingly difficult to provide financially for large families, have also contributed to this demographic change.

During this time of declining kindergarten, elementary, and high school enrollments, nursery school enrollment for three- and four-year-olds has more than doubled. Preschool children account for approximately 16.7 million new students, and by 1990 there will be an estimated 24.1 million preschoolers (Daniels, 1978).

It appears that nursery school and preschool enrollments will continue to escalate as the numbers of working mothers increase and more children are enrolled in programs like Head Start. It has been projected that over 10 million working mothers will enroll their children in some form of preschool program by 1990 (Daniels, 1978).

Another possible reason why preschool programs will continue to grow is the commitment by the federal government to serve minority children and those children who have been classified as being handicapped. As an example, Public Law 94-142 stipulates that each three- to five-year-old child in a state who is served by a school program can generate a special $300 entitlement.

Furthermore, preschool children from minority backgrounds have now become majority populations in twenty of the nation's largest cities (Daniels, 1978) and can no longer be ignored. Kallan (1975) and others have continually stated that the present educational system often ignores well established knowledge about human behavior that could be applied to the benefit of preschool disadvantaged children. Established developmental information, offered by individuals such as Piaget and Gesell, as well as work in the psychosocial and psychosexual progression of personality by Erickson and Freud, has often been considered of minor importance or completely disregarded in the development of curricula for this population.

Most professionals, however, are in agreement that an individual's eventual success in life depends largely upon what he learns before the age of five. The hypothesis that advocated waiting for a child to mature before introducing educational experiences is currently being viewed as the wasting of critical time in a preschooler's life. Many educators have suggested that to not educate a child before the age of five may result in irreparable damage to the child, particularly the disadvantaged preschooler. Intervention programs, when used appropriately, can do much to intellectually stimulate the disadvantaged preschool child and decrease the educational deficits the child will eventually face when he is asked to perform with his school-age peers.

Societal conditions that create the need for earlier intervention and comprehensive preschool programs continue to exist. Cull and Hardy (1975) have stressed that one of the most significant problems facing us today is how to program for youth who have been physically, psychologically, and socially marred by deprivation and disadvantagement. It also seems obvious that these conditions will continue to exist to some degree for specific populations no matter what forms of compensatory education are developed.

For years the majority of preschool programs did not attempt to teach the disadvantaged preschool child. A notable exception was Project Head Start, which was designed to help preschoolers from low income families get an early advantage in school life by promoting positive health, nutrition, motivation, and social attitudes. Although Head Start and model educational projects did much to serve the disadvantaged preschool population, comprehensive curricula, evaluation techniques, and innovative methodology were all but absent in most grass roots preschool programs. The majority of programs that were developed to serve the disadvantaged preschool child did little more than act as day care programs, run by noncertified teachers and providing minimal parent education programs. To many professionals, serving this population of children was considered an educational luxury that could only be supported by federal programs and direct grants.

Many professionals argued that to teach the disadvantaged child is an arduous task that requires parental cooperation. They emphasized that parents of these children often do not possess favorable educational attitudes and that what is accomplished within the school program is virtually eliminated at home. Other professionals isolated the motivational factor as being a major obstacle to educating this population of children. They coined terms such as *culturally disadvantaged* to strengthen their statements that many of these children would not be easily assimilated into the culture of their time and would inevitably end up as frustrated, anxious, and bitter youth and adults.

This book has been developed around the philosophy that the disadvantaged preschool child is an individual in need of a wide range of educational services. Only recently has federal legislation directed funds toward disadvantaged preschool children and made the education of these special children a priority. It is important to reiterate that with the few exceptions of the federal model projects launched in the early 1960s, preschool disadvantaged children have been largely ignored and few public and nonpublic programs have been available to serve them.

In this source book the authors present a review of the varied areas that constitute educational programming for the disadvantaged preschool child. Emphasis is placed on curriculum areas involving cognitive development, socialization skills, motor development, and language skills, as well as skills in music, art, and the industrial arts. The preacademic area, which has often not been included in traditional preschool programs, receives special emphasis in this source book because the authors believe that without these critical skills the preschool child may never learn to be competitive with his peers. Section III presents a sample curriculum developed by the authors to offer representative objectives and activities in these areas.

Of equal importance is the area of parent involvement (discussed in Section IV) which, for too long, has been relegated to secondary or tertiary status in the development of an educational program for a child. It is critically important at this time to discuss parent involvement, especially in light of the mandate of Public Law 94-142, which requires parent participation in the development of a handicapped student's individualized education program (IEP).

Intervention strategies, in terms of past and recent demonstration projects ranging from Head Start to the Portage Project, are also discussed and presented in terms of current research findings. The majority of early intervention strategies can be categorized in terms of one or a combination of four major intervention models. The four models—the behavioral model, the normal developmental model, the cognitive developmental model, and the cognitive learning model—are discussed in terms of their development, implementation, and educational applications.

The book concludes with a section on classroom organization, scheduling and teaching strategies, and suggested curriculum materials and resources, which have been accumulated from a wide variety of sources and from numerous interviews with personnel who are presently teaching disadvantaged preschool children. A list of references is provided to supplement the reader's interest in this critical educational area.

It is extremely important that those individuals who use this source book understand that *a culturally disadvantaged child is not disadvantaged by his culture*. All children are enriched by their own culture. Culture only becomes a disadvantage when a child from a minority or poverty background is assessed according to a middle class or different societal standard.

Chapter 2
Definitions and Characteristics of Disadvantaged Preschool Children

It has been conservatively estimated that at least 50% to 60% of the children in the IQ range of 70 to 80 come from disadvantaged homes. Similarly, there are strong indications from demographic studies that a disproportionately large number of children who reside in economically depressed areas attend special education classes for the mildly retarded or are receiving some form of special education throughout most of their school years. A high incidence of children with poor self-concept and delayed language development is pervasive in preschool programs for the disadvantaged, and the psychological characteristics that are commonly used to describe mildly retarded populations often parallel the characteristics attributed to disadvantaged children.

In 1969, the Joint Commission on Mental Health of Children supported the view that children from the lowest socioeconomic groups were handicapped by multiple problems that affected their cognitive, physical, and emotional development. The commission emphasized that these problems begin in early childhood and steadily worsen as the child grows older. In essence, these children do not outgrow these problems, and without careful and planned intervention the difficulties become worse.

Much effort has been expended in applying fruitless labels to disadvantaged preschool children. These have included terms such as *socially retarded, economically deprived, culturally disadvantaged,* or related descriptive terminology which incorporates a range of disabilities. While the process of labeling children is an inappropriate educational procedure that promotes self-fulfilling prophecies, it continues to function as a means of identifying specific populations of children. The authors are in agreement with those

7

professionals who strongly oppose the use of labeling; nevertheless, it is important to review how the definitions of groups of children have been derived, because their derivation is a direct reflection of how society views these children.

CULTURAL DEPRIVATION

The majority of definitions that describe the preschool disadvantaged child refer to the factor of cultural deprivation. What is meant by the term *cultural deprivation* has been outlined by Miller (1967):

1. [We] begin with the observation that many children have difficulties in school. They have trouble learning to read and write. They are not especially well-behaved, and they subsequently drop out of school. These are our primary data and control observations as educators and psychologists.
2. [We] then note that many of these children come from underprivileged homes and impoverished environments, that their parents lead marginal social and economic existences, and that the children suffer accordingly. We label the entire cluster of deprivations that these children seem to have in their home environment "cultural deprivation."
3. And we then go on to conclude that cultural deprivation *causes* school problems (pp. 38–39).

Rosenham further states that, in fact, we have two separate sets of circumstances: school behavior and impoverished environments. They commonly occur among the same children. But are we sure that one necessarily causes the other? Many educators have argued strongly that because these children are underprivileged (and some call the status of being underprivileged "culturally deprived") the environment in which they live must have an overwhelming effect on their school behavior.

A classic definition by Riessman (1962) describes the culturally deprived child as:

Physical and visual, rather than aural
Content-centered, rather than form-centered
Externally oriented, rather than introspective
Centered on a problem, rather than on an abstraction
Inductive, rather than deductive
Spatial, rather than temporal

Riessman's description is further supported by the fact that disadvantaged children do not do well in school. Dusewicz (1975) reports that disadvantaged children in general have to rely on meager environmental backgrounds, which do little to encourage the development of cognitive skills. The deficit in this skill area takes its toll early in the child's life, when he is unprepared to cope with the demands of his first school experience. This condition of entering school with lower cognitive abilities places the child at a disadvantage that often increases over time. This tendency to "never catch up" results in what has been called a cumulative deficit, which eventually leads to educational and, at times, societal failure.

Listing other characteristics of the disadvantaged child, Miller (1967) has written:

> . . . he quite often comes from a broken home;
> . . . he is non-verbal and concrete-minded;
> . . . he is often hungry;
> . . . he lacks stable identification figures;
> . . . as a result of constant migration, he lacks stable community ties;
> . . . his color handicaps him and provides him with a negative self-image;
> . . . he is physically less healthy than his middle-class peers;
> . . . he is handicapped in the expression and comprehension of language;
> . . . he tends to be extroverted rather than introverted (p. 40).

Kallan (1975) has defined the disadvantaged child as a child of any race (white, black, or a mixture of many ethnic cultures) whose place in society is determined by his socioeconomic environment. Many of these children come from poverty backgrounds, with the poverty level being defined as an annual family income of less than $3,000.

It has been suggested (Cull and Hardy, 1975) that one out of every three children enrolled in our school system is culturally deprived or disadvantaged, or a delayed or retarded reader. It is important to emphasize that the *culturally deprived* child has not been deprived of culture but may have been reared in a culture that is different from that of his middle class peers. The culturally deprived child tends to be more nonverbal than his middle class peers and to orient spatially through the physical world rather than the world of abstract reasoning.

It is important to initially state that the majority of information concerning past and current definitions of the disadvantaged preschool child was compiled during the mid to late 1960s when federal money was available to conduct select, model preschool projects for the disadvantaged. It is equally important to state that while new projects have added general information to the compendium of knowledge currently available, relatively little information has evolved since the 1960s concerning innovative curricula, teaching strategies, or educational methodology for this population of students.

Riessman (1962) and Kaplan (1966) have often used the terms *culturally deprived, educationally deprived, disadvantaged, underprivileged,* and *lower class* interchangeably. Whatever terminology is finally selected to describe those individuals considered disadvantaged, two common characteristics usually exist to identify this generic group: 1) they are typically from the lower socioeconomic group within the community, and 2) they are noticeably deficient in cultural and educational-academic strengths.

LOW SCHOOL ACHIEVEMENT

It has also become clear that there is a high correlation between low school achievement, low income, and minority group status. This has led many educators to view any student who falls below a predescribed school standard and fulfills the low income and minority group criteria as being disadvantaged. Frost and Hawkes (1966) offered a definition that appears to reflect the varying views of what constitutes a disadvantaged population when they stated that disadvantaged students are "children with a particular set of educationally associated problems, arising from residing extensively within the culture of the poor." This view was supported by Noar (1967), who defined disadvantaged children as individuals who have too little of everything, including living space, quality food, personal attention, medical and nursing care, and energy and endurance. These children often have inadequate time to sleep, little curiosity, and far too little information about themselves and the world in which they live. They often experience severely limited success, have low self-respect and self-confidence, and seldom have reasons to try to succeed in accomplishing tasks. They may be described as children with too little money, too little clothing, and too little time to play and to learn the academic subjects. The result is often a child whose overall development is delayed and is accompanied by a considerable amount of unhappiness. With all of these recurring problems confronting the disadvantaged child, he is often unready to go to school because he does not understand how school can make his life better. As a consequence, the student's readiness for school programs often falls well below that of his nondisadvantaged peers and the expected standards of the school itself, and he quickly becomes and accepts being an academic failure.

While physical and genetic factors have an obvious and important role in the developmental delay of these children, readiness for school appears to be the critical factor in whether these children will be successful in society. Frequently readiness for school is influenced by the environment of the child's home (Krajicek and Tearney, 1977). If the child has not experienced a home life that nurtures prereadiness and basic academic skills, the student is at a disadvantage as soon as he steps inside the school building. Consequently, the limited experience of these children has played a major role in inhibiting their ability to be successful. In 1966, Israel and others described the disadvantaged child as one who is "handicapped by limited experiences." This definition appears to still hold true today.

HIGH RISK FACTORS IN THE DISADVANTAGED CHILD'S PROFILE

It is often stated that children are at high risk because of influences that may occur prenatally, perinatally, neonatally, postnatally, or environmentally. The high risk concept and accompanying theories have led to an increasing awareness of the need for early identification, especially as one reviews the developmental or physical problems that may occur early in the child's normal development and maturation process. Many factors have been considered as relevant components in the profile of a disadvantaged child. These factors have been categorized by Lansford (1977) as including whether the child is from a single-parent family and if there is a young mother (under 17 years of age).

Many disadvantaged children are premature or very sick as newborns and have experienced extended periods of hospitalization. They often come from large families whose low economic class is coupled with additional high risk factors. Family interaction, particularly observed mother-child interaction, is often not as prevalent as one might expect in a comparable middle class family constellation. At times there are recorded incidents of child abuse of a sibling as well as historically poor relationships between the child's mother and her mother. Recently, there has been documentation of psychiatric problems on the part of one or both parents, as well as an inability to cope with the stress of today's society.

SUMMARY

It becomes clear that it is extremely difficult to define and conceptualize the term *disadvantaged* in a precise manner. Many authorities attempt to describe rather than define the disadvantaged, based upon certain common elements that appear more often in environments that produce a high incidence of this type of child. Descriptions of these impoverished environments have included the following components:

1. A low annual income level
2. An underutilization of available community resources
3. A rate of unemployment considered to be high within the community in which the family is residing, with minimum living and sanitary conditions
4. Large families with inadequate room and living space and an overwhelming lack of privacy
5. Inadequate education and inability to search out educational opportunities
6. Excessive reliance on welfare and governmental programs
7. A pervasive attitude of hopelessness and a feeling that there is little chance of change

The need to provide appropriate educational programming for the preschool disadvantaged child is of critical importance; those individuals in society who have been classified as disadvantaged will raise children who are themselves disadvantaged unless the deprivational pattern is broken. Without educational support only the very strong can break the cycle.

Chapter 3
Legislative Mandates

CREATING A LEGISLATIVE FOUNDATION

During the early 1960s several significant governmental programs and acts of federal legislation that related directly to disadvantaged and underprivileged young people were initiated. Although none of these original programs directly addressed the needs of the three- to five-year-old preschool child, they did lay the foundation for future programs, such as Project Head Start. The majority of these programs and legislation were embodied in the 1962 Welfare Amendments, the 1963 Vocational Education Act (select sections only), the Manpower Development and Training Program, and provisions of the Economic Opportunity Act of 1964. Other federal acts that dealt directly or in part with the disadvantaged or the culturally deprived child included the Kennedy Mental Health Act and the Juvenile Delinquency and Youth Census Act.

1962 Welfare Amendments

The 1962 Welfare Amendments (Public Law 87-543) altered the public welfare provisions of the Social Security Act and were administered by the Bureau of Family Services of the Welfare Administration. These specific amendments constituted the first extensive modification of the public assistance program and emphasized the concept of public assistance as a program designed to reeducate welfare families. A major goal of the program was to make as many as possible of its welfare families self-supporting, with the amendments aimed especially at those families receiving welfare aid under the Aid to Families with Dependent Children (AFDC) Program. Special emphasis was also given to educating the children in those families who were receiving public assistance so that their children in turn would not fall into the pattern of public dependency. Some of the major components and provisions of these amendments are discussed below.

Aid to Families with Dependent Children–Unemployed Persons (AFDC–UP) Under AFDC–UP the federal government shared in the assistance payments to families with children under 18 years of age, where the family was in need of support because of the father's unemployment.

Community Work and Training (CWT) Program This program was aimed at providing constructive work and training experiences to heads of households and other adults who were receiving public assistance. The CWT Program provided many adults with appropriate training and significantly increased their chance for future employment. In addition, it increased the morale and attitude of those individuals who were part of a program that provided financial support and experience at a time in their lives when they could find no employment.

Special Demonstration Projects The 1962 Amendments also provided special demonstration programs, specifically those involved with youth, and were originally designed to keep young teenagers in public assistance families enrolled and achieving within the public school programs. The subsidized employment, which was part of this program, was allowed to continue only as long as the students continued in high school or in a high school equivalent vocational program. It has been suggested that this specific program helped to develop strong and appropriate work habits and attitudes toward future private employment.

Day Care Centers During World War II mothers were encouraged to find acceptable employment that was connected with the war effort. As an assistance to mothers endeavoring in this effort, day care centers were opened in most urban areas of the country. After the war, however, much of the financial assistance that had been available for these centers was eliminated. As a result of the withdrawal of this federal financing, many public day care centers ceased to operate. The rationale for this elimination, while fundamentally based on economic reasons, was also predicated upon the idea that it was unnecessary for mothers to work. In essence, the unavailability of day care centers covertly encouraged mothers to stay home with their children.

The 1962 Welfare Amendments, by providing federal funds for the establishment of day care centers, contributed to the reversal of this post–World War II pattern. The recent resurgence of day care centers, reflective of the increasing numbers of working women with children who need day care and of working women who are heads of single-parent families, has continued to strengthen.

1963 Vocational Education Act

The 1963 Vocational Education Act (Public Law 88-210) was enacted shortly after the assassination of President John F. Kennedy. Many have suggested that the enactment of this law was in part a response to the President's strong commitment to educational programs for young children. The act clearly stated that any disadvantaged person was eligible for vocational education whether he was attending school, out of school, or in need of training or retraining. The major provisions of the 1963 Vocational Education Act, which were directly applicable to disadvantaged youth, are described below.

Residential Vocational Schools   This section of the act provided for the building of select experimental residential vocational schools. The schools were built, completely equipped, and further maintained with federal funds up to a maximum of $2,000 per student each year. The schools were operated by state and local school authorities. The students eligible to attend these schools were boys from urban slum areas whose environmental conditions were characterized as being intolerable or severely impoverished.

Work-Study Provisions   Under the 1963 Vocational Education Act, and in the same section of the act that provided for residential vocational schools, several million dollars were allocated for the development of a nationwide work-study program for needy youths between the ages of 15 and 21 who were enrolled in full-time vocational programs. The employment situations, which paralleled the work-study program, were public service-type employments and were limited to a maximum of $350 per academic year or $500 per year if the young person was a resident student.

Area Vocational Schools   A large amount of the funds allotted under the Vocational Education Act was for the construction and equipping of area vocational schools. In essence, this allocation constituted recognition by the federal government that, in many parts of the country, small, poorly supported, and inefficient educational units existed that were ineffective in promoting vocational and technical education. Requests from school districts seeking financial support through this provision became very competitive during the mid 1960s.

The Commissioner's Role   This component of the act allowed the Commissioner of Education to allocate 10% of all vocational education funds for the purpose of research in the field of vocational and technical education. This was an attempt to provide an incentive to develop demonstration programs and initiate research that would in turn generate new ways to involve severely disadvantaged youth, who were found to be concentrated at the lower end of the intelligence scale.

The Manpower Development and Training Act of 1962 (MDTA) and the 1963 Amendments to this Act

This act was the principal adult Manpower Development and Youth Training Program of the federal government for out of school youths who were already a part of the labor force. As with most federal programs, this one quickly became difficult to put into operation because of its inability to transcend the bureaucratic problems in trying to establish federal cooperation between the Labor Department and the Department of Health, Education, and Welfare. Furthermore, the considerable state and local cooperation required to ensure that all certification and training carried on at the local level by state agencies and local education bodies was in agreement hindered efficient application of the MTDA's provisions.

Labor Department Youth Opportunity Centers The Department of Labor, using MDTA funds, earmarked a multimillion dollar budget to open special youth opportunity centers in the slums of more than 100 urban areas across the country. These centers were staffed with men and women who were qualified to deal with the "drop-out" student as well as other marginally educated youth who needed special training and handling in order to be placed in jobs.

Economic Opportunity Act of 1964 (The Anti-Poverty Program)

Several parts of the Economic Opportunity Act, also referred to as the Anti-Poverty Program or the Poverty Bill, had special significance to those working with the disadvantaged child. These sections included provisions that allowed for Job Corps, work-training programs, work-study programs, urban and rural community action programs, adult basic education programs, work experience programs, and volunteer programs (e.g., Volunteers in Service to America (VISTA)).

Job Corps The Job Corps was originally aimed at students between the ages of 16 and 21. These students were enrolled in a camp-type program, which included extensive vocational training to provide the skills needed to perform useful work in the community. The enrollees of this program lived in training centers in both rural and urban areas. In many instances, educational programs and vocational training were provided through local public education agencies or private vocational institutions. The Job Corps program, perhaps because of its continued bureaucratic and financial problems, received extensive publicity and poor press during the mid 1960s.

Work Training Program The Work Training Program was mandated under Title I and was designed to offer unemployed young men and women, ages 16 through 21, a chance to escape poverty by providing them with an opportunity to work and receive training. Students, both in school and out of school, were eligible to apply for the program. Many of the young students who enrolled in this program began to develop new relationships within the community, since many of their jobs were public service–oriented work projects.

Work-Study Programs The Work-Study Program was a reconstitution of the pre-war National Youth Administration Program, which allowed many students to work while they completed their college education. It was limited to those college-level education students who required financial assistance in order to enroll in a college or to continue in a college program once enrolled.

Community Action Program (CAP) and Adult Basic Education Programs Outside of the vast Job Corps, work-training, and work-study programs, the Community Action Program (CAP) allocated money to be spent for urban and rural programs and earmarked funds for basic adult education in communities with large concentrations of impoverished students. CAP was another attempt at working through the community to combat poverty at its very core. This program was one of the first to recognize the possibility of new types of special education programs that could provide assistance to disadvantaged youth and could be funded under the Poverty Bill.

Family Unity Through Jobs   This part of the Poverty Bill was administered by the Welfare Administration and was developed to implement adequately the 1962 Welfare Amendment Program of Community Work and Training (CWT). The program, while predominantly male centered, also allowed for AFDC mothers to seek employment, especially those who could benefit from the basic education work training that was available under Title V.

Volunteers In Service To America (VISTA)   The VISTA Program was the new name for President Kennedy's previously proposed domestic Peace Corps. The state and local communities were expected to draw on VISTA individuals to help staff the teaching and administration positions that were needed as part of the local training programs for some of the Community Action Programs. The volunteers, whether they were through state or federal programs, received a financial allowance as well as living allowances during their service to the program.

Juvenile Delinquency and Youth Census Act

The Juvenile Delinquency and Youth Census Act of 1961 (Public Law 87-274) provided short term training grants and technical assistance to urban communities for development of techniques to control juvenile delinquency and to promote youth development. Many of those children who originally were enrolled in programs for disadvantaged preschool children ended up receiving services funded through this act.

THE PROVISION OF FUNDING

The Anti-Poverty Program, which stemmed from the Economic Opportunity Act of 1964, came at a time when the Office of Economic Opportunity was organized to provide new and innovative educational programs for the deprived. During this era, poverty was characterized as the enemy of education and a war on poverty was declared. Many programs were developed during this time to benefit disadvantaged children under the premise that poverty stands between children of all ages and learning. While many of the Office of Economic Opportunity educational programs centered upon the adolescent, specifically those who were dropping out of school and trying to find jobs, little was done for the young disadvantaged child (Rees, 1968).

By the mid 1960s the increasing number of educational programs was to a large extent the result of many of the social trends outside the school systems themselves. Of prime importance was the dramatic increase in federal funds allocated for education in general, bolstered by a public outcry to provide funding for programs for children with special needs. The Anti-Poverty Program had begun the provision of funds in a direct way to experimental school programs through the Office of Economic Opportunity and had also influenced the allocation of general educational financial resources. In essence, poverty had become a popular professional target for research and pilot program development (Miller, 1967). Major pieces of legislation that would result in programming for disadvantaged children were evolving.

Elementary and Secondary Education Act (ESEA)

In 1965, the landmark legislation of the Elementary and Secondary Education Act (ESEA) (Public Law 89-10; revised 1970, Public Law 91-230) marked the greatest degree of federal fiscal involvement in the nation's schools up to that time. The basic core of this new proposal was a series of supplementary centers for the demonstration of educational practices that were considered to be innovative. Major emphasis was given in ESEA to what is now called Title I, passed in 1966 and later referred to as the Act to Help Disadvantaged Children. Designed to encourage and to support the establishment, expansion, and improvement of special programs, including the construction of school facilities where needed, Title I provided for compensatory or "catch up" education for children from poverty areas or poor families. While Title I was primarily designed to support inner city and urban schools, Title III of ESEA was primarily aimed at developing new, creative, and innovative programs.

At this particular time, various school districts were eligible to receive payments for programs designed to meet the special educational needs of children who came from concentrated disadvantaged areas. In these areas, school districts designed a variety of special education services and programs, including those which all children in need of such services could benefit from and participate in.

Additional examples of the services that were developed during this era included educational radio and television programs, mobile educational services and equipment, remedial education, and preschool or after-school programs. Additional instruction and personnel, equipment and facilities, and other components of education that were necessary for improving the education of disadvantaged children were also made available.

Additional Efforts

Before the passage of the Educational Aid Bill, the Office of Economic Opportunity had spent considerable funds on the education of the disadvantaged, predominantly the older disadvantaged individual, in areas outside of the schools. Most notable among these efforts was the Job Corps. The Economic Opportunity Office also was permitted to support programs of remedial education but was restricted from entering the realm of the regular curriculum within the schools. At the end of 1966, a combined effort on the part of the Office of Economic Opportunity and the U. S. Office of Education was responsible for creating a significant number of experimental projects geared toward helping the disadvantaged student. The term *compensatory* suddenly entered the professional vocabulary of educators and quickly replaced the use of labels such as underprivileged and disadvantaged (Miller, 1967).

While the many federal acts, in addition to ESEA, passed to provide funding for various forms of community education programs and projects to benefit the disadvantaged are too numerous to discuss here, specific mention of a few is warranted.

The Child Nutrition Act of 1966 (Public Law 89-642) supplied schools in low income and poverty areas with equipment for storing, transporting, preparing, and serving food to children. This act was supported by the National School Lunch Act (Public Law 87-688), which allocated funds to educational agencies to enable them to provide nutritious school lunches. In 1968, the Early Childhood Assistance Act offered further support, particularly to handicapped children, through the Bureau of Education for the Handicapped.

Private Funding

In addition to federal funding, many private foundations supported various phases of community education that were involved with disadvantaged children and allowed local education agencies or school districts access to their foundation support. Among the more commonly known foundations to provide assistance programs, the following should be recognized: the Corning Foundation, Corning, New York; the Dan Forth Foundation, St. Louis, Missouri; the Ford Foundation, New York, New York; the Meyer Foundation, Washington, D.C.; the Rockefeller Foundation, New York, New York; the Sears, Roebuck Foundation, Chicago, Illinois; and the Whirlpool Foundation, Benton Harbor, Michigan. While there are many other local and equally prestigious foundations, the above organizations have, over the past years, strongly supported all phases of community education programs for disadvantaged individuals.

STRENGTHENING MANDATES

Continued strengthening of legislation to benefit the disadvantaged and refinement of previous legislation has been the hallmark of the 1970s.

In 1974, Head Start, revitalized through the Economic Opportunity and Community Partnership Act (Public Law 93-644), provided direct federal grants to private and public organizations and school agencies for administering and planning Head Start programs. These programs were to provide medical, educational, nutritional, and social services to preschool children from low income families. Noteworthy is the stipulation that 10% of children enrolled in Head Start programs must be handicapped, and programs must provide services to meet these children's special needs. Head Start's 475-billion-dollar fiscal 1977 appropriation included services that totaled 29 million dollars for 36,133 handicapped children. These children represented 13% of the total enrollment.

It is important to reiterate that the 1966 Title I of ESEA related specifically to the deprived. It placed major emphasis on the special needs of the disadvantaged and helped draw attention to the direct relationship between poverty and educational deprivation. It was through the implementation of Title I that the federal government began to make available large sums of money with the stipulation that local education agencies, following the guidelines of Title I, would determine how to spend this money in accordance with their students' particular needs. However, criticism has been voiced concerning the local management of funds since the implementation of that act. Reasons for this criticism have included suggested improprieties in leadership, inappropriate spending of money, inadequate planning of programs, and lack of evaluation measures.

Of equal importance are the questions that have been raised concerning the allotment of funds on the basis of the number of children from low income families; charges have been made that certain groups misrepresented the number of children within a prescribed category. The criticism has sparked the introduction of several bills to amend Title I so as to provide the means for a basic transition for the allocation of funds from the potentially misleading criteria of poverty level incomes (the original basis) to assessments of educational need. It has been suggested that the original fiscal formula, used until the mid 1970s, was based upon discredited economic data and the assumption that being economically poor is equivalent to being educationally disadvantaged.

Most recently the Education for All Handicapped Children Act (Public Law 94-142) provided formula grants to states for the funding of direct services to handicapped children, based on the number of students the state reported as being served annually in special education programs. Included as part of the Education for All Handicapped Children Act funding were preschool incentive grants, awarded to states based on the number of handicapped preschool children between the ages of 3 and 5 receiving special education. In the school years 1976–1977 and 1977–1978, states were receiving a total of 12.4 million dollars to serve 195,848 preschool handicapped children. HEW's Bureau of Education for the Handicapped estimated Congress would have had to appropriate 58.7 million dollars for the current school year in order to provide a 300-dollar incentive grant for every preschooler served as authorized under Public Law 94-142.

In 1978, President Carter took a significant step toward helping minorities by increasing the national education budget. Compensatory education for the disadvantaged (Title I of the Elementary and Secondary Education Act), under the Carter Administration's proposal will receive 3.38 billion dollars. This is an increase of 650 million dollars, representing a 23% increase over fiscal 1978 and 47% more than fiscal year 1977. This major step, in addition to proposed funding increases in bilingual education, Indian education, and community schools, represents a substantial financial increase for major areas of education for the first time in seven years. Ernest L. Boyer, U.S. Commissioner of Education, has remarked that for the first time in many years educational programs, specifically through the increase in Title I expenditures, can benefit approximately 900,000 more children than ever before.

FUTURE DIRECTIONS

After a review of this specific information, it quickly becomes obvious that the federal government has played a major role in trying to develop programs aimed at supporting disadvantaged children and youth. While little has been done for the preschool disadvantaged child, the time appears right for this to be a new thrust on the part of not only governmental agencies but private foundations as well. The information garnered from a review of the preceding programs for the disadvantaged should provide a foundation upon which to develop more comprehensive, fair, efficient, and less bureaucratic programs to serve the disadvantaged preschool child.

Section II
CURRICULUM
DEVELOPMENT

Chapter 4
Evaluation Strategies

There has been a growing national interest in the early assessment, screening, and diagnosis of the preschool-age child. While recognition of the need for early intervention has resulted in an increase in the number of identification instruments, there is almost universal agreement that no one instrument or battery of instruments can accurately and consistently predict the multiplicity of problems that many preschool disadvantaged children exhibit. It also has become evident that no clear-cut age levels can be identified to indicate when certain instruments are no longer appropriate for a particular population and when other systems should be automatically substituted. Furthermore, many assessment techniques used during the early years of a child's life may be classified as preschool instruments, although these same instruments are used with older children who are suspected of having a variety of handicaps.

After a brief review of the inherent difficulties in screening and assessing the disadvantaged preschool child, this chapter presents to the reader selected evaluation procedures that have been used successfully with children who are entering the preschool years. The instruments are discussed in relation to five domains in particular: cognitive abilities, language development, social/emotional development, and motor skills. Many of the instruments cited have been developed for handicapped populations or those children considered at risk for future educational problems.

COMBATING DISCRIMINATORY ELEMENTS IN EARLY ASSESSMENT

In recent years, class action suits and other litigation directed at the illegal and biased placement of minority children in special education classes have come to the forefront as representative of major educational problems. Arguments in many of these suits have suggested that placement of minority and disadvantaged children was based primarily on results obtained from testing procedures that did not accurately measure these children's learning abilities. Often, minority children's cultural, linguistic, and socioeconomic backgrounds were not taken into consideration. Instruments were frequently standardized on white, English-speaking, middle class student populations and contained many culturally loaded questions that were extremely difficult for the child who lived in an impoverished environment to answer.

Ross, Deyoung, and Cohen (1971) and Weintraub (1972) supported the views of many educators when they stated that minority children's test results do not always accurately indicate their learning abilities. Most recently, the percentage of culturally or linguistically different children who have been enrolled in public preschool classes has escalated. In some areas of the United States, such as the southwest, minority populations who speak languages other than English comprise major preschool populations. For many of these children, being culturally different has meant placement in special education classes. Public Law 94-142 has directly addressed this issue and made it illegal to place children (in this case handicapped children) on the basis of a sole evaluation criterion or without consideration of the student's native language or major mode of communication.

Culture-Fair and Culture-Free Tests

The proposed panacea, "culture-fair" or "culture-free," tests, has been less than successful. The culture-fair concept is based on the assumption that test items are selected on the basis that all children have had an opportunity to familiarize themselves with the materials or ideas being discussed and that there is equal motivation for all students to respond to the questions. Obviously this is not only very difficult to achieve but is also nearly impossible to control when evaluating the disadvantaged preschool child whose experiences at best date from no more than five years earlier and traditionally reflect the environmental surroundings into which the child was born.

The Goodenough **Draw-a-Man Test** (Goodenough and Harris, 1963), based on the concept that all children have an opportunity to see men, is an example of a culture-free test. The child's performance is scored on the basis of the amount of material he provides in his drawing. However, regardless of test content, whether test performance, within itself, is culture-bound is always debatable.

Norm- and Criterion-Referenced Instruments

With all the real and anticipated problems inherent in testing any child, there is a critical need to accurately assess young children so that individualized education programs may be planned more effectively. To this end, many instruments have been developed from a criterion-referenced or norm-referenced basis. Criterion-referenced measures provide the teacher with information concerning what specific skills a student has or does not have as part of his repertoire. Because skills are often based on a continuum of subskills, the evaluator can zero in on deficit areas and plan instruction accordingly. In addition to providing the teacher or evaluator with information that may lead to a prescription for subsequent instruction, criterion-referenced measures also can provide the teacher with an evaluation of the effectiveness of her instruction and offer immediate feedback regarding the performance of a student on a specific learning task.

Norm-referenced measurement provides information concerning how a student is progressing as compared to the performance of his peers on the same measure. The standardized achievement test is a common norm-referenced instrument. It becomes obvious that norm-referenced instruments communicate little about an individual's performance levels or actual skills.

Whichever instruments are selected, be they criterion or norm referenced, there is still the added problem that few exist specifically for use with the disadvantaged preschool child. In an attempt to alleviate the disparity between good and poor criterion-referenced instruments, many educators have resorted to developing their own forms of instrument, which have surfaced as the "checklisting" system.

Checklists

The checklist, which has been predominantly used in special education to assess behavior, offers a straightforward and effective way of obtaining information about a student. Checklists are currently being used as a means of rating children entering preschool programs to assess whether or not they have mastered some of the very basic self-care skills normally associated with children of their age. Parents are often given developmental checklists to fill out which ask the parent to indicate whether or not the child has performed each of the listed behaviors at some time in the past or as part of his everyday activities. An example of a developmental checklist is the **MEMPHIS Comprehensive Developmental Scale** (Quick, Little, and Campbell, 1974), which was designed to assess personal-social abilities of preschool children. This specific scale samples 60 skills that are arranged in developmental order, ranging from simple to complex, with one month's credit being given for each task the child successfully performs. Using this information, a developmental age is calculated.

The usefulness of checklists and rating scales, as of any instrument that relies on informant information, depends highly on the reliability of the sources being consulted. Unfortunately, many checklists are often completed by individuals who are unaware of a child's actual abilities, especially those abilities exhibited during non-school hours.

The two major purposes for using behavior checklists appear to be *description* and *prescription*. If diagnosis or screening is the major aim, any checklist that comprehensively and accurately rates the behaviors in question is appropriate. A prescriptive checklist additionaly enumerates the means for remediating or treating any identified deficiency.

At the end of this chapter, a table of checklists that were developed primarily for use with the handicapped is presented. It is important to note that many of these checklists are widely used with nonhandicapped students as well and may be of particular interest to the teacher of the preschool disadvantaged because of their developmental genesis.

EVALUATION TESTS IN USE

The most widely used and cited evaluation instruments are discussed in this chapter. While all efforts have been made to select those instruments that are particularly useful with the disadvantaged preschool child, it should be noted that many are employed to evaluate a variety of student populations.

Instruments that assess cognitive abilities, language development, social/emotional development, motor skills, and behavior are described, and tables listing instruments by name, developer or author, and suggested age range for use are provided. Assessment systems that look at multiple behaviors in a variety of domains, such as the **Denver Developmental Screening Test,** the **Alpern-Boll Developmental Profile** and the **McCarthy Scales of Children's Abilities,** are discussed, as are those instruments that have been traditionally used as screening tools for this population of disadvantaged children.

Cognitive Abilities

When considering the measurement of the cognitive abilities of young children, traditional evaluation instruments, such as those developed by Binet (Stanford-Binet) and Wechsler (The Wechsler Preschool and Primary Scale of Intelligence), are often discussed. While these are perhaps two of the most widely used tests of intellectual functioning, numerous other instruments exist that can provide valuable information in this domain. Before discussing other instruments, some basic knowledge concerning these two tests, so frequently applied to assess preschool disadvantaged children, is useful.

The **Stanford-Binet Intelligence Scale,** which can be used with preschool children as young as two years of age, yields both a mental age (MA) and an intelligence quotient (IQ). It contains a different set of items at each age level, with no particular attempt to assess the same domains of behavior at each age level.

The second instrument commonly used to assess intelligence in the preschool child is the **Wechsler Preschool and Primary Scale of Intelligence (WPPSI).** The WPPSI can be used to assess children from 4 to 6½ years of age and is different from the Binet in that its items are organized by content areas into eleven subtests. Preschool children who are evaluated with the WPPSI are administered tasks that attempt to elicit the use and understanding of language (defining words). The performance of verbal analogies and the answering of factual questions require the child to perform tasks that use little or no expressive language. For this reason, the WPPSI has been widely employed with many disadvantaged preschoolers, who are often severely delayed in the area of language development. The WPPSI, unlike the Stanford-Binet, does not yield a mental age score, but it does yield verbal, performance, and overall IQ scores. These scores relate the child's performance to other children of the same age. It has been suggested that the WPPSI is the most appropriate test for young children who are already suspected of functioning at a low level. Thus, for children suspected of being at high educational risk, such as the preschool disadvantaged child, the WPPSI appears to be a most efficacious selection.

Many traditional tests of intelligence that assess the cognitive area are still in use today. Most notable are the **Gesell Developmental Schedules,** developed by Arnold Gesell and his staff at Yale University. This instrument consists of qualitative measures of motor development, language development, adaptive behavior, and personal-social behavior. For years, this instrument has been the standard that professionals have used to determine the developmental ages of children.

Other well established instruments that are used to measure preschool development include the **Merrill-Palmer Preschool Performance Test,** the **Minnesota Preschool Scale,** and the **Cattell Infant Intelligence Scale.**

Infant tests are often used to assess the beginning preschool child who may appear to be deficient in a variety of developmental areas. The **Bayley Scales of Infant Development** have recently been used interchangeably with the Cattell, because the tests appear to be highly correlated and similar. The Bayley Scales include a mental scale designed to assess sensory-perceptual abilities, memory, learning and problem-solving abilities, discrimination, the ability to respond on tests of early object constancy, and the beginnings of verbal communication. Results are expressed as a Mental Development Index. In addition, a motor scale measures the degree of control of the body as well as the coordination and fine control of the hands and fingers. The results of this scale are expressed as a Psychomotor Index. It has been suggested that the Bayley presents advantages over the Cattell in that it is more recent and provides a greater variety of items. It also has separate mental and motor scales. The Cattell, however, does take less time to administer and can be combined with the Stanford-Binet to present a thorough picture of the child. Other tests, such as the **Kuhlmann-Binet Infant Scale** and the **Griffiths Mental Development Scale,** while currently in use, appear to suffer from a lack of predictive validity.

The **Columbia Mental Maturity Scale** is another instrument used for preschool-age children as well as children up to the age of twelve. It is especially useful for children with language delay or associated problems, because it is composed of tasks requiring only that the child indicate by gesture which of several stimuli does not belong with the others. In a similar manner, the **Leiter International Performance Scale** can be used to evaluate children from the preschool level to the young adult years. It was originally developed for deaf persons and is especially useful in situations that require a measure of cognitive function exclusive of language. The Leiter Scale tests visual and spatial abilities, using tasks that involve block design, picture completion, and color matching. The Leiter is not widely used in the United States because its norms are not appropriate for American children, having been standardized on a Hawaiian population of Chinese and Japanese children.

One of the instruments used to provide a culture fair measurement of children is the **Institute for Personality and Ability Testing (IPAT) Culture Fair Intelligence Test.** This series of tests is composed of three scales, with Scale 1 being for use with children from ages four to eight. However, the concept of any test being culture fair is open to question, and this, coupled with the relative oldness of the test, has discouraged its wide use during recent years.

Another instrument, which has been used increasingly for very young children who present varying degrees of severe handicaps, is the **Ordinal Scales of Psychological Development** developed by Uzgiris and Hunt in 1975. While the predominant use of this scale has been with the most profoundly delayed youngster, it has been adapted for use as an assessment instrument in some preschool programs. The instrument is a scale based upon a Piagetian framework, which implies a hierarchical relationship between accomplishments at different levels, so that higher skills are derived from and incorporate lower skills. The scales of this instrument are not necessarily concerned with incremental progress. The areas of psychological development reviewed by this instrument include: 1) visual pursuit, localization, and object permanence, 2) development of means for obtaining desired environmental events, 3) development of operational causality, 4) development of motor imitation, 5) development of vocal imitation, 6) construction of object relations in space, and 7) development of schemes for relating to objects. It can be quickly deduced that many of these areas are absent from the repertoire of most disadvantaged preschoolers.

Table 1 offers the reader a quick analysis of the many instruments currently being used in the preschool area to assess cognitive functioning. Not all instruments presently available are discussed, but those most widely used or reported in the literature are listed. Many of the instruments can be used for other areas, including those discussed in the following pages. It is important to remember that no single instrument in itself can accurately predict the level at which a child is functioning and that any assessment should be supported by as much other information as is available.

Table 1. Instruments that assess cognitive abilities

Test or procedure	Developer(s) Author(s)	Age range
Stanford-Binet Intelligence Scale	Binet	2 years to adult
Wechsler Preschool and Primary Scale of Intelligence (WPPSI)	Wechsler	4 to 6 1/2 years
Gesell Developmental Schedules (Revised Scale)	Gesell et al.	Birth to 5 years
Merrill-Palmer Scale of Mental Tests	Stutsman	Preschool
Minnesota Preschool Scale	Goodenough et al.	Preschool
Infant Intelligence Scale (CIIS)	Cattell	Birth to 30 months
Bayley Scales of Infant Development	Bayley	Birth to 30 months
Kuhlmann-Binet Infant Scale	Kuhlmann	Birth to 30 months
Griffiths Mental Development Scale	Griffiths	Birth to 4 years
Columbia Mental Maturity Scale	Burgemeister, Blum, and Large	3 to 12 years
Leiter International Performance Scale	Leiter	Preschool to adult
IPAT Culture Fair Intelligence Test	Cattell and Cattell	4 to 8 years (Scale 1)
Ordinal Scales of Psychological Development	Uzgiris and Hunt	Birth to 3 years

Language Development

Language problems associated with preschool disadvantaged children are often reported in the literature. Most recently, language handicaps of young children enrolled in compensatory programs, such as Head Start, far outnumber any other type of problem exhibited by the child. With the growing recognition of the role language plays in helping to assimilate the disadvantaged preschool child into the mainstream of school have come other dilemmas. For example, as a child grows older the assessment of his language development becomes more difficult, because it is often associated with impaired intellectual functioning. In essence, it becomes an issue of the chicken or the egg theory: Which one created the other? Researchers have reported that by the time a normally developing child reaches preschool, he typically has mastered the majority of all the syntactic structures in language. When a child appears to not have the important prerequisite skills, a language evaluation is usually performed, which often indicates what is wrong with the child's

Table 2. Instruments that assess language development

Test or procedure	Developer(s) Author(s)	Age range
Houston Test of Language Development	Crabtree	6 to 36 months
Mecham Verbal Language Development Scale	Mecham	Birth to 15 years
Peabody Picture Vocabulary Test (PPVT)	Dunn	2 1/2 to 18 years
Illinois Test of Psycholinguistic Abilities (ITPA)	Kirk, McCarthy, and Kirk	2 1/2 to 10 years
The Bzoch-League Receptive-Expressive Emergent Language (REEL) Scale	Bzoch and League	Birth to 36 months
Early Language Assessment Scale	Honig and Caldwell	3 to 48 months
Expressive Language Test	Reyes et al.	2 to 4 years
Receptive Language Test	Marmor	1 to 3 years
Communication Evolution Chart from Infancy to Five Years	Anderson, Miles, and Matheny	3 months to 5 years
Fokes Developmental Scale of Language Acquisition	Fokes	Birth to 7 years
Observational Rating Scale of Language	Kolstoe	5 1/2 to 14 years
Oral-Aural Language Schedule	Mecham	
Pattern of Normal Language Development	Lillywhite	Birth to 6 years
Preschool Language Scale	Zimmerman, Steiner, and Evatt	2 to 6 years
Rating Scale for Evaluation of Expressive, Receptive, and Phonetic Language Development in the Young Child	D'Asaro and John	4 weeks to 72 months
Reynell Developmental Language Scales (experimental edition)	Reynell	1 to 5 years
Test of Preschool Language Proficiency	Graham	3 to 5 years
Preschool Preposition Test	Aaronson and Schaefer	3 to 5 years
Hannah/Gardner Preschool Language Screening Test	Hannah and Gardner	3 to 5 1/2 yers
Speech and Language Test for Preschool Children	Fluharty	2 to 6 years

language development but is rarely prescriptive in nature. Tests like the **Houston Test of Language Development** and the **Mecham Verbal Language Development Scale** are examples of such instruments, which have been developed with varying degress of accuracy. Unfortunately, many instruments are not sensitive to the child who makes rapid increases in language ability;

yet "one-time" evaluations tend to act as the framework for educational programming.

Evaluation in all areas, particularly in the area of language, should be ongoing and supplemented with a careful monitoring system. The rationale behind this is that the young child rapidly grows in language sophistication. It is often said that the disadvantaged child's school program may be his only chance to model appropriate language patterns and behaviors.

As with intelligence testing in the cognitive area, there are many instruments available that purport to provide information concerning the progress of a child in the language domain. Perhaps the most widely known instrument for use with preschool children is the **Peabody Picture Vocabulary Test (PPVT),** which was designed to be a quickly administered instrument, can be used with individuals ranging in age from 2½ to 18 years, and requires no spoken responses. This instrument is primarily used as a receptive language measure, although some professionals have used it as an intelligence test since it can yield an IQ. The validity of using the PPVT as an intelligence test has been highly questioned; those instruments mentioned previously in the cognitive area are better used for this purpose.

Another instrument commonly used to assess the language area is the **Illinois Test of Psycholinguistic Abilities (ITPA),** which was developed for children ranging from 2½ to 10 years of age. While this test provides valuable information about a student's language ability, it is a very time-consuming and cumbersome instrument that requires specific training on the part of the examiner. Some of the ITPA subtests have been questioned in terms of whether or not they really measure what they purport to assess. Of special importance is the information that only children with IQs between 84 and 116 were used initially in the instrument's normative sample, a fact that generates major questions concerning its use with disadvantaged children whose IQs may not fall within that range.

The instruments described in Table 2 represent those most commonly used to evaluate the preschool disadvantaged child in the language area. Some of these instruments are in the form of rating scales that attempt to measure both expressive as well as receptive language.

Social/Emotional Development

The social/emotional area is often neglected in the assessment of very young children. Little time is spent in investigating how effective an individual is in adapting to the natural and social demands of his environment. For the disadvantaged preschool child, this is a most critical assessment area because how this type of child adapts to his peers and the pressure of his surroundings may very well indicate how he will function in future years.

The most widely used test for assessing social development is the **Vineland Social Maturity Scale,** which uses an interview with an informant, such as the parent, to obtain information. This information attempts to question how an individual manages his practical needs and assumes responsibility. The scale contains items reflective of self-help, self-direction, communication, locomotion, and socialization skills and was standardized on a sample population ranging in age from birth to thirty years. As with most social/emotional instruments, it assesses behaviors that might be considered cognitive or communicative, since it is almost impossible to separate intelligence, social, and language behavior. The child's total score can be converted into a social age and a social quotient.

The **California Preschool Social Competency Scale** measures a child's social communication skills as well as his ability to interact with others and the degree of his independence. Items on this scale include: Using Names of Others, Taking Turns, Initiating Group Activities, and Dependence Upon Adults.

The **Cain-Levine Social Competency Scale** is another instrument that has been adapted for use with preschool populations, especially children five years of age or older. This instrument was originally developed for evaluating the social competency of the moderately retarded and was designed as a behavior rating scale. It contains forty-four items that are divided into the four major areas of self-help, initiative, social skills, and communication. As on the Vineland, competency behaviors are assessed through an interview technique, and the test's greatest value lies in its recognition and evaluation of a student's progress, rather than comparing the child with others.

Many of the other social and emotional scales currently in use have also

Table 3.   Instruments that assess social/emotional development

Test or procedure	Developer(s) Author(s)	Age range
Vineland Social Maturity Scale	Doll	Birth to 18 years
California Preschool Social Competency Scale	Levine, Elzey, and Lewis	2 1/2 to 5 1/2 years
Cain-Levine Social Competency Scale	Cain-Levine and Freeman	5 to 13 years
TARC Assessment System	Sailor and Mix	3 years to adult
Behavioral and Neurological Assessment Scale (II)	Brazelton et al.	Birth to 3 years
Behavior Problem Checklist	Quay and Peterson	Birth to 4 years
Rimland Diagnostic Check List	Albert and Davis	Birth to 4 years
Behavior Checklist	Ogilvie and Shapiro	3 to 6 years
Quantitative Analysis of Tasks	White and Kaban	1 to 6 years
Behavior Management Observation Scales	Terdal et al.	Birth to 4 years
Preschool Attainment Record	Doll	Birth to 7 years
Behavioral Categorical System	DeMyer and Churchill	2 to 5 years

been developed for handicapped as well as nonhandicapped populations. Examples of these include the **TARC Assessment System,** the **School Self-Control Behavior Inventory,** and the **Children's Minimal Social Behavior Scale.** Other instruments presently used with preschoolers, or adapted for use with this population, are listed in Table 3.

Motor Skills

The assessment of motor skills, especially those defined as perceptual motor skills, has drawn a significant amount of interest when assessing the preschool disadvantaged child. It is well documented that perceptual motor functioning is a crucial skill area that interrelates closely with the daily educational tasks that a child is asked to perform. Perhaps the best known assessment technique for evaluating the perceptual motor area is the **Frostig Developmental Test of Visual Perception.** This instrument has been used extensively in Head Start and similar programs where there are children considered to be at educationally high risk. This instrument was designed for evaluating children from 4 to 8 years of age and can be administered individually or to groups. Five areas are assessed: 1) eye-motor (hand) coordination, 2) figure-ground discrimination, 3) form constancy, 4) position in space, and 5) spatial relations. Frostig has also designed select remediation techniques to accompany her evaluation instrument, and, although there has been some criticism as to the relationship between Frostig exercises and what they actually accomplish aside from doing better on the Frostig test, the instrument is widely used in many preschool programs as well as in kindergarten and first-grade classes.

Another instrument used for assessment in the perceptual-motor area is the **Purdue Perceptual-Motor Survey (PPMS).** Although the PPMS norms were initially developed after testing children 6 to 10 years of age, it has been extensively used in many preschool programs. The PPMS is based upon a developmental theory that presents a child moving through a series of stages, such as those postulated by Piaget. It was designed to focus on an individual's perceptual-motor development and has five categories of performance, eleven subtests, and twenty-two test items. The student is assigned a score ranging from 1, which is the lowest level of performance, to 4, which is the highest level of performance, for each individual task. The five areas of performance evaluated are balance and posture, body image and differentiation, perceptual-motor match, ocular control, and form perception. The PPMS can be given by teachers and is administered individually. Similar to the Frostig, the results can be used to prescribe developmental and remedial activities.

The Frostig and the PPMS are assessment instruments that focus on perceptual-motor skills from a framework that integrates perceptual functioning with motor performance. It becomes readily apparent that, in order for many academic and preacademic tasks to be learned, these critical skill areas must operate in concert. There are times, however, when it may be necessary to evaluate independently either perceptual functioning or motor performance. For example, a student may be penalized in his assessment if a severe motor problem affects his overall performance score on a visual perception test. It therefore becomes apparent that some instruments need to be used and selected on the basis of how well they isolate visual and motor components. As might be expected, the task of separating components in the visual-motor area is quite difficult, since both vision and motor are typically blended within many tasks. One instrument designed to address this very problem is the **Motor-Free Visual Perception Test (MVPT),** which presents a child with a series of plates that involve selected visual images. The motor response is significantly decreased because the child only needs to nod his head as the evaluator points to components of the drawings.

Other instruments, such as the **Developmental Test of Visual-Motor Integration (VMI),** can be used to assess the degree to which visual perception and motor behavior are integrated. In this specific instance, the child is asked to use paper and pencil to copy select geometric forms. Skill deficits are noted, and remedial instruction is planned on the basis of these results. The VMI was designed primarily for use at the preschool and early primary levels, although it can be administered to children from 2 to 15 years of age.

The **Adams County Checklist for Perceptual-Motor Deficiency,** which assesses gross motor skills, balance, eye-hand coordination and visual skills, the **Perceptual Forms Test,** which assesses general visual-motor performance, and the **Southern California Perceptual Motor Tests,** which assess balance, right-left discrimination, imitation of postures, crossing the midline, and bilateral motor coordination, are other examples of perceptual-motor assessment instruments.

In addition to those instruments that assess the visual-motor area, instruments predominantly used to assess basic movement skills are available. For example, the **Bruininks-Oseretsky Test of Motor Proficiency (BOTMP)** assesses running speed, agility, balance, bilateral coordination, strength,

Table 4.   Instruments that assess motor skills

Test or procedure	Developer(s) Author(s)	Age range
Frostig Developmental Test of Visual Perception	Frostig	4 to 8 years
Purdue Perceptual-Motor Survey (PPMS)	Roach and Kephart	6 to 10 years
Developmental Test of Visual-Motor Integration (VMI)	Beery	2 to 15 years
Bruininks-Oseretsky Test of Motor Proficiency (BOTMP)	Bruininks-Oseretsky	4 1/2 to 14 1/2 years

upper limb coordination, speed and dexterity, and response speed. The BOTMP is often used to provide a comprehensive assessment of motor development, although it can provide a general survey of motor proficiency as well as a specialized assessment of particular fine or gross motor skills. The results of the evaluation are presented as age equivalents and as percentile ranks. **The University of Connecticut and Mansfield Training School Motor Skills Test** can also be used in this area; it assesses crawling, rolling, walking up and down stairs, running, grasping, jumping, and numerous other skills associated with the gross motor domain.

Table 4 provides a sample of tests that have been used in programs for disadvantaged preschool children. Each year revisions of existing measures as well as innovative instruments are being developed. It is important that those individuals who are involved in assessing the specific area of visual-motor skills keep abreast of this new information.

Behavior

The evaluation of a preschool child's behavior, aside from the information that may be generated from tests involving the social/emotional domain, should also be considered when developing a program for the child. As an example, the **Behavior Developmental Profile** was designed to measure the development of deprived as well as handicapped children. It is best used to help program for preschool children within the home setting and includes three major scales: Communication, Motor, and Social.

Other assessment instruments or their components, such as the **Washington Guide to Promoting Development in the Young Child** and the **Alpern-Boll Developmental Profile,** are listed in Table 5 and provide screening information that has often proved valuable in developing educational plans for disadvantaged preschool children.

Assessment/Screening Systems

There are many assessment instruments currently available that evaluate more than one domain. These are often defined as assessment systems and traditionally comprise the major tests or subtests most preschool children are

Table 5.   Instruments that assess behavior

Test or procedure	Developer(s) Author(s)	Age range
Behavior Developmental Profile	Marshalltown	0 to 6 years
Washington Guide to Promoting Development in the Young Child		1 to 52 months
Alpern-Boll Developmental Profile	Alpern and Boll	Birth to preadolescence

given. Perhaps the most widely administered multifactor system is the **Denver Developmental Screening Test,** which can be used with children ranging in age from birth to 6 years. The areas of development assessed are gross and fine motor skills, language, and the personal-social domain. While the Denver is widely used and appears to have a high reliability and validity, its major drawback seems to be its inability to be accurate in terms of predictive validity with minority children. A positive aspect of this instrument is that it requires the evaluator to observe the child's behavior directly rather than relying solely on the information of a reporter.

Similar to the Denver is the **CCD Developmental Progress Scale,** which evaluates the student's developmental status in three areas. These areas, motor skills, communication-interpersonal skills, and self-sufficiency skills, represent a combination of two motor areas of the Denver. The CCD scale seems to be more appropriate for older children, while the Denver is best for younger students. Like the Denver, the CCD scales rely on parent reporting as well as direct observation.

The **Alpern-Boll Developmental Profile,** previously discussed as a behavioral assessment instrument, was developed in 1972. Also considered as an assessment system, this profile organizes information obtained from the parents or those familiar with the child to formulate a developmental age. The areas addressed include physical, self-help, social, academic, and communication skills. As an example, the socialization component measures the student's interpersonal relationship abilities, with items pertaining to playing in the neighborhood without supervision and recognizing how other people feel by naming emotions such as fear, anger, or sadness.

Unlike tests that consist of a great amount of "mental" content, the **McCarthy Scales of Children's Abilities (MSCA)** provide separate indices of a student's performance on a series of perceptual-performance, verbal, quantitative, memory, and motor tasks. This system was developed for use with children 2½ to 8½ years of age and can be used with children from various ethnic, regional, and socioeconomic groups. The MSCA have been validated in terms of their ability to predict school achievement, although the caution is again offered that no system can be completely accurate when assessing young children because of the child's ability to rapidly change.

The **Cooperative Preschool Inventory,** while having limited norms on lower class children, offers assessment of achievement in areas of concept, activation-sensory, activation-numerical, and personal-social responsiveness, and associative vocabulary.

The **Boyd Developmental Progress Scale** focuses upon practical and useful developmental skills that are suspected of emerging at a given age and are related to daily living skills. This was one of the systems developed in the early 1960s in an attempt to describe pictorially developmental progress and to avoid the errors and misinterpretations involved in quotient scores or age equivalents.

The Boyd is a screening device that can be administered by either a teacher or other professional and can lead to a better understanding of the strengths and weaknesses of the child after evaluating the student, interviewing the parent, or both.

A more recent instrument, which is currently being used in programs for the severely handicapped as well as in preschool programs, is the **Lexington Developmental Scale.** This is a teacher-oriented tool that evaluates an individual's progress over time and can be used as a basis for curriculum planning. This instrument is available for use with two age ranges: birth through 2 years, and 2 through 6 years. The five major areas addressed by this instrument include motor, language, personal-social, cognitive, and emotional domains. All but the emotional area are scored on the basis of a developmental age while emotional development is scored on the basis of a five-point scale because of the lack of adequate norms in this area. Of special interest to the teacher is that two types of items are included on the scale, one type being

Table 6. Assessment/screening systems

Test or procedure	Developer(s) Author(s)	Age range
Denver Developmental Screening Test	Frankenburg and Dodds	Birth to 6 years
CCD Developmental Progress Scale	Boyd	Birth to 8 years
McCarthy Scales of Children's Abilities (MSCA)	McCarthy	2 1/2 to 8 1/2 years
Cooperative Preschool Inventory		2 to 6 1/2 years
Boyd Developmental Progress Scale	Boyd	Birth to 8 years
Lexington Developmental Scale	Irwin et al.	Birth to 2 years; 2 to 6 years
System of Comprehensive Health Care Screening and Service	Scurietis and Headrick	Birth to 4 years
Preschool Multiphasic Program	Belleville and Green	Birth to 4 years
Pediatric Multiphasic Program	Allen and Shinefield	4 years +
Rapid Developmental Screening Checklist	Giannini et al.	Birth to 5 years
Guide to Normal Milestones of Development	Haynes	Birth to 3 years
Alpern-Boll Developmental Profile	Alpern and Boll	Birth to preadolescence

behavioral, which may be scored when observed once, and the other experimental, which reflects information that is best obtained through observation over a period of time or from past records.

Table 6 offers examples of assessment systems currently being used in many preschool disadvantaged programs. Those systems, which were originally developed for handicapped populations, appear to offer the teacher new ways of assessing the disadvantaged child and should be considered when developing evaluation programs.

Other Screening Tools

Table 7 lists other screening instruments that have been suggested as being useful in evaluating disadvantaged preschool children (Krajicek and Tearney, 1977). The **Denver Articulation Screening Exam (DASE)** evaluates children ranging in age from 2½ to 7 years in their ability to reproduce 30 sounds intelligibly. It is limited to looking at possible articulation problems, not the more general speech and language skills. The screening time for this test is approximately 5 minutes.

The **Denver Audiometric Screening Test (DAST)** screens children 3 years and older for serious hearing loss (25 dB or less). It uses pure tone audiometry and can identify children with hearing loss during the preschool years. The screening time for this procedure is approximately 5 to 10 minutes.

A prescreening tool, the **Pre-Screening Developmental Questionnaire (PDQ),** is another assessment instrument that is presented to the parents or guardian of the child. It requires a response to ten age-appropriate developmental questions about the child's abilities. The parent merely has to answer yes or no to each question. Negative responses are followed up with more precise developmental screening tools, such as those mentioned previously in this chapter.

Table 7. Other screening tools

Test	Developer(s) Author(s)	Age range
Denver Articulation Screening Exam (DASE)	University of Colorado Medical Center	2 1/2 years to 7 years
Denver Audiometric Screening Test (DAST)	University of Colorado Medical Center	3 years and older
Pre-Screening Developmental Questionnaire (PDQ)	University of Colorado Medical Center	1 month to 6 years
Denver Developmental Screening Test (DDST)	Frankenburg and Dodds	1 month to 6 years
Denver Eye Screening Test (DEST)	University of Colorado Medical Center	6 months or older

SUMMARY

The majority of the test instruments mentioned in this chapter are normed and well established. Additional information for these measures can be located in reference material developed by Oscar Buros in his *Mental Measurement Yearbook*. Several instruments that are mentioned are neither normed nor widely used but have been included to give the reader a perspective of the different types of evaluation tools that are available. A further description of some of these instruments can be located in Johnson and Bommarito's handbook on *Tests and Measurement in Child Development*. The reader is advised to be careful in selecting tests that are not normed or criterion referenced, and it is always wise to review their strong and weak points in publications on test information such as those described above.

SAMPLE CHECKLISTS

Title: AAMD Adaptive Behavior Scale (1974 revision)
Source: American Association on Mental Deficiency
5201 Connecticut Avenue, N.W.
Washington, D.C. 20015
Areas: Eating, toilet use, cleanliness, appearance, care of clothing, dressing and undressing, travel, other independent functioning, and 29 other skill areas

Title: Basic Skills Children from the Ages of 0-5 Years Should Acquire (Allessi and Gutman)
Source: Mary Free Bed Hospital and Rehabilitation Center
235 Wealthy, S. E.
Grand Rapids, Michigan 49503
Areas: Cognitive, affective, and motor skills

Title: BMT Assessment Instrument: Global Evaluation Scale (Watson)
Source: Luke S. Watson, Jr.
Behavior Modification Technology, Inc.
Box 597
Libertyville, Illinois 60048
Areas: Self-help skills, motor coordination, undesirable behavior, language, miscellaneous skills

Title: Camelot Behavioral Checklist (Foster) and
Skill Acquisition Program Bibliography (Tucker)
Source: Camelot Behavioral Systems
P.O. Box 607
Parsons, Kansas 67357

Areas: Self-help, vocational and numerical skills, physical development, and communication

Title: Commonwealth Plan for Education and Training of Mentally Retarded Children: COMPET (Pennsylvania Departments of Education and Public Welfare)

Source: Department of Education
         Box 911
         Harrisburg, Pa. 17105

Areas: Gross motor, fine motor, visual-motor, auditory, and tactile/kinesthetic skills, self-concept, communication, conceptual development, math, toileting, and 10 other skill areas

Title: Guide to Early Developmental Training

Source: Wabash Center for the Mentally Retarded, Inc.
         2000 Greenbush Street
         Lafayette, Indiana 47904

Areas: Balance and posture, perceptual-motor skills, locomotion, body image, cognitive development, language development, eating, and 3 other skill areas

Title: Learning Accomplishment Profile: LAP (Sanford)

Source: Kaplan School Supply Corporation
         600 Jonestown Road
         Winston-Salem, North Carolina 27103

Areas: Gross motor, fine motor, social, and self-help skills, cognitive development, language

Title: Meyer Children's Rehabilitation Institute Early Childhood Education Program Developmental Scales

Source: Meyer Children's Rehabilitation Institute
         444 S. 44th Street
         Omaha, Nebraska 68131

Areas: Expressive language, receptive language, visual-motor-perceptual skills, memory and general information, personal/social development, and other skill areas

Title: Minnesota Developmental Programming System (Bock, Hawkins, Jeyachandran, Tapper, Weatherman)

Source: Warren H. Bock
         Outreach Training Program
         301 Health Service Building
         St. Paul, Minnesota 55108

Areas: Gross and fine motor skills, eating, dressing, toileting, grooming, receptive language, expressive language, and 10 other skill areas

Title: Prescriptive Behavioral Checklist for the Severely Retarded
               (Popovich)
Source: University Park Press
               233 E. Redwood Street
               Baltimore, Maryland 21202
Areas: Eye-hand coordination, self-help skills, and language development

Title: Steps to Independence: A Skills Training Series for Children with
               Special Needs (Baker, Brightman, Heifitz, and Murphey)
Source: Research Press
               2611 North Mattis Avenue
               Champaign, Illinois 61820
Areas: Self-help readiness skills, basic motor skills, motor activities, eat-
               ing, dressing, grooming, housekeeping, and behavior prob-
               lems

Title: The TARC Assessment System (Sailor and Mix)
Source: Wayne Sailor Personnel Training Program
               Kansas Neurological Institute
               3107 W. 21st Street
               Topeka, Kansas 66604
Areas: Self-help, motor, communication, and social skills

Chapter 5
Considerations in
Program Planning

EDUCATIONAL PLAN FORMULATION

Following an initial assessment stage, it becomes necessary to interpret diagnostic findings and to formulate an educational plan for the child. This educational plan should be developed in concert with the professionals who will teach the child as well as the parents and those individuals who have evaluated the child. Once a plan is developed, curriculum areas and activities can be arranged in accordance with the plan that best serves the needs of that child.

Considering Learning Characteristics

Before planning any curriculum for this population of children, it is advisable that the teacher or individual charged with the responsibility of carrying out curricular objectives be familiar with the learning characteristics of typical 3- to 5-year-olds. For example, it is during this stage that the young child is learning the basic principles that govern the actions of objects and persons in the world (Horitz, 1978). This is also a time when he is expected to emulate societal behaviors that are considered acceptable, such as demonstrating appropriate sex-related roles, inhibiting antisocial behavior, and cooperating freely during social activities. Perhaps more than at any other time this is when the preschool-age child is forced into participating in a growing number of experiences that do not involve his immediate family. The rate of physical growth tends to slacken somewhat during this stage, while cognitive growth and language development appear to escalate rapidly.

Of critical importance is the realization that young children who are not considered disadvantaged bring to the school a variety of experiences and traditionally may have had far more opportunities than their disadvantaged peers to learn new skills and behaviors. Nondisadvantaged preschool children generally have an abundance of natural curiosity, typified by the stage during which they ask numerous "why" questions. They also are eager to be exposed to new experiences and seem to be in a continual state of cognitive exploration.

Language becomes more sophisticated during this stage, and it is quite common for the child to use adult-like grammatical forms and imitate the adult vocabulary he hears around him. This is also the time when children do not articulate as well as possible, have the need to talk quickly, and often do not listen to the responses of others. Bloom (1975) has suggested that children who come from environments in which adults listen to them and respond to what they are saying tend to develop better language skills than children who do not come from this type of environment.

Cognitive exploration usually is evident; the child seems to be figuring out how the world works. Piaget and Inhelder (1969) have suggested that activities encouraging exploration of spatial relationships and concepts, in addition to experiences that help the child follow complex relationships, are especially suited to the cognitive needs of the preschool child at this time.

It is important to reiterate that the disadvantaged preschool child traditionally comes from an environment that is characterized by low annual income of parents, high rate of unemployment, underutilization of human resources, poor housing, poor sanitary conditions, large families, inadequate living space, inadequate education, excessive reliance on welfare, and an overall attitude of hopelessness. Numerous studies, such as those cited by Bereiter and Engelmann (1966), dramatically point out that disadvantaged preschool children from lower socioeconomic backgrounds are severely delayed or retarded in almost every intellectual ability. Furthermore, they are at least one or more years behind their normal age-peers in language development, and, without intervention, this disparity appears to widen.

Balancing the Behavioral Domains

A strong preschool program can provide more than the expected academic and societal prerequisites for the disadvantaged child. It can also act as a sociocultural bridge between the background and environment of the child and the realities and demands of the school and society. It should be strongly emphasized that the preschool program must not act in any way to regulate or inculcate different social norms in its students but should include the richness and uniquenesses of the child's culture because it helps the student understand the demands for achievement and accomplishment that are an integral part of today's society.

In developing this program, there must be a careful balance between the social, cognitive, cultural, and emotional domains. The program must also address students' cultural discontinuities, especially where intensive enrichment may be warranted. Some individuals may wish to develop their program around certain established curriculum models that emphasize certain domains over others. For this reason, a brief summary follows of some curriculum models that have been relatively successful when used with the disadvantaged preschool child.

CURRICULUM MODELS

It is interesting to note that, before the mid 1960s and the Head Start movement, the majority of preschool and early childhood programs concentrated on using or modifying three existing models. The following models, many of which are still in use today, represent the major emphasis that was placed on preschool programming during that era.

Cognitive Developmental Model

The cognitive developmental model was perhaps one of the earliest models that attempted to promote positive attitudes toward school by improving oral language abilities, memory, discrimination learning, problem-solving ability, concept formation, general information, and comprehension. This model looks upon a child's development of cognitive abilities as occurring in a rather predictable sequence as proposed by Piaget and others (see Piaget and Inhelder, 1969). Ispa and Matz (1978) have reported that the utilization of a model based upon cognitive developmental theory is still in existence today, as demonstrated by programs like the High/Scope's First Chance model demonstration project supported by grant OEG-0-74-2720 from the United States Office of Education. Programs such as these have been highly influenced by what Ispa and Matz (1978) define as some basic concepts about how children learn.

> Given at least a minimum amount of emotional security, children are intrinsically motivated to exercise their emerging abilities . . . [through] an opportunity to make choices, experience success, and pace themselves.
> Intellectual development occurs through active transactions with adults, peers, real materials, and events.
> Language development proceeds naturally in an environment where children are encouraged to communicate their needs and ideas in day-to-day social interactions.
> A variety of media including gesture, drawing, construction, and dramatic play are involved in symbolic functioning.
> A setting designed to foster active learning and intrinsic motivation will also enhance children's self-esteem and promote positive social interaction among children and adults (pp. 167–168).

Perceptual-Motor Developmental Model

The perceptual-motor developmental model is best exemplified by the type of activities taught in a classic Montessori curriculum, with visual discrimination and visual motor integration being key elements. As in the Montessori program, sensory training and psychomotor learning, through the manipulation of materials, are stressed. The cardinal principles of this approach are to teach the student independence and self-control coupled with a strong degree of concentration. Ultimately this purports to allow the child to feel better about himself and exhibit a greater degree of self-confidence and maturity as well as an overall readiness for formal school learning.

Academic Skills Developmental Model

The academic skills developmental model attempts to get at the very core of why disadvantaged children fail by teaching them in a concentrated and intensive way the basic skills they need to achieve successfully in future grades. The model assumes that disadvantaged children fail in school mainly as a result of ineffective instruction, which often ignores their need to master language, reading, and arithmetic skills before the first grade. These academic skills are stressed so the students will not be at a disadvantage when they are brought together for the first time in a first grade with peers who have been taught this information in other preschool programs or who have learned it as a result of being taught at home. This model is best illustrated in the curriculum work done by Bereiter and Engelmann(1966) and is perhaps one of the most widely replicated programs for working with disadvantaged preschool children.

Deprivation Model

Few models have been adopted since those mentioned above with the exception of the *deprivation model,* which surfaced as the necessity for parent involvement and the home environment became evident. This model was developed to counteract the destructive effects poverty appeared to be having on the development of young children. With this type of model, the preschool setting, which had always been the site of the intervention program, and the teacher's role, which had always been as the agent to carry out the intervention, were modified to establish the *parent, not the teacher,* as the agent primarily responsible for much of the instruction the child would require. The home of the child became as important as the preschool classroom, and many activities were carried out and implemented at both sites (Miller and Dyer, 1975).

NEED FOR NEW CURRICULUM MODELS

It becomes patently obvious that there is a critical need to develop sensible curricula involving philosophies from many sources and many models for the disadvantaged preschool child. A totally eclectic approach need not be taken, *but each child should have a program that considers his individual needs.* The disadvantaged child who is not directly taught readiness or prereadiness skills in all areas, particularly in the academic areas, soon becomes lost in the mainstream of first grade and is often socially promoted until the degree of his delay becomes so obvious that he requires a special form of education. It is extremely important to remember that the teacher or individual working with the disadvantaged preschooler can develop a program and activities that encapsulate both content and process objectives suitable for this type of child without sacrificing herself to a curriculum that is significantly dependent upon drill, pressure, and a rigid adherence to rules. Unquestionably, the emphasis should be based upon how well a child can utilize his abilities in the cognitive, behavioral, and social domains. As a brief review, Appleton, Cliffton, and Goldberg (1975) have categorized these abilities as:

Cognitive
1. Attention skills such as persistence, curiosity, and exploration;
2. Perceptual skills, including the ability to notice discrepencies and learn from observation; and
3. Conceptual skills, such as the anticipation of consequences, taking the perspective of another person, planning and carrying out activities, developing strategies for problem-solving, and the acquisition of basic knowledge.

Behavioral Abilities
1. Motor skills such as manipulation of objects and control of body position;
2. Control skills, including the ability to carry out instructions and to inhibit impulsive behavior; and
3. Self-care skills such as toileting, eating in a regular manner, and so on.

Social Skills
1. The understanding and use of language;
2. The ability to use adults as resources by getting their attention and help at appropriate times; and
3. The development of such personal attributes as feeling of self-worth, independence, ability to express feelings, warmth, flexibility, and cooperation (p. 161).

(From *Review of Child Development Research*, F. D. Horowitz, ed. University of Chicago Press. Copyright 1975.)

It is not just *what* we teach the child that will make him successful or less than successful in school but it is also *how* we teach him. It is best to remember that children must be interested in what they are learning and there must be a purpose to why certain learning areas are emphasized above others. The preschool disadvantaged child, like other children, needs time to learn new concepts, and each child may have his own time table for learning. Perhaps the most important ingredient in teaching the preschool child is that he must be able to put to use what he is learning. It is therefore contingent upon the teacher to develop meaningful and functional objectives and activities that encourage this learning process.

Section III
THE CURRICULUM: BEHAVIORAL OBJECTIVES AND SUGGESTED ACTIVITIES

Chapter 6
Using The
Sample Curriculum

The sample curriculum provided in this section was developed to offer representative objectives and activities in those educational areas that are considered of primary importance when educating the disadvantaged preschool child.

FORMAT

The areas, which include cognitive development, socialization skills, motor development, language skills, music, art, industrial arts, and preacademic skills, are presented in a lesson plan format that the teacher may or may not wish to follow. Of critical importance is that each objective and activity should be evaluated according to the system of evaluation described in Chapter 4 or one with which the teacher feels confident.

The curriculum is presented in a format (see Figure 1) that allows the teacher to use her own teaching style and creativity as she strives to meet the individual needs of her students. For example, in the Activity column, a presented activity can be taught exactly as it is described, or the teacher can adapt or modify it according to the student's skill level. The Adaptations/ Modifications column has been developed to allow each child to enter or perform an activity without having to be penalized for a lack of experiences while at the same time offering enough challenge to motivate him. The column in which appropriate Materials are suggested lists those materials that the teacher should have available in order to carry out the specific objectives. Chapter 21, ''Curriculum Materials and Resources,'' provides a comprehensive listing of additional educational media that the teacher may wish to consider for possible inclusion in her instructional plans.

This sample curriculum should be supplemented by those objectives and activities the teacher develops as she begins to generate individual program plans for her students. It is hoped that the objectives and activities presented in

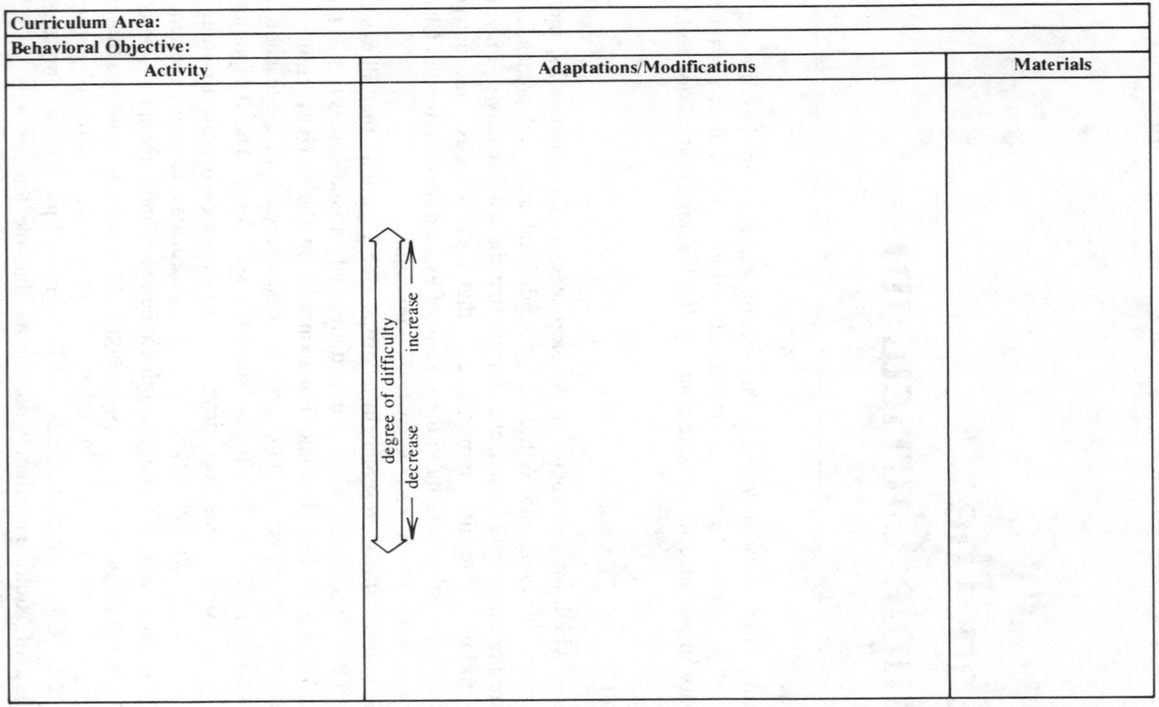
Curriculum Area:
Behavioral Objective:
Activity
Adaptations/Modifications
Materials
degree of difficulty
decrease
increase

Figure 1. Curriculum lesson plan format. (Acknowledgment is given to Dr. David Compton and Project SELF (Special Education for Leisure Fulfillment) for development of this format. Project SELF is funded by a grant from the Bureau of Education for the Handicapped, Division of Innovation and Development.)

this section will serve as a framework upon which to develop a comprehensive educational program for each child.

EVALUATION OF SAMPLE
CURRICULUM OBJECTIVES AND ACTIVITIES

While there are many norm-referenced instruments that can be used to evaluate a student's progress, such as those mentioned in Chapter 4, it becomes increasingly clear that the teacher will need additional information if she is to accurately assess whether or not her student is progressing. The writing of the sample objectives in the following curriculum in behavioral form is an attempt to define behavior in a way that can be evaluated and clearly demonstrated by the student. While the development of additional objectives and their accompanying activities is left to the expertise and imagination of each teacher, it is suggested that she may wish to evaluate these objectives using a diagnostic checklist type of system. Such a system offers a means of systematically recording and analyzing behavior and comparing it to a criterion previously set by the teacher or individual working with the child. Bender, Valletutti, and Bender (1976b) have suggested that checklists of this type be developed on the premise that the teacher sets a recommended performance level as part of each objective in the student's educational plan. For example, we may wish for a student to complete an activity three out of the four times he participates in it. The teacher may therefore set the criterion level as being three out of four times, or 75%.

There must also be ample opportunity for the student to demonstrate whether or not an objective has been learned to avoid the possibility of accidental occurrence. It is therefore the responsibility of the teacher to assign a required number of observations to authenticate that the behavior has indeed been learned. For many of the objectives in the sample curriculum that follows, there may be a different number of observations required for each activity. Some may only require four or five observations during a predetermined amount of time, while others may involve constant checks resulting in a great number of observations.

Once the student successfully performs an objective, it can be compared to the required performance level initially established by the teacher. This will result in a percentage of how close to criterion the student has mastered the task. Bender, Valletutti, and Bender's (1976b) simplified formula for developing this percentage is outlined below:

$$\text{Student Performance Level} = \frac{\text{Successful Student Performance}}{\text{Recommended Observations}}$$
$$\times\ 100\ =\ \underline{\hspace{2cm}}\%$$

For example, if a student is being asked to discriminate between large and small objects with 100% accuracy, the teacher may wish to observe him in this activity 4 times. If the student successfully discriminates large from small 2 out of the 4 times she observed him, he would have attained a 50% (2/4) performance level and would need continued work in this area.

It is important that the teacher carefully monitor her student's progress over a period of time. It is therefore suggested that, whatever instrument is selected to evaluate student progress, its administration be repeated on a scheduled basis so the information generated from these measurements can provide feedback to the teacher on how to modify or change the objectives of her program.

The checklists that have been mentioned at the end of Chapter 4 can provide models for developing additional checklists that may be more responsive to the requirements of the spec'fic curriculum the teacher may develop or be using. It is critical, however, that, whatever system is ultimately utilized, the evaluation instrument parallel the curriculum objectives and be used as an individual assessment for each student.

Chapter 7
Cognitive Development

There are numerous definitions for cognition and all include the ability to remember, see, or hear likenesses and differences, and to determine the relationship between ideas and things (Bluma et al., 1976). Cognition takes place within the individual; therefore, measurement can only occur on the basis of what the child says or does.

COGNITIVE ABILITIES AND ENVIRONMENTAL FACTORS

Numerous studies (Caldwell, 1976; Yarrow, Rubenstein, and Pederson, 1975) have cited the disastrous effects inadequate care has had on cognitive development. As a contrast, other studies and reports past (Rheingold and Bayley, 1959) and present (Ramey et al., 1978) have supported the view that successful social-environmental interventions may improve the cognitive abilities of children. The effects of maternal behavior on cognitive development have also been widely reported in the literature (Elardo, Bradley, and Caldwell, 1975; Engel and Keane, 1975). Maternal involvement with the child, provision of age-appropriate toys, and awareness of the child's needs have been suggested as being positively related to cognitive development. Other studies, such as one by Ainsworth and Bell (1974), have demonstrated that the children of middle class mothers who talk to them and work with them as infants, i.e., allowing them to explore and experience new situations, tend to do well on measures of cognitive development.

DEFICIENCIES IN LEARNING MODES
OF DISADVANTAGED PRESCHOOL CHILDREN

The storage of any information that a child has, whether the storage be for recall or reproduction, is termed memory. It is this memory ability that allows the child to name (label) and remember objects and symbols, such as safety logos and traffic signs, long before he can identify the letters of the alphabet or simple sight words. Traditionally, curricula involving the cognitive area emphasize activities ranging from the beginning awareness of one's self and one's environment to the awareness of objects, numbers, and the accompanying concepts. Repeating stories and the ability to compare objects, places, and things are also typical components of preschool curricula in this area. When disadvantaged children are given intelligence tests that purport to measure cognitive areas, they have typically scored 5 to 15 points below the expected average (Bloom, Davis, and Hess, 1965). Often their deficiencies result from, and are indicative of, a poor educational foundation in the areas of prereadiness and readiness skills. Those differences that are significant tend to fall in the area of school success–related subjects. That is to say that the preschool disadvantaged child often has not been exposed to the cognitive skills already mastered by his nondisadvantaged peers.

Equally important is that many preschool-age disadvantaged children are at least one year or more behind in language development, vocabulary size, sentence length, and use of grammatical structure. As early as 1963, Weaver indicated that many preschool disadvantaged children were functioning at the level of average children who were a year or more younger. The disadvantaged preschool child also tends to have great difficulty in his ability to manipulate symbols as he uses his verbal and reasoning abilities. This inability is considered to be a factor leading to poor academic achievement throughout the student's school years (Lavin, 1965).

While much has been said about the deficiencies in the learning modes of the disadvantaged preschool child, there are several areas of performance in which these children exhibit little or no delay or retardation. Among these are the ability to recall and employ immediate memory spans and to master specific rote-type learning tasks. Often, performance on items like these does not rely on previously learned strategies or concepts as do tests of reasoning. Some educators have concluded that the ability to learn tasks such as the above-mentioned is an indication that the disadvantaged child does not necessarily lack the fundamental capacity to learn but actually lacks the opportunity for an enriched learning environment.

Today, it is much more accurate to state that a child who is considered disadvantaged may very well have lacked exposure to an appropriate learning situation staffed with skilled teachers, and has yet to recognize the importance of school. The disadvantaged preschooler is often restricted not only in the opportunities for learning but also in the way he learns. Techniques such as exploration, trial and error, imitation, and participation are all methods through which a disadvantaged child can learn, but often there are only minimal opportunities for these types of interactions within the home. Children also learn through pain and pleasure as well as by communicating their needs or feelings. Again, the disadvantaged preschool child is often restricted in communicating his needs, and does so mainly in crisis situations.

APPROACHES TO LEARNING
IN THE PRESCHOOL CHILD'S ENVIRONMENT

Exploration

Exploration, one of the ways through which a child can learn, can be encouraged by providing a variety of materials and objects to the child and encouraging him to explore and play with them. Objects of varying sizes, shapes, weights, textures, etc., can provide opportunities for a young child to compare objects and to explore materials. Outdoor exploration can also be encouraged, specifically by taking walks through the neighborhood so the child is able to expand his awareness of the scope of his environment.

Trial and Error

A trial and error approach is an attempt to profit from learning to do a task successfully or learning from the mistakes encountered while trying to complete the task. Trial and error approaches often help a young child accept his mistakes as a step toward accomplishing a specific goal. It is always advisable to provide young children with experiences that allow them to use a trial and error approach in specific situations, since this tends to be one of the more common ways that most individuals learn.

Pain and Pleasure

Learning through experiencing pain and pleasure is a concept that is often used in the behavioral sciences. It is clear that pain is one of our most vivid experiences, and young children quickly learn to avoid situations that may cause pain. Similarly, pleasure or pleasurable experiences tend to encourage a student to search for similar pleasurable experiences. Pain and pleasure experiences help to develop a child's observation abilities, and are critical components of the learning process.

Imitation

Those students who learn through the process of imitation must have the opportunity to imitate good models. The very early studies in human behavior have offered strong proof that children learn by observing and then imitating. What is especially important to realize here is that the young, disadvantaged preschool child can achieve success in this area without having to verbalize any specific responses. This mode of learning may be particularly relevant for those children who are restricted or delayed in language development. Cognitive skills can also be fostered by encouraging children to join in ongoing activities, songs, games, and stories because much incidental learning is achieved even by the child who does not have an active role.

CURRICULAR OBJECTIVES AND ACTIVITIES

The following sample curricular objectives and activities range from beginning awareness of self and the environment of the child to the ability to make comparisons, repeat stories, recognize likenesses and differences, and relate events in sequential order.

Curriculum Area: Cognitive Development

Behavioral Objective: The child discriminates between *large* and *small*.

Activity	Adaptations/Modifications	Materials
Seat the student at a table, desk, or other work area. Place a number of blocks (5–6) on the table in front of the student. Call the student's attention to the fact that some blocks are small and some are large. Ask the student to sort the blocks, placing the large blocks in one pile and the small blocks in another. Praise the student's efforts.	Using 12 blocks, graduated in size from small to large, ask the student to arrange them according to size. Using 8 blocks, graduated in size from small to large, ask the student to arrange them according to size. Using 5–10 blocks, assorted large and small, ask the student to sort them according to size. Using 4 blocks, assorted large and small, ask the student to sort them according to size. Using 2 blocks, one large and one small, show the student the difference in size. ← increase decrease → degree of difficulty	Chair Desk or table 10 blocks, large and small Assortment of blocks, graduated in size from large to small

61

Curriculum Area: Cognitive Development

Behavioral Objective: The child identifies and names the parts of his face and body.

Activity	Adaptations/Modifications	Materials
Stand in front of a mirror with the child. Touch the various parts of your body and face, naming each body part or facial feature as you touch it. Encourage the child to imitate your actions and repeat the names of the body parts. Repeat the activity until the child can correctly point to and name the parts of his face and body.	Stand in front of the child; touch a part of your body, name it, and move it in some way (wave your hand, tap your foot). Ask the student to touch a part of his body, to say its name, and to make it move. Give the student a life-size doll or puzzle; point to the various body parts and say the name of each. Ask the child to imitate your actions, first using the doll or puzzle and then on his own body. Give the student a doll or stuffed toy; point to the doll's eyes, your eyes, and the child's eyes, and say "eyes." Encourage the child to say "eyes." Repeat for the other parts of the body. Show the child large color pictures of faces; point to the eyes, say "eyes," and ask the student to imitate your behavior and say "eyes." Repeat the activity for nose, mouth, ears, forehead, and cheek.	Mirror Doll Life-size doll Body parts puzzle Pictures of faces

degree of difficulty increase ← → decrease

62

Curriculum Area: Cognitive Development		
Behavioral Objective: The child names common objects.		
Activity	Adaptations/Modifications	Materials
Seat the student at a desk or table. Place a variety of familiar objects on the table in front of the student. Point to each object and ask the student, "What is this?" Praise the student if he correctly names the object. If he fails to do so, point to the object, name it, and ask the student to repeat the name of the object after you say it. Repeat the activity for each object until the student can name each one.	Place familiar objects into a "mystery box." Ask the student to reach in, choose an object, and name it. Ask the student to close his eyes. Place a familiar object in his hand, and ask the student to name the object. Take a walk in the neighborhood, pointing to objects and asking the student to name them. Walk around the classroom, pointing to objects and asking the student to name them. Beginning with one object and adding one object at a time, complete the activity. Using one object at a time, complete the activity.	Chair Desk or table Familiar objects Mystery box (a box with a hole cut in the cover so a child's hand can fit through it to choose the object)

degree of difficulty — increase ← / decrease →

63

Curriculum Area: Cognitive Development

Behavioral Objective: The child names objects and identifies their purpose.

Activity	Adaptations/Modifications	Materials
Seat the child at a desk or table. Place a number of familiar objects on the table in front of the child (for example, comb, toy, pencil, scissors). Ask the child to identify which object is used for a particular purpose; for example, "Which one do you play with?" or "Which one do you use to cut paper?" As the child points to the appropriate object, ask him to say the word "toy," "scissors," etc. Correct any incorrect responses; praise correct ones.	*degree of difficulty decrease →* *← increase* Repeat the activities with the child playing the part of the teacher and you the child. Identify some objects correctly and some incorrectly. Praise the child for correcting your errors. Show the child a picture of an object, and ask him to pantomime its use until the other children guess what the object is. Show the child familiar objects (for example, hammer, spoon, vacuum cleaner, broom), and ask him to "act out" how they are used and describe what he is doing (for example, "I'm eating with a spoon"). Repeat the activity, beginning with one object and adding new ones, one at a time, until the child can name each object and identify its purpose. Repeat the activity, beginning with one object and adding new objects, one at a time, until the child can name each object.	Common objects Pictures of common objects Desk or table

64

Curriculum Area: Cognitive Development

Behavioral Objective: The child recites or sings rhymes and songs from memory.

Activity	Adaptations/Modifications	Materials
Sing or recite a nursery rhyme. Do this on a daily basis. After you have done this three or four days, ask the child to sing along with you. Once he is able to sing the entire rhyme with you, encourage him to sing it alone. Praise the child's efforts.	*degree of difficulty* ← increase / decrease → Put on a class "talent" show, and ask each child to sing a song or recite a rhyme from memory. Act out a rhyme or commercial jingle. Ask the children to guess what you are acting out and recite it to you. Make a tape recording of each child singing a jingle or reciting a rhyme or series of words he has memorized. Play the recording as a "radio" show. Ask each child to choose a commercial jingle and sing it for his classmates (McDonalds's, Coke, 7-Up, Libby's, etc.). Recite one-line songs or jingles. Ask the child to repeat it after you until he is able to do so independently. Play records or tapes of nursery rhymes or songs during rest period or quiet time. Encourage the student to listen and sing along quietly.	Tape recorder Records of rhymes or songs Tapes of rhymes or songs Record player

Curriculum Area: Cognitive Development

Behavioral Objective: The child repeats the details of a story told to him.

Activity	Adaptations/Modifications	Materials
Read a story to the child. Use many gestures, changes of tone and voice, and facial expressions to make the story interesting and memorable to the child. Ask questions about the story: "Who were the characters?" "What were they doing?" "What color was the house?" etc. Reread parts of the story to help the child remember details he has forgotten.	Encourage the child to use a tape recorder and tell a story about himself. Play the story for the class. Ask a group of children to act out a familiar story, and have the other children try to guess what the story is. Play "Something Is Missing": read a familiar story, stopping frequently and asking the child to tell "What is missing." Help the child compose a language experience story about a recent experience or trip. Emphasize correct sequence and detail. Read current events stories from newspapers and magazines, and ask the child questions about the stories read. Read simple, short stories and repeat them often until the child can relate the details and answer questions about the story. Read stories a page at a time in an "installment" fashion to allow the child time to absorb the details of the story.	Stories Tape recorder Paper for language experience chart Magic markers Newspaper articles

degree of difficulty

← increase   decrease →

66

Curriculum Area: Cognitive Development

Behavioral Objective: The child relates his experiences in sequential order.

Activity	Adaptations/Modifications	Materials
Take the child on a field trip to a zoo, park, playground. While on the trip, call attention to and describe sights and sounds of interest. Upon returning to school, encourage the child to describe the trip, step by step. Assist the child in his efforts to put the events in order by saying, "First you . . . , next you . . . , then you . . . , and last you . . . ." Praise the child's efforts.	Plan activities for the child that require following an exact sequential order (art activities, recipes, model or craft kits). Upon completion, ask the child to explain what he has done in the correct order. Ask the student's parents to tell you of any pleasant experiences the child has recently had. Find out the details, and encourage the student to share his experience with the class. Help him tell the story in sequence by providing prompts, such as "first," "next," "last." With felt cutouts of a familiar story, ask the child to tell the story in order, using the cutouts as prompts to his memory. Praise his efforts. Repeat the activity using the daily class schedule as the experience rather than a field trip. Ask the child to list the daily activities, beginning with arrival and ending with dismissal. Develop language experience stories to describe class activities or trips. Read them with the child and ask him if he can guess "what comes next."	Experience chart paper Magic marker Felt cutouts of story characters Art projects Recipes Model kits Craft kits

degree of difficulty ← increase   decrease →

Curriculum Area: Cognitive Development		
Behavioral Objective: The child sorts objects and matches them in pairs.		
Activity	Adaptations/Modifications	Materials
Seat the child at a table or desk, or on the floor. Place a laundry basket containing pairs of socks in front of the student. Demonstrate sorting and matching the socks into pairs. Explain to the child that you want him to sort and match the socks. Offer assistance if necessary, and praise the child's efforts.	Place a selection of hinges on a table in front of the child. Ask the student to sort the hinges into matched pairs. Use the hinges in an art, craft, or industrial arts project. Place pieces of jewelry that comes in pairs (for example, earrings, cufflinks, barrettes) in front of the child. Ask the child to sort the jewelry into matched pairs. Place a pile of clothing in front of the child. (Use articles that come in pairs, such as, gloves, mittens, shoes, and socks.) Instruct the student to sort through the pile and find matching pairs of gloves, mittens, socks, and shoes. Praise the child's efforts. Play "Shoe Detective": Ask each child to remove his shoes, and place them in a pile in the middle of the floor. Mix the shoes up, and instruct the children to become "shoe detectives" and find their shoes in the pile. Repeat the activity, using two pair of socks that are very different in color, for example, one pair of white socks and one pair of red. degree of difficulty: ← increase / decrease →	Table or desk Chair Pairs of socks Children's shoes Gloves Mittens Shoes Earrings Cufflinks Barrettes Hinges

68

Curriculum Area: Cognitive Development		
Behavioral Objective: The child sorts or groups objects into categories.		
Activity	Adaptations/Modifications	Materials
Show the child pictures and objects of food. Point to each food item or picture of food and name it. Go through the pictures and items, and this time say, "Apple—an apple is food," "Bread—bread is food."	Set up a "Grocery Store" game: Give the child pictures of or objects found in a grocery store. Ask the child to pretend he is the stock clerk and arrange the items for his store. Encourage the child to name objects and categories as he works. Give the child pictures of objects that belong to a category not previously worked on. Encourage and assist him as he tries to name the new category (for example, fruit, hats). Give the child pictures of animals and furniture, and ask him to sort them according to categories. Repeat the activity, using pictures and items of clothing, furniture, means of transportation, animals, plants, money, etc. Repeat the activity, using one picture or object at a time. As the child identifies the picture or object, add a new one.	Pictures of objects Objects

degree of difficulty — increase ← / decrease →

Curriculum Area: Cognitive Development		
Behavioral Objective: The child identifies categories within categories.		
Activity	Adaptations/Modifications	Materials
Seat the student at a desk or table. Give the student silverware. Say, "This is silverware. Can you see any differences among the silverware?" Point out that forks, knives, and spoons are silverware but are also forks, knives, and spoons. Ask the child to sort out the silverware into piles of knives, forks, and spoons. Offer assistance if necessary, and praise the child's efforts.	*degree of difficulty — decrease → / ← increase* Give the student a selection of silverware and kitchen utensils (for example, wooden spoons, measuring spoons, meat forks), and ask the student to categorize them. Give the student forks, knives, spoons, salad forks, steak knives, and serving spoons. Ask the student to separate them into piles of forks, knives, and spoons, and then into groups of specific types of forks, knives, and spoons. Give the student three forks, three knives, and three spoons, and ask him to separate them into piles of forks, knives, and spoons. Give the student a fork, knife, and spoon. Point out the differences and similarities; they are all silverware, but each is different.	Silverware Kitchen utensils

Chapter 8
Socialization Skills

Socialization skills have been defined as those appropriate behaviors that involve interacting and living with other people (Shearer and Shearer, 1972). Socialization behaviors are especially observable during the preschool years as the young child works and plays with his peers, siblings, playmates, and members of his immediate and extended family. As the child begins to interact socially, he begins to develop specific capabilities that affect his ability to handle different types of societal expectations. In essence, the development of appropriate socialization skills dictates how successful a child will be in adjusting to his environment and to society.

While children learn through many active ways, including imitation and participation, they also learn by observing how others react to situations with which they are unfamiliar. Many socialization skills, such as smiling and cooperating, are common to most cultures, but many others are indigenous to specific cultures. For example, the preschool child who interacts in a family that encourages conversation at meals may not parallel the same age child who is from a culture in which there is rarely any communication at meal time. It is important to consider that, while certain cultures do not necessarily stress socialization skills, the teacher of the preschool handicapped child must decide which socialization skills will be critical acquisitions for the child as he advances into the primary grades. The young preschool child who has delayed socialization skills and is then thrust into a large social group with a mixture of children from different backgrounds will soon find himself at a disadvantage. Often he will feel left out or frustrated because he has not developed the interpersonal skills the other children possess.

PLAY AND PEER INTERACTIONS

When the child enters the preschool world, new experiences, relationships, and avenues for learning immediately become available. Attachments to the teacher and to peers often develop in a multiplicity of ways. The child begins to develop play strategies, but initial play or play interaction may be of an isolated rather than an interactive nature. Conversations are apt to be in the form of monologues, which are not responsive to what others are saying. In essence, the preschoolers are in a world by themselves where the teacher often acts as mediator of problems that arise from peer rivalry, during activity selection, or because of territorial conflicts.

This stage is often characterized by the child's becoming aware of his body; he often becomes quite modest about exposing it. Privacy becomes a central issue to the child even if he comes from a home that is devoid of privacy. Many fears surface during these preschool years, especially those concerning the child's vulnerability to death. Preschoolers often resort to the security of playing at being a baby and ask to be called "pet" infant names that reinforce this feeling of security. It is only after the child feels somewhat sure of himself and his role in the preschool that he begins to play coopera- tively with other children.

LaVeck (1978) has suggested that three important aspects of social rela- tionships evolve during the preschool years. The first is *sympathy,* which in many ways is an empathetic reaction to someone else's stress, such as when another child cries and there is need to comfort and offer consolation. Second is *leadership,* which often surfaces at the preschool level and provides evi- dence that even the young child quickly learns to assess situations and make decisions. Third is *aggression,* which typically involves disputes over pos- sessions such as *who* is going to play with *whom* and using *what* rules. It is interesting to note that aggression, which is almost totally physical with the younger preschool child, quickly turns to verbal aggression as the child grows older and becomes assimilated into the primary school setting. Peer interac- tions begin to be fostered at this time, although procedures need to be de- veloped by the teacher to encourage and maintain these exchanges. Nordquist (1978) reported that teacher attention, peer attention, peer modeling, and physical and spatial features were often related to peer interactions. These events can be controlled, in part, by the teacher to ensure some degree of continued peer interaction.

ROLE PLAYING

Murphy and Leeper (1974) have stressed that it is essential that young chil- dren be able to identify themselves with grown-ups whose standards are high and whose approach to life is worth copying. Thus, it is important that the preschool disadvantaged child learn to imitate a variety of socialization skills that are realistic and that will be highly regarded and accepted by society in general. While there is universal agreement among adults that children need to learn such societal behaviors as self-control, there are differences of opinion as to how to encourage the development of these skills. Handling situations with which all children come in contact, such as the ability to become aggressive, feel hurt, or angry, must be taught in an organized fashion so that the young child learns that there are reasons for why people have different feelings and why people react to situations in different ways.

Avoiding Use of Punishment

When a young preschool child reacts or acts in a way that is not socially acceptable, it is the teacher's responsibility to help the child learn alternative and more appropriate ways of handling the situation. Punishment, angry words, hitting, or spanking rarely have a place in an early childhood program because they tend to make the child angry and resentful and will result in other inappropriate behaviors (Murphy and Leeper, 1974). Punishment, more specifically, tends to leave the child with confused feelings. Several established facts demonstrate why punishment is ultimately not effective:

1. It is more effective to promote desirable behaviors than to punish undesirable ones. Young children tend to associate punishment with select situations and often will become petrified about participating in any situation that even faintly resembles one in which they might have been punished.
2. Children learn to dislike people who punish them, and the idea that punishment will build a respect for people is often not valid. The child soon learns to avoid these individuals rather than being able to accept what they are trying to do.
3. Children will do most anything to avoid punishment. They may resort to lying, cheating, or other behaviors that may help them from being caught in an act for which they know they will be punished.
4. Recent studies have indicated that punishment, especially with young children, may cause a high degree of anxiety. This increased anxiety in turn leads to their being ineffective in other school-related areas.
5. Perhaps one of the most negative effects punishment can have on the preschool child is that the child may imitate the punishment he has received with other children or his siblings.

Generally punishment should not be advocated, except in extreme circumstances; it is often a short lived type of consequence that rarely alters the child's behavior over time. There are also many children at the preschool level who are immune to punishment because it has been such a traditional part of how they are treated in their environment. This is especially true for the preschool disadvantaged child whose impoverished background has made him accept punishment as a way of life.

It is therefore imperative that a teacher who observes a child behaving inappropriately set the example of how to react to the situation. It is important to remember that a young child tends to model the behavior he is able to observe. Thus the child who is angry and upset needs comforting at that particular time, or he needs to witness someone who is angry and upset being comforted by the teacher. It is also suggested that the teacher be firm but, at the same time, avoid being a "dictator," for whom the child fearfully follows what is being required of him but then is unable to generalize the expected behavior to other situations. The teacher should also explain why a behavior is unacceptable so the child will realize what he has done wrong. This explanation should be accompanied by reassurance that, although the teacher does not approve of his behavior, she still loves or cares for him personally.

Providing Reinforcement

A positive way by which a teacher can show concern and love for a young child is to use a system of physical contact or reinforcement. Reinforcement can be provided in numerous ways, including verbal approval, nonverbal approval, or physical contact. For example, *verbal approval* can consist of telling the child that he has done a good job, or telling him you are happy about the way he performed a specific task. Single words like "great," "good," or "fantastic" all serve to let the child know you feel he is performing the way you think he should.

For other children, verbal praise does not act as well as *nonverbal approval*. In this instance, just smiling or winking at a child allows him to know you value what he is doing; your eyes can also let the child know that you are watching him and that his performance meets your expectations of him. It is quite common to see a child perform even at a higher level after this form of reinforcement, because he has been told through your nonverbal approval that he is doing fine.

Perhaps the major type of reinforcement that can be used in a class setting, without drawing special attention to the child, is that which incorporates *physical contact*. This may simply involve patting a student on the shoulder or sitting next to the student while he is doing a task. It is important during this type of reinforcement to touch the student and perhaps allow him to know by this touch that you feel he is doing a good job. Occasional hugging or holding a student's hand often provides the closeness the preschool disadvantaged child may be missing in his home environment. While the authors do not advocate assuming a parent surrogate role, it is important that the teacher recognize when a child does need this extra support and praise and, whenever possible, provide it. It is the teacher's responsibility to help the child feel comfortable in his learning environment and to offer support through all of the emotional, psychological, and educational systems provided by the ongoing preschool program.

Parent-Teacher Cooperation

It is most important that the teacher who finds specific approaches or methods that work well with a particular child share this information with the parents and others who play roles in the young child's life. Cooperative exchange between school and home regarding the development of socialization skills is critical. Often, the young child is treated one way in a school situation and a different way at home, leading either the parent or the teacher to say that the child's behavior is erratic, when, in essence, inconsistent handling has encouraged the behavior.

TEACHING SOCIALIZATION SKILLS THROUGH PLAY

Much has also been written about the process of teaching socialization skills through the medium of play. Smilansky (1968) has advocated that young children should be given suitable play materials and opportunities to play in a noninterfering atmosphere. In essence, you allow the child to minimize his fears and anxieties by releasing his emotional energy through play activities. It is Smilansky's belief that a free and permissive atmosphere often allows children to reveal their preferred type of play activity and provides the teacher with information she may use at a later time to reinforce specific preacademic or socialization skills.

When incorporating play activities into a curriculum, it is important to realize that most preschool children, particularly the disadvantaged preschool child, enjoy all types of physical movement and display a sharp interest in physical phenomena such as animals and plants, as evidenced by their continual gravitation to activities of this nature. Preschool is also the age at which children begin to play social games involving pretend playmates and friends, although the level of pretending depends upon the culture group as well as the level of sophistication of the individual student. It is interesting to note that many children from a wide range of socioeconomic levels, and most specifically those children of high or middle socioeconomic backgrounds, tend to enjoy movement games that are highly competitive, involve activities that incorporate investigation, and promote analysis of why things occur. Children from a disadvantaged background often are more interested in concrete types of simple movement activities and frequently need to be coaxed into developing an interest in tasks that have traditionally been considered creative in nature.

Most recently, however, the disadvantaged child has been credited with creatively dealing with his home environment. Many times this youngster has had to resort to using the materials and objects in his immediate world rather than incorporating the commercially made or prepared materials that more affluent children may have available to them. It is not uncommon to see these children playing games that appear to have no codified set of rules but rules that are flexible and change constantly. In essence, their creativity has many times been a forced function as a result of their lack of traditional resources.

The socialization process of young children can be strongly enhanced by play activities, provided the child has suitable play materials and opportunities to play in a permissive, noninterfering atmosphere (Smilansky, 1968). If the atmosphere is appropriate, the child learns to minimize his fears and anxieties by using play as a release and, in addition, may improve his physical skills, which ultimately may make him more acceptable to his peers. Unfortunately, the disadvantaged preschool child does not always want to participate in social games such as "Let's Pretend" and is often quite satisfied to remain relatively quiet in the classroom. Many of these children are afraid to take a chance at interacting with others in games that they do not know, and their fear of failure is often the paramount reason for lack of play involvement.

Social-Dramatic Play

It has often been suggested that social-dramatic play is a major means of naturally meeting the needs of the culturally disadvantaged child. This type of play requires the child to utilize his past experiences and previously learned knowledge and incorporate them in almost life-like situations. This is a time when the child can express, through action and words, how he feels and what he has learned about certain situations. It is imperative that disadvantaged preschool children be allowed the opportunities for this type of play because they often have had few opportunities for it in their own environment.

Social-dramatic play is a voluntary social play activity in which preschool children can participate. It can be a main avenue in meeting the needs of the culturally disadvantaged child. By its very nature, social-dramatic play requires the child to use his potential, as well as his knowledge, to perform in life-like situations. In essence, he learns to play his role by drawing on his past experiences of observing situations that involved other people, without having to rely on a great fund of new knowledge, which is often absent from the disadvantaged preschool child's educational repertoire. Most young preschool children enjoy social-dramatic play, and it is easily integrated into nursery schools and kindergarten programs. Too often, however, the utilization of play to teach new or reinforce previously taught concepts is relegated to the end of the year, holiday time, or special occasions during the school term. It would appear that a more successful approach would be to incorporate social-dramatic play into all teaching areas because it will allow the disadvantaged child to broaden his concept formation as well as promote language development through interaction with his peers, adults, and others he may either observe or interact with in society. While this specific area seems to be such a critical one for integration into the preschool program, it is surprising that few studies mention social play when discussing the teaching of the disadvantaged preschool child. Again, like other subjects mentioned in curricula for the preschool disadvantaged child, social-dramatic play must be *taught* to the child.

The development of social relationships can be reinforced through social-dramatic play. Often parents' expectations of their child do not transcend what their expectations were for themselves or what their parents' were for them, and, therefore, developing a social relationship component to the curricula may be very difficult. The teacher must carefully explain to the parents why she is teaching certain play activities to their child without offending the parents or having them feel that their child's lack of specific skills is a reflection on their own upbringing or the way they have raised their child.

Smilansky (1968) lists several indirect influences associated with social-dramatic play. These include:

1. Providing for normal emotional relationships essential for healthy identification
2. Providing for conceptual, informational, and verbal means essential for understanding human behaviors and social relationships
3. Developing the power of abstraction and imagination
4. Encouraging possible social relationships of the child with both parents and peers, based on tolerance and self-discipline

During dramatic play activities children often know exactly what role they want to act out. The older preschool child typically demands realistic props for his imaginary play (LaVeck, 1978). This is also the time when many imaginary playmates materialize and children begin to stretch the truth to suit their immediate needs. It is often difficult for the preschool child, especially the disadvantaged preschool child, to perceive the consequences of inappropriate behavior. Extenuating circumstances for activities or situations that have not materialized are often not accepted.

The parents' pattern for social behavior and social relationships often plays an instrumental role in how well the child responds to social-dramatic play. Without question the parents' interaction between themselves, between parents and their children, and between parents and other adults in their environment will be mirrored in some way by the child's behavior. The degree of imitation of what one sees is often underestimated and yet may account for many of the atypical behaviors that young children often exhibit at the most inopportune time.

With some degree of teacher-parental cooperation and intervention, social-dramatic play can provide many of the skills the preschool child will need if he is to survive in the school world.

CURRICULAR OBJECTIVES AND ACTIVITIES

If a primary goal of the preschool program is to facilitate the overall growth of the child in behavioral, attitudinal, and emotional development, it is contingent upon the teacher to make sure that the child receives maximal programming to promote his social integration into the school society. This social learning can be enhanced by promoting positive social contacts with peers as well as with those adults with whom the student interacts. As mentioned previously, it is important that the teacher know when to praise the child and to do so only under circumstances that warrant it. Role playing and social-dramatic activities should also be capitalized upon because they do much to promote successful social interactions. The following curricular objectives and activities have been designed to facilitate efforts toward these goals.

Curriculum Area: Socialization Skills		
Behavioral Objective: The child shares toys and takes turns.		
Activity	Adaptations/Modifications	Materials
Plan an art activity. Seat the children at tables or desks. Pass out materials to only half of the children. Ask each child with art materials to choose a child with none as his partner in the art project. Encourage the pairs of children to work together, sharing materials with each other and taking turns using materials such as scissors and glue. Commend the children on their art projects, stressing the roles of cooperation and sharing that helped the children create their art projects.	Encourage parents and guardians to plan activities and situations that will encourage the child to share and take turns (for example, playing board games with the family, sharing toys with a sibling or friend). Assist the children in preparing sandwiches for lunch or a snack. Seat the children at a table; give each child a plate and some children two sandwiches, others two beverages. Tell the children to share what they have with someone who needs it and they in return will share what they have. When each child has a sandwich and a beverage, eat lunch. Praise the students for sharing. During daily class activities, remind the student to share and take turns. Encourage this by planning activities that foster sharing and taking turns. Play games such as "Follow the Leader" or "Simon Says" that require leaders. Encourage the children to take turns at being the leader.	Art materials Tables or desks Chairs Plates Cups Napkins Sandwich filling Bread Beverage Napkins Knives (for cutting sandwiches)

degree of difficulty   ← increase   decrease →

Curriculum Area: Socialization Skills

Behavioral Objective: The child treats the belongings of others with respect.

Activity	Adaptations/Modifications	Materials
Take the child on a tour of the classroom and school building. Point out and name the furnishings in the school and classroom. Explain to the child that the furnishings belong to the school but the children are allowed to use them. Impress upon the child that since the furnishings belong to others, the children must be especially careful when using them. Stress that when others let us use their property, we should be responsible enough to care for it.	Discuss vandalism: Talk about it; read articles from the newspaper or magazines about property damage. Use examples the child will understand, such as broken windows or damaging boarded up houses. Explain that vandalizing property is against the law and should never be done. Ask each child to bring into the classroom a toy, game, book, or record he would like to share with his classmates. Encourage children to ask others if they may use items belonging to others during a supervised play period. Remind children to be especially careful when using the property of others. Bring into the classroom toys, games, books, and records that belong to you. Explain that these belong to you and you would like to share them with the children. Encourage the child to share your things and to be especially careful with them. At home, encourage parents to share games, books, and magazines with the child. Remind him that he may use these shared items as long as he treats them with care. decrease → degree of difficulty ← increase	*The School's* Games Books Magazines Records Educational equipment School furnishings *The Teachers's* Games Books Records Magazines *The Child's* Games Books Personal property Newspaper articles

Curriculum Area: Socialization Skills		
Behavioral Objective: The child waits when necessary.		
Activity	Adaptations/Modifications	Materials
At various times during the school day (for example, between activities, before school begins, or time before lunch) tell the child he must wait. Say, "You must wait 5 minutes before it will be time for lunch" or "You must wait 2 minutes and then you may go out for recess." At the end of the allotted time say, "The 2 minutes have passed. I liked the way you waited and you may go to recess (lunch, art, a new activity)."	*degree of difficulty* ← decrease · increase → Role play visits to the doctor, dentist, bakery, beauty shop. Pretend that there will be a 5-, 10-, 15-minute wait, and role play waiting patiently. Plan a cooking activity that requires timing like baking a cake or cooking hard boiled eggs. Set a timer, and encourage the child to watch the timer and try to judge how much time is left. Explain that waiting is sometimes necessary. Have a countdown at bus time or dismissal. Say, "There are 5 minutes until bus time (or dismissal); get your things together," "Now you have 4 minutes," "3 minutes," "2 minutes," "1 minute" until dismissal time. Praise the child for waiting patiently. When two children want the same toy or game, give the game to one child and tell the other he must wait. Set a specific length of time (5 minutes, 10 minutes), and instruct the child that he may play for 10 minutes and then share the toy with the other child who will wait 10 minutes and then play for 10 minutes.	Toys Games Timer Cooking equipment Cooking supplies

Curriculum Area: Socialization Skills

Behavioral Objective: **The child behaves courteously.**

Activity	Adaptations/Modifications	Materials
As part of daily classroom activities and during conversations with the student, use "Please," "Thank you," and "Excuse me" at appropriate times. Discuss with the student the fact that well mannered persons use these polite expressions as part of their working vocabulary. Encourage the child to include "Please," "Thank you," and "Excuse me" at appropriate times in his conversations. Praise the student's efforts.	Take the child on a shopping trip (for groceries, school supplies, etc.). Purchase items and point out the salesperson's courtesy ("May I help you?" and "Thank you") when waiting on you. Encourage the child to be a courteous consumer by saying "Will you please help me?" and "Thank you."	
	Role play situations that require good manners and courteous responses (for example, asking a sales clerk for help, asking a policeman for directions, asking a peer or sibling to share a toy). Praise the child's courteous responses.	
	Encourage parents and guardians to use "Please" and "Thank you" in conversations with their children, and ask them to encourage the child to imitate their use of "Please" and "Thank you."	
	Ask the child to hand you something, saying "Please hand me the papers" and saying "Thank you" once he does so. Reverse roles, with the child asking for something saying "Please" and "Thank you." Comment on his use of verbal courtesies.	

degree of difficulty ← increase   decrease →

Curriculum Area: Socialization Skills

Behavioral Objective: The child introduces himself to others.

Activity	Adaptations/Modifications	Materials
On the first day of school or as you greet the children at the door, encourage the child to introduce himself to you and his peers. Demonstrate how to do this by saying, "Hello, my name is _____," Encourage the child to respond to your introduction by saying, "Hello, my name is _____." Practice on a daily basis during classroom activities.	degree of difficulty <- decrease increase -> Instruct the student that should he ever get lost or need help, he should seek out a policeman, introduce himself, and explain his problem. Role play this situation. At recess, lunch, and other interclass activities, encourage the child to introduce himself to other children. Praise his good manners and friendliness. Role play situations in which it would be inappropriate for the student to introduce himself. For example, he should not introduce himself to strangers or salespeople. Emphasize the situations in which the student should *not* introduce himself to others. Role play situations in which it would be appropriate for the child to introduce himself to others, for example, the first day of school, meeting new children on the playground, meeting the parents of his friends.	

83

Curriculum Area: Socialization Skills		
Behavioral Objective: The child works cooperatively as a member of a group.		
Activity	Adaptations/Modifications	Materials
Assign each child to a work project team consisting of four children. Give each project team a group activity or chore to complete (pass out papers, clean art tables, wash paint brushes). Supervise the team as it works, encouraging each child to complete his share of the assignment and to cooperate with his fellow workers. Praise the child's efforts.	*degree of difficulty* — decrease / increase Develop an assembly line art project. Assign each child a specific task and set up the project in the order of assembly. Start with the first child at the first assembly point. As he finishes, he passes the project to the next station until the project is completed. Praise the finished project and the students' cooperative efforts. Assign classroom jobs to work teams of two or three people. Demonstrate how teamwork can make the work go more quickly and efficiently. Spot check to see that children are sharing the work and helping each other. Ask parents or guardians to allow the child to participate in group family activities like folding laundry, preparing a simple meal, setting the table, making cookies, etc. Develop a buddy system. Assign two children to work together on a project or game or to share a toy and play together.	Toy or game Art project materials

Curriculum Area: Socialization Skills		
Behavioral Objective: The child participates in play activities with others.		
Activity	Adaptations/Modifications	Materials
As part of the daily classroom schedule, set aside specific times during each school day as group play periods. On work tables or on the floor, put out games and toys that allow two or more children to play (for example, lotto games, checkers, Lego, Missing Match-Ups, Lincoln Logs, etc.). Explain to the children that they must choose what they wish to play with and share it with the other children who want to play with the toy or game. Supervise to see that the children are sharing games and playing together. Comment on how well the children are playing together and sharing the activities.	Encourage the child's parents to enroll him in play programs at neighborhood playgrounds, a YMCA, a YWCA, a Boys' Club, a Girls' Club, etc., that promote group involvement. Organize a field day. Include activities requiring team cooperation, such as three-legged races, relays, wheelbarrow races, and team sports. Assign each child a different partner or team for each event. Stress teamwork and group cooperation. Praise the child's efforts. Organize a game of dodgeball. Divide the children into teams, and stress the importance of team spirit, group cooperation, and playing as a member of a team. Praise the child for good sportsmanship. Encourage the child's parents to allow him to invite friends to his home to share his toys and games. Set up a lotto game. Show the children how to play the game, and explain the rules. Encourage groups of children to get together and form lotto teams. Organize a lotto competition.	Lotto games Checkers Lego Missing Match-Ups Lincoln Logs Play equipment for field day activities

degree of difficulty ← increase | decrease →

Curriculum Area: Socialization Skills

Behavioral Objective: The child uses park and playground facilities and equipment appropriately.

Activity	Adaptations/Modifications	Materials
Take the child to a park or playground. Demonstrate the appropriate uses of the play equipment, being sure to tell the child the name of each piece of play equipment (for example, "This is a swing," "this is a sliding board," "... a see saw," etc.) as you use it. Encourage the child to imitate your actions and use the play equipment in an appropriate manner. Go to a park or playground often, offering the child an opportunity to practice using a variety of play equipment.	Ask parents or guardians to encourage the child to use neighborhood playgrounds or parks. Stress that adequate supervision is essential to the child's safety when using neighborhood facilities. Play "Follow the Leader" on the playground. As part of the game use the playground equipment (for example, slide down the sliding board, climb up one side of a jungle gym and down the other) in an appropriate manner. Let the child be the leader; encourage him to use the play equipment. Set up an obstacle course. As part of the course include playground equipment. Walk through the course with the child a few times. Once he knows the sequence of the obstacles on the course, encourage the child to use it as part of recess or gym. During recess time, assist the child as he practices using one piece of play equipment at a time. ← degree of difficulty → (increase / decrease)	Playground with play equipment Park Materials for an obstacle course (tires, clean trash cans, large boxes, etc.)

86

Curriculum Area: Socialization Skills

Behavioral Objective: The child recognizes community helpers and relates to them in appropriate situations.

Activity	Adaptations/Modifications	Materials
Plan out an art activity around community helpers. Construct costumes from brown paper grocery bags to represent the uniforms of various community helpers. Cut arm and neck holes, and slit the bags down the front so the student can wear them as costumes. Paint the bags so they resemble the uniforms community helpers wear (white for doctor or nurse, blue for policeman, yellow or black for fireman's slickers, green (or other appropriate color) for trash men, etc.) Add, by glueing on or painting, the details of brass buttons, badges, insignias, or other identifying items. Encourage the children to wear the costumes and role play the parts of the community helper their costume represents. Praise the child's efforts.	Take a walk in the community; point out, name, and (if possible) visit community helpers. Comment on situations in which the child might need the community helpers' help.	Pictures of community helpers
	Role play situations in which the child might interact with community helpers (for example, doctor for check-up, policeman for a lost child). Repeat the activity, playing situations the student is likely to experience.	Bulletin board Chart paper Magic marker Art materials Paper grocery bags Tempera paints Paint brushes Glue Buttons Badges
	Take the child on field trips to places where community helpers work (police station, fire station, dentist's office, hospital, etc.). After each field trip, develop language experience stories and draw pictures for a bulletin board.	
	Invite firemen, policemen, doctors, nurses, lawyers, trash collectors, and other community helpers to come to the school and discuss their jobs with the children. Encourage the child to ask questions.	
	Construct a community helpers bulletin board. Name each one, his job within the community, the services he provides, and situations in which the child might come into contact with him.	

degree of difficulty ← increase decrease →

87

Curriculum Area: Socialization Skills

Behavioral Objective: The child obeys the rules and laws of the classroom, home, and community.

Activity	Adaptations/Modifications	Materials
Discuss rules and laws. Stress that rules and laws are necessary to maintain order in the classroom, home, and community. Talk about the class, and, with the help of the child, explain why some rules exist and develop any new rules the children feel are necessary. Stress that rules must be obeyed and people who break the rules must accept the consequences. Praise the child for following rules of the classroom.	Encourage parents or guardians to develop "house" rules, including the child in the making of the rules. Remind the child that people who break rules usually get punished in some way. Read stories or newspaper articles in which people break rules or laws and accept the consequences of their behavior (for example, *Little Toot, Curious George Rides A Bike*). Discuss the rules or law, why it was made (for safety, protection), and what happens when rules or laws are broken. Invite a policeman to speak to the class about laws. Ask him to stress the fact that as a responsible student, member of a family, and part of the community it is the child's responsibility to be aware of rules and laws and to obey them. Role play situations in which children follow the rules and also break the rules. Discuss the consequences of breaking the rules.	Stories such as *Little Toot, Curious George Rides A Bike* Newspaper articles

degree of difficulty ← increase   decrease →

88

Chapter 9
Motor Skills

The motor domain has long been considered a crucial area for teaching those prerequisite and primary skills that enable a young child to interact with his environment. Motor activities also provide the child with the opportunity to explore objects and relationships to individuals, peers, and other objects and materials. This area is primarily concerned with the coordination of movements that involve the large and small muscles of the body. Traditionally, those movements involving the large muscles of the body are referred to as gross motor skills and those movements utilizing the smaller muscles are referred to as fine motor skills. Many times fine motor activities that involve small muscle movement are refinements of select gross motor skills.

PROVIDING A MEANS OF EXPRESSION

While many professionals have suggested that motor skills are often the foundation for cognitive and language skills development, an equally critical reason for their inclusion in a preschool curriculum for the disadvantaged is their ability to provide an alternative means for a child to express himself when he may not be fluent or experienced in the other domains.

FOSTERING EXPLORATION

Without some degree of proficiency in the motor area, a young child often will avoid engaging in exploration activities as well as those very beginning motor skills involving such activities as grasping, holding, and manipulating the objects of his environment.

Often, the preschool disadvantaged child has not been exposed to the gross and fine motor activities that have been made available to his nondisadvantaged preschool peer. He will therefore need help in developing and coordinating his motor movements if he is to successfully participate in the daily activities that would be part of any preschool or kindergarten program.

This ability to have freedom of movement, whether in gross motor or fine motor areas, is essential to the development of the child. The absence of these skills may create physical barriers to succeeding in the future grades as well as leading to the development of social barriers if the child cannot interact in play or skill activities with his peers.

ENCOURAGING INDEPENDENCE

As the preschool child learns to develop and master his motor skills, he also begins to gain more independence and freedom to perform tasks with a minimal amount of directions and supervision. This type of freedom is especially critical to the child from a disadvantaged background who often has difficulty gaining independence away from his home environment.

Chapter 4, "Evaluation Strategies," provides an analysis of selected instruments that address the perceptual-motor area and have been closely aligned to tasks in the fine motor domain. Instruments that measure gross motor activities should also be used to determine the student's level of functioning so that appropriate activities can be planned. For example, the child needs to gain competence in the balance and posture area; this provides him with a base for understanding and moving within his environment. Without some of these skills, the child would have difficulty in exploring new objects and the relationship of objects to himself. The child who cannot master tasks, such as those that involve such objectives as pushing, catching, and throwing, soon begins to accept the fact that his environment is restricted and begins to avoid further exploration.

CURRICULAR OBJECTIVES AND ACTIVITIES

The motor development objectives and activities that follow have been divided into two major parts. The first part addresses those skills associated with the fine motor area, while the second part addresses the gross motor area. It must be emphasized that these are merely samples of motor behaviors; it is the responsibility of the teacher to decide which additional areas and accompanying developmental levels her individually designed activities and objectives should address.

Curriculum Area: Motor Development—Fine Motor Skills		
Behavioral Objective: The child reaches for and grasps objects.		
Activity	Adaptations/Modifications	Materials
Seat the child at a table or desk. Place small objects, such as blocks, Matchbox cars, or crayons, on the table in front of the child. Demonstrate reaching for an object, grasping it, and picking it up. Replace the object. Ask the child to imitate your actions by reaching for an object, grasping it, and picking it up. Praise the child's efforts and reward him for picking up objects by allowing him to play with what he picked up. Repeat the activity using a variety of objects.	Walk to a mailbox within the community. Show the child a letter you want to mail. Tell him he may mail the letter if he can open the mailbox slot. Demonstrate. Lift the child so he can reach the mailbox slot handle, grasp it, open the slot, insert the letter, and release the handle. Take the child outside. Blow soap bubbles into the air. Demonstrate reaching for and grasping the bubbles. Tell the child to chase the bubbles, to reach for them, to grasp them, and to see how many he can catch and break. Stand in front of the child, facing him. Tell him to reach for your hands, grasp them, and hold them. Praise the child for following your instructions. If necessary, demonstrate first and ask the child to imitate your actions. Place a favorite toy or object in front of the child and within his reach. Demonstrate reaching for and grasping the object. Ask the student to do the same, using the cue words "reach" and "grasp." Praise the child's efforts.	Table or desk Chair Small objects and toys Bubble soap (for blowing bubbles) Wand for blowing bubbles Mailbox Letters to mail

degree of difficulty — increase ← / decrease →

Curriculum Area: Motor Development—Fine Motor Skills

Behavioral Objective: The child picks up and plays with small toys and playthings found in the classroom.

Activity	Adaptations/Modifications	Materials
Seat the child at a table or desk. Place a number of small toys and playthings on the table in front of the student (blocks, beads, pegs, small cars, doll dishes). Demonstrate using a pincer grasp (thumb and forefinger together) to pick up each object. Praise the child's efforts, and allow him to play with the toys he has picked up.	As part of group play activities, show the child how to play games with small pieces (bingo, dominoes, checkers, pick-up sticks, Chinese checkers). Demonstrate picking up the small objects used in the games. Ask the child to imitate. Play the games with the child. Review safety rules that govern using small toys or games with small pieces. Remind children *not* to put small things into their mouths, ears, or nose. Stress this each time the children play with small objects. Play pick-up sticks with the child. Play a modified version of "Show and Tell": place a number of small toys and playthings on a table in front of the child. Tell the child that you are going to name an object and you want him to pick it up and show you the object you named. Praise the child's efforts. Place a number of medium-size toys and playthings on a table in front of the child. Demonstrate picking up and playing with each object. Once the child is able to pick up the medium-size toys, use smaller toys until the child is able to pick them up using a pincer grasp. Allow the child to play with the small toys and playthings.	Small toys and playthings Medium-size toys and playthings Table or desk Chair Games with small pieces (bingo, dominoes, checkers, pick-up sticks, Chinese checkers)

degree of difficulty ← decrease | increase →

Curriculum Area: Motor Development—Fine Motor Skills		
Behavioral Objective: The child picks up and holds a pencil correctly and makes marks on a piece of paper.		
Activity	Adaptations/Modifications	Materials
Seat the child at a table or desk. Give the child a primary pencil and a piece of paper. Demonstrate the proper way to hold a pencil (the pencil rests on the third finger and is held in place by the thumb held in opposition to the index finger). Place the pencil in the child's hand and position it properly. Guide the child's hand so that he makes marks on the paper. Praise his efforts. Remove your hand and encourage the child to make marks on the paper. Praise the child.	_degree of difficulty_ ← increase decrease → Use a Spiro-graph or Spiro-tot game with the child. Encourage the child to pick up the pencil independently, hold it correctly, and make marks on a paper without your help. Repeat the activity, using nontoxic, water-soluble magic markers. Repeat the activity, using colored chalk. Repeat the activity, using colored pencils to keep the child interested in making marks on paper. Wrap clay around the pencil so it is easier for the child to grasp the pencil while making marks.	Table or desk Chair Paper Primary pencil Clay Colored pencils Colored chalk Magic markers Spiro-graph game Spiro-tot game

Curriculum Area: Motor Development—Fine Motor Skills

Behavioral Objective: The child strings beads, spools, and other objects.

Activity	Adaptations/Modifications	Materials
Tie a knot at the end of two heavy shoe laces. Give the child one of the laces and keep the other. Place a number of spools in front of the student. Pick up a spool and string it onto your lace. As you are doing this, tell the child what you are doing. Ask the child to string a spool onto his lace; assist him if necessary. Praise his efforts, and instruct him to put all the spools onto his lace. When this is done, knot the end. Use the finished product as a decoration for the room or as a necklace for the child.	*degree of difficulty* ← increase / decrease → Using embroidery needles and thread, string cranberries and popcorn to use as holiday decorations. Use food coloring to dye macaroni various colors. Use different shapes of pasta to make bracelets and necklaces by stringing different shapes and colors on heavy thread, light string, or jewelry wire. Show the child the jewelry you made and ask him to make one for himself or to give as a gift. Offer assistance when necessary. Create patterns using different colors and shapes. Ask the child to string beads, copying your patterns. String wooden beads according to color (all red, all yellow, all blue, etc.). String wooden beads according to shape (all round, all square, all triangles, etc.). String large wooden beads on heavy laces.	Large wooden beads Beads, different colors Beads, different shapes Shoe laces String Jewelry wire Food coloring Pasta, various shapes Cranberries Popcorn Embroidery needles Thread

94

Curriculum Area: Motor Development—Fine Motor Skills		
Behavioral Objective: The child fits puzzle pieces, pegs, and other playthings into their corresponding forms.		
Activity	Adaptations/Modifications	Materials
Seat the child at a table or desk. Give the child a pegboard and a box of pegs. Demonstrate fitting one peg into one hole. Ask the child to imitate your actions. Instruct him to complete the pegboard. Praise him for doing a good job.	During playtime, use games like Lego, Lincoln Logs, and Tinker Toys that have interlocking parts that must be fitted together. Encourage the child to use a variety of toys. For birthday celebrations, place candles and candle holders in front of the student. Demonstrate fitting one candle into each holder. Tell the student to imitate your actions and put the candles on the cake. Give the child puzzles (begin with five-part wooden puzzles and work up to those with more pieces). Demonstrate how to work the puzzle. Encourage the child to do so, and offer help when needed. Glue small knobs (available at hardware stores) onto puzzle and form board pieces to aid the child in removing and replacing puzzle pieces. Use oversized pegs and pegboards or pegs with knobbed tops for children who have difficulty holding regular-size pegs. Use form boards that require placing shapes into corresponding forms but have no interlocking pieces. ← increase / decrease → degree of difficulty	Table or desk Chair Pegs and pegboard Wooden puzzles Form boards Small knobs (available at hardware stores) Candles and candle holders Lego Lincoln Logs Tinker Toys

Curriculum Area: Motor Development—Fine Motor Skills		
Behavioral Objective: The child uses eating utensils in an appropriate manner.		
Activity	Adaptations/Modifications	Materials

Activity	Adaptations/Modifications	Materials
Prepare a snack for the child. Set a place for him at the table, with a fork and spoon as well as whatever dishes are necessary. Use a fork to eat foods such as string beans, carrots, or french fries. Demonstrate using a fork by putting food on the fork, lifting the fork to your mouth, eating the food from the fork, taking the fork back to the plate of food, refilling the fork, and repeating the steps. Give the child his fork and ask him to imitate your actions and eat, using his fork. Offer assistance if necessary. Follow the same steps, using a spoon with foods such as applesauce, pudding, or ice cream. Encourage the child to eat his snack, using his fork and spoon.	← increase / decrease → degree of difficulty

Include the children in the preparation of a class luncheon. Use foods that can be eaten with a spoon or fork. Do not prepare finger foods. Encourage the children to use their utensils to eat the meal they prepared.

Cut pictures of foods from magazines, and make collages of foods that can be eaten with a spoon and those that can be eaten with a fork.

Prepare a class luncheon. Include foods that must be eaten with a fork or spoon: Spaghetti-o's, applesauce, or fruit cocktail for spoons; french fries, vegetables, or cake for forks.

If the student has difficulty handling eating utensils, modify them for ease of handling by wrapping tape around handles so they fit the child's hand.

During snack time, discourage finger feeding and encourage the child to use eating utensils. | Forks
Spoons
Food for snacks
Magazines
Scissors
Paste
Heavy tape |

Curriculum Area: Motor Development—Fine Motor Skills

Behavioral Objective: The child paints, using a brush and paints.

Activity	Adaptations/Modifications	Materials
Cover tables or desks with newspaper. Place large pieces of drawing paper on the table. Place large paint brushes, water, pans, and paint in containers (margarine tubs work well, cardboard or Styrofoam egg boxes can be used to hold many different colors) on the table. Seat the child at the table, within reach of the paints, brushes, and paper. (You may want the child to wear a smock to protect his clothing.) Demonstrate dipping the brush into the paint and then applying the paint to the paper. Encourage the child to do the same. Remind the child to rinse his brush in the water before using another color paint. Praise his efforts. Use pictures as room decorations or part of an art bulletin board.	As a group project, paint a mural, e.g., a Halloween or Thanksgiving mural, to decorate the classroom. Draw simple pictures of objects (Christmas trees, pumpkins, apples, animals, leaves, etc.). Give the child paints and ask him to paint within the outline of the picture. On large paper trace the child's body. Draw in the details (eyes, hair, ears, clothes), and assist the child as he paints "himself." Cut out the paintings and hang them in the classroom. See if the children can guess whose picture is whose. Repeat activity, using one color of paint. Gradually increase the number of colors used. Give the child sponges cut into shapes and thick tempera paint. Demonstrate dipping the sponge into the paint and pressing the sponge onto the paper. Encourage the child to imitate your actions and make pictures or designs.	Table or desk Chair Newspaper Large paint brushes Water pans Paint containers (margarine tubs, egg cartons) Paints Large paper Magic marker Sponges cut into shapes

degree of difficulty ← increase   decrease →

97

Curriculum Area: Motor Development—Fine Motor Skills		
Behavioral Objective: The child colors, using crayons.		
Activity	Adaptations/Modifications	Materials
Seat the child at a desk or table. Give the child a primary crayon and a large piece of paper. Show him how to hold the crayon so that he can make marks on the paper. Once the crayon is positioned properly in the child's hand (crayon resting on the third finger with the thumb held in opposition to the index finger), guide the child's hand to help him make marks on the paper. Remove your hand and encourage the child to draw on his own. Praise his efforts.	Give the child coloring books. Encourage him to color the pictures during art time at school and leisure time at home.	Desk or table Crayons Paper Records Record player Magic markers Pictures from coloring books Coloring books
	Give the child large, simple pictures from coloring books. Demonstrate coloring in the pictures. Ask the child to do the same.	
	Using a thick magic marker, draw shapes on a piece of paper. Give the child crayons, and ask him to color in the shapes.	
	Draw shapes on a piece of paper. Ask the child to copy the shapes. Praise his efforts.	
	Give the child a crayon and paper. Play music and ask the child to "draw the music" on his paper as he listens to it.	
	Give the child a crayon and paper. Help him draw or scribble on the paper.	

degree of difficulty — increase ← → decrease

98

Curriculum Area: Motor Development—Fine Motor Skills

Behavioral Objective: The child pastes paper onto paper and objects onto paper.

Activity	Adaptations/Modifications	Materials
Seat the student at a desk or table. In front of the student place a piece of construction paper, paste, and shapes cut from paper. Demonstrate applying paste to the back of a shape and pasting the shape to the construction paper. Give the student a selection of shapes, and tell him to paste them onto the construction paper. Use the completed papers as room decorations or as part of a bulletin board or display about shapes.	*(degree of difficulty — decrease / increase)* Make mosaic pictures and designs by pasting or glueing seeds, beans, rice, macaroni, and berries onto heavy paper (cardboard, tagboard). Make an assemblage of natural items (pine cones, twigs, dried flowers, acorns, small stones) by pasting or gluing the objects on cardboard or tagboard. Make a collage using paper and objects (for example, pictures of food as well as dried food items, or pictures of toys and small pieces of toys). Collect pictures from magazines of something the child is interested in (cars, animals, food). Paste the pictures in a scrapbook. Use tissue paper, crepe paper, rice paper, cellophane, foil wrapping paper, and Kleenex to create a collage. Paste the papers onto construction paper; twist and shape the papers to create interesting textures. Cut pictures out of magazines. Paste them onto construction paper, overlapping the pictures to create a collage effect. Pre-paste shapes and ask the child to place them on paper. Comment on how well he pasted the papers together.	Desk or table Paste Paper shapes Construction paper Glue Cardboard Tagboard Different types of paper Scrapbook Natural objects Magazines Pictures from magazines Seeds Beans Rice Berries Macaroni

Curriculum Area: Motor Development—Fine Motor Skills

Behavioral Objective: The child uses scissors to cut paper.

Activity	Adaptations/Modifications	Materials
Seat the child at a desk or table. Place a pair of primary scissors on the table in front of the child. Demonstrate picking up the scissors, placing your thumb and index finger, in the finger holes. Demonstrate opening and closing the scissors in the cutting motion. Give the child the scissors, and ask him to practice holding the scissors properly and opening and closing the scissors. Praise the child's efforts.	Demonstrate cutting simple shapes that are drawn on construction paper or light cardboard. Use the shapes for holiday decorations, party place cards, or name tags for field trips. Give the child magazines, and tell him to look through the magazine and cut out pictures of food, cars, red things, faces, etc. Use the pictures for scrapbooks, bulletin boards, or other art projects. Draw circles and ovals on construction paper. Demonstrate cutting out the same shapes. Ask the child to do the same; offer assistance when necessary. Use the cutout shapes for collages or other art projects. Draw triangles, squares, and rectangles on construction paper. Demonstrate cutting out the shapes. Ask the student to do the same; offer assistance when necessary. Use the shapes for collages. Draw cutting lines (using a heavy black marker or crayon) on drawing paper. Demonstrate cutting on the lines. Assist the child in cutting on the lines—use the strips in weaving activities. Give the child primary scissors and scraps of construction paper. Tell him to cut the paper into small pieces. Use the pieces as confetti or for making paper mosaics. Using double-handled (teaching) scissors, assist the child in opening and closing the scissors in the cutting movement.	Desk or table Scissors Double-handled scissors Primary scissors Construction paper Magic marker or black crayon Magazines

degree of difficulty

← decrease   increase →

100

Curriculum Area: Motor Development—Gross Motor Skills
Behavioral Objective: The child hits play equipment in an appropriate manner.

Activity	Adaptations/Modifications	Materials
Demonstrate the use of play equipment that requires hitting a ball or other object (bat and ball, tennis racket and tennis ball, croquet mallet and ball, etc.). Assist the child as he tries to imitate your actions and hits play equipment in an appropriate manner. Encourage the child to practice using the play equipment during recess, physical education, and free-play time. Play games using the equipment.	Play croquet on the playground or in the room. Use corrugated cardboard tunnels in place of hoops when playing indoors. Organize a modified game of baseball. Use a plastic bat and a volleyball so the child can hit the ball easily, and simplify the rules. Construct a "Paddle Ball" game: hang a baseball-size wiffle or "Nerf" ball from the ceiling by a thin wire or cord. Give the child a plastic bat, and assist him as he tries to hit the hanging ball. Praise his efforts. Encourage the child to play "Paddle Ball" during free-play time. Blow soap bubbles, and ask the child to "hit" them and break them. Give the child piles of clay, and ask him to pound it into different shapes. Get a punching bag or roly-poly punching toy. Demonstrate hitting the toy or bag and encourage the child to do the same.	Punching bag Roly-poly punching toy Bubble soap Wand to blow bubbles Clay "Nerf" ball Thin wire or cord Plastic bats Volleyball Tennis racket (child size) Tennis balls Croquet game (child size)

degree of difficulty

← increase   decrease →

Curriculum Area: Motor Development—Gross Motor Skills

Behavioral Objective: The child maintains his balance during play activities.

Activity	Adaptations/Modifications	Materials
As part of daily classroom activities, include exercises or games that involve gross motor movements. Using masking tape, outline a large circle on the floor. Ask the children to stand on the circle. Tell the children to extend their arms to the side to be sure there is enough space between them as they stand on the line. Stand in the center of the circle and demonstrate exercises (for example, hopping, jumping, standing on one foot, bending forward and backward, touching your toes, and reaching for the sky). Ask the child to imitate your actions. Give the children turns at being the leader and choosing the exercises.	Play "Twister"; use a commercial game or make your own by glueing cloth cutouts of footprints on an old shower curtain or sheet of heavy plastic. Supervise the children as they play, offering assistance when necessary. Practice walking on a balance beam. Encourage the child to use the balance beam during free play or physical education activities. Play "Follow the Leader." Include activities that involve balancing, hopping on one foot, skipping, and jumping over obstacles. Play music and do activities that involve balancing; creative movement ("Let's be birds flying," "... trees swaying in the breeze") as well as exercises. Play "Simon Says." Include actions that involve balancing: standing on one foot, hopping, and running in place. Seat the child on a chair. Place art or play materials on a table far enough away from the child so that he must balance his body as he reaches for the toy or art material. Draw shapes and lines on the playground (use chalk) or in the classroom (use masking tape). Walk over the shapes, using your arms to maintain your balance. Encourage the child to imitate your actions and walk over the shapes at recess or free-play time.	Chalk Masking tape Chair Table Art materials Play materials (puzzles, toys) Records Record player Balance beam "Twister" game Shower curtain or plastic sheet Cloth cutouts of footprints Glue

degree of difficulty — increase ← / → decrease

102

Curriculum Area: Motor Development—Gross Motor Skills		
Behavioral Objective: The child marches.		
Activity	Adaptations/Modifications	Materials
Play a record of marching music. Demonstrate how to march. Stand the children in a line, and ask them to march with you. March in a line around the room as the music plays. Praise the child's efforts at marching.	*(degree of difficulty: decrease → / increase ←)* Phone the local high school, and arrange for the child to watch the marching band as it practices its routines. Give the children rhythm band instruments. Have them wear their paper "band uniforms" and march as they play a rhythm on their rhythm instruments (set the rhythm by beating a drum so the children can match your beat). During art activities, make band uniforms (coats from grocery bags and paper hats). When they are completed, play marching music and encourage the children to pretend to be a marching band and march to the music. Beat a drum and ask the child to march to the beat of the drum. Clap your hands and march in place to the rhythm of the claps. Ask the child to do the same. Play "Simon Says." As one of the commands, ask the child to march in place.	Rhythm instruments Drum Brown paper grocery bags Art paper Tempera paints (to paint bag uniforms and hats) Records of marching music Record player Scissors

Curriculum Area: Motor Development—Gross Motor Skills

Behavioral Objective: The child jumps.

Activity	Adaptations/Modifications	Materials
Place a box with low sides on the floor in the classroom. Demonstrate jumping into and out of the box. Ask the child to do the same. Play "Jack in the Box." Say, "Jack, jump in the box," and "Jack, jump out of the box." Encourage the child to jump in and out of the box as part of the game of "Jack in the Box."	Use a trampoline to practice jumping. Show the child how to jump over a rope. Ask two children to hold the ends of the rope. Begin with the rope flat on the floor. Tell the child to jump over it. Raise it gradually so the child must jump a little higher at each turn. Hold a hula hoop a few inches from the floor, and ask the child to jump through the hoop. Raise or lower the hoop to suit the child's abilities. Play "Simon Says." As one of the commands say, "Simon says, jump," or "Simon says, do jumping jacks." Recite the poem "Jack be nimble, Jack be quick, Jack jump over the candlestick." Place a cardboard model of a candlestick on the floor, and let the child act out the rhyme and jump over the candlestick. Using masking tape, mark out squares on the floor. Demonstrate jumping into and out of the square. Ask the child to do the same. Praise his efforts. Demonstrate jumping in place. Ask the child to jump in place as you do.	Box with low sides Rope Masking tape Cardboard model of Jack's candlestick Hula hoop Trampoline

←— increase   decrease —→

degree of difficulty

Curriculum Area: Motor Development—Gross Motor Skills		
Behavioral Objective: The child hops.		
Activity	Adaptations/Modifications	Materials
Read the child stories about rabbits, *Peter Rabbit, Peter Cottontail, The Easter Bunny*, or make up your own. After the story, assign the children parts. Ask them to act out the story, encouraging the children to hop around like rabbits. Praise the children for being such good rabbits.	Mark out a hopscotch court (with chalk for outdoors, masking tape for indoors). Show the child how to play hopscotch, and encourage him to play during recess or play time.	Chalk Masking tape Ladder Tires Record of "The Bunny Hop." Record player Stories about rabbits
	Lay a ladder on the ground or floor, and ask the child to hop over the rungs of the ladder. Stand close enough to assist children who lose their balance.	
	Lay tires on the floor, and show the child how to hop in and out of the tires. Use the tires as part of an obstacle course or as a physical education activity.	
	Play a record of "The Bunny Hop." Demonstrate how the Bunny Hop is done, and encourage the child to join you as you do the Bunny Hop.	
	Play "Hop Tag"; follow the rules of tag, except that players must hop rather than run.	
	As one of the commands in "Simon Says," say, "Simon says, hop on one foot."	

degree of difficulty ← increase / decrease →

105

Curriculum Area: Motor Development—Gross Motor Skills

Behavioral Objective: The child rides a tricycle.

Activity	Adaptations/Modifications	Materials
Seat the child on a tricycle. Show him how to hold the handlebars, both for support and to steer the tricycle. Place the child's feet on the pedals and move his legs in a pedaling motion. Encourage the child to pedal and steer the tricycle independently. Walk behind or beside the child, and offer assistance when necessary.	Encourage the parents to help the child ride his tricycle at home or in the neighborhood, with supervision. Place obstacles on a Mystik tape path. Show the child how to steer the tricycle around the obstacles. Encourage the child to steer around the obstacles independently. Mark out paths on the floor with brightly colored Mystik tape. Seat the child on a tricycle and show him how to follow the path while pedaling the tricycle. Encourage the child to follow the path while riding the tricycle during play time. Put tricycles on the playground or in the classroom. Encourage the child to ride the tricycle during recess or free play. Seat the child on a tricycle and place his feet on the pedals. Attach a rope to the front of the tricycle and pull the child on a tricycle around the room. Seat the child on a tricycle and place his feet on the pedals. Stand on the back of the tricycle and slowly push the tricycle around the room or playground.	Tricycles Rope Mystik tape (colors) Boxes, blocks to use as obstacles

degree of difficulty

increase ← → decrease

106

Curriculum Area: Motor Development—Gross Motor Skills		
Behavioral Objective: The child participates in activities utilizing playground equipment.		
Activity	Adaptations/Modifications	Materials
Take the child to the school playground or neighborhood park or playground. Point out, name, and demonstrate the safe and appropriate use of playground equipment. Ask the student to practice using playground equipment in a safe and appropriate manner. During recess or outings to parks and playgrounds, encourage the child to use the play equipment.	Encourage the child's parents to take him to a nearby playground and to supervise and join the child as he uses the playground equipment. Play "Follow the Leader" on the playground. As part of the game, use each piece of equipment (slide down the slide, swing on a tire, etc.), and encourage the child to "Follow the Leader." Take turns allowing the child to lead you and his classmates through the playground equipment. Set up obstacle courses on the playground. Include playground equipment as obstacles (for example, climb up one side of the jungle gym and down the other, or walk around the swings, climb through hanging tires). Encourage the child to use the obstacle course during play time or recess. Use playground equipment during recess.	Playground with play equipment

degree of difficulty

← increase   decrease →

107

Curriculum Area: Motor Development—Gross Motor Skills

Behavioral Objective: The child pulls toys and other movable objects.

Activity	Adaptations/Modifications	Materials
Organize a towel pull. Seat two children on a mat on the floor facing each other. Give the children a long towel or piece of terry cloth, and ask each child to grasp an end of the towel so the towel is stretched between the two children. Instruct one child to lie back on the floor. Tell the other child to pull on the towel until the other child is raised to a sitting position and the child who is pulling is lying back on the floor. Repeat the action of pulling the towel in an alternating pattern, with the children lifting and lowering each other to and from the floor. Supervise closely so the children do not get hurt.	*(degree of difficulty: increase ↑ / decrease ↓)* Organize wagon relay races. Divide the children into teams; mark out a race course and stand half of each team at each end of the course. At each end of the course place a block for each team member. Have one child pull a wagon from one end of the course to the other. He places a block in the wagon and the next child in line pulls the wagon to the other end of the course and places a block in the wagon. Repeat until each team member has had a turn. The first team to finish is the winner. Organize a wagon race. Set up two teams; divide each team into pairs. One of each pair sits in a wagon, and the other pulls the wagon. Each pair must race to a prearranged point and back until each team pair has had a turn. The first team to finish wins. Store building blocks and toys in wagons or containers that can be pulled. After using blocks, encourage the child to pull the wagon around the room as he collects the blocks and toys that need to be put away. Place pull toys or wagons in the classroom. Demonstrate grasping the string or handle and pulling the toy or wagon. Ask the child to do the same. Encourage the child to use pull toys and wagons during recess or free-play activities.	Large towel Mat Pull toys Wagons Blocks

Curriculum Area: Motor Development—Gross Motor Skills		
Behavioral Objective: The child throws balls and other play equipment.		
Activity	Adaptations/Modifications	Materials

Activity	Adaptations/Modifications	Materials
Organize a beanbag throwing game. Place a tire or small child's wading pool a few feet from a masking tape line on the floor. Stand on the line, and toss a beanbag into the tire or pool. Give the child a beanbag, and ask him to imitate your actions. Praise the child's efforts. Give each child three beanbags, and encourage him to try tossing the beanbags into the tire. Keep score if the children wish to compete against each other.	Play "Frisbee" with the child on the playground. Play dodge ball on the playground. Set up a magnetic dartboard in the classroom (never use sharp or pointed darts). Demonstrate how to use the dart game. Ask the child to imitate your play. Supervise dart games. Set up teams and competitions if the children are interested. Divide the class into two teams. Place two tires on the floor. Give each team three beanbags. Each team member throws the three beanbags and scores one point each time the beanbag lands in a tire. The team with the highest score wins. Clear an area in the classroom or playground. Demonstrate throwing play equipment (balls, frisbees, beanbags, nerf balls, magnetic darts (never sharp ones), etc.). Encourage the child to practice throwing the play equipment. Play catch with the child—he throws the ball and you catch it—to let the child practice throwing.	Beanbags Frisbees Balls Magnetic dart game Tires or small wading pool "Nerf" balls

degree of difficulty ← increase / decrease →

Curriculum Area: Motor Development—Gross Motor Skills		
Behavioral Objective: The child catches balls and other play equipment.		
Activity	Adaptations/Modifications	Materials

Activity

Mark off a large circle (use chalk outdoors, masking tape indoors). Tell the children to stand on the line and form a circle. Stand in the center of the circle, and bounce a large ball to the child. Go around the circle so each child gets a turn to catch the ball. Ask the child to catch the ball and throw it back to you. When the child is learning to catch, call his name before you throw him the ball. Once the child is able to catch well, throw the ball at random and try to surprise the child by catching him off guard.

Adaptations/Modifications

← increase

decrease →

degree of difficulty

Form teams and play games that require catching play equipment.

Play games that require catching: dodge ball, beanbag toss, or frisbee.

Stnad two children facing each other with about 2 feet between them. Give them a large ball and ask them to throw it to each other and catch it. As the children get better at catching, increase the distance between them.

Give each child a ball. Play music (marches, disco, popular) and bounce a ball in time to the music. Encourage the child to do the same.

Demonstrate bouncing a large ball and catching it. Give the child a ball, and ask him to imitate your actions. Chant rhymes or count to help the child develop a rhythm as he bounces the ball.

Play catch with the child. Use different size balls, "Nerf" balls, beanbags, and Frisbees.

Seat two children on the floor facing each other. Give the children a ball, and ask them to take turns rolling the ball to each other and catching it.

Materials

Chalk
Masking tape
Balls
Beanbags
Frisbee
Record player
Records

110

Chapter 10
Language Skills

Communication has often been called the link between a child and his environment. As one begins to analyze the area of communication, the role language plays in the success of a preschool disadvantaged child becomes quickly apparent.

It is often reported that one of the greatest accomplishments of a child during the period from birth to six years of age is his development of a system of language. During this time span, children develop a system of language that enables them to interact successfully with their peers as well as with the adult society. The disadvantaged child, however, does not always develop these competencies and is often found to function at the level of average children who are a year or more younger than his chronological age. This is especially important to remember, as there is wide recognition that a close relationship between language and cognitive abilities exists.

ENVIRONMENT IN LANGUAGE ACQUISITION

Children require a great amount of language input before they will produce what is considered to be language output, or expressive language. The facilitation of this output is enhanced by an environment that provides appropriate models, realistic expectations, and ample opportunities to express one's self. Young children, whose needs in the area of language are continually anticipated, have little need to develop communication skills, and, similarly, environments that do not reinforce communication skills will in essence not stimulate their reoccurrence. Obviously, an environment that is conducive to language learning will stimulate language and allow the disadvantaged child to experience success in this area.

Many studies have been conducted to assess the differences that determine why some children develop language early and others experience a language delay. One hypothesis is that the language environments of children with low verbal test scores were different from those children with high verbal test scores (Schumaker and Sherman, 1978). Further investigation revealed that environments that encouraged language development were characterized by the way the mother used speech at home in addition to her use of vocabulary, praise, corrective feedback, prompts, and how she presented instructions concerning everyday tasks. The language environment has also been examined in light of its effect on receptive language abilities, and results indicated that children from disadvantaged homes were not proficient in their ability to listen and, consequently, appeared not to be concerned or interested in school tasks. This is especially important to remember in that many theorists have suggested that a child must first understand speech before he can effectively use it.

DEFICIENCIES IN THE DISADVANTAGED PRESCHOOL CHILD'S ENVIRONMENT

Bereiter and Engelmann (1966) identified the learning situation that promotes language for the preschool disadvantaged child as being either a classroom or home. Here language becomes a "self-consistent representation of reality that deals in true and false statements" (Bereiter and Engelmann, 1966). It is these true and false situations that many preschool disadvantaged children often lack exposure to, which, when combined with a lack of reality situations, result in the child being unaware of societal expectations. A most important fact is that many professionals (Deutsch, 1965; Bereiter and Engelmann, 1966; Anderson, Hemenway, and Anderson, 1969; Risley, 1972) have arrived at the conclusion or have suggested that preschool disadvantaged children continue to fall further behind as they proceed through school. They are especially deficient in language arts, and this deficiency reduces their future chances of success in other academic areas.

Lack of Family Conversation

The disadvantaged preschool child often comes from a family that fails to provide the educational advantages or prerequisites the child needs to be ready for a formal school setting. One involvement that is typically lacking is *family conversation,* which provides a forum for answering and asking questions as well as the opportunity to extend the child's vocabulary. It also provides an opportunity for the child to explain his points of view and to discuss incidents or occurrences that are meaningful to him. Frost and Hawkes (1966) refer to a study by Bernstein of the language behavior of families which is especially interesting in light of what we now know about children from disadvantaged environments. He distinguishes between two types of language: one being *restricted* and the other being *elaborated.*

The restricted language environment is characterized by:

—Short, grammatically simple, often unfinished sentences with a poor syntactical form, stressing the active voice.

—Simple and repetitive use of conjunctions (so, then, because).

—Little use of subordinate clauses to break down the initial categories of the dominant subject.

—Inability to hold a formal subject through a speech sequence; thus a dislocated informational content is facilitated.

—Rigid and limited use of adjectives and adverbs.

—Constraint on the self-reference pronoun; frequent use of personal pronoun.

—Frequent use of statements where the reason and conclusion are confounded to produce a categoric statement.

—A large number of statements/phrases which signal a requirement for the previous speech sequence to be reinforced: ''Wouldn't it? You see? You know?'' etc. This process is termed ''sympathetic circularity.''

The family that employs an elaborated language system uses language that is characterized by:

—Accurate grammatical order and syntax regulate what is said.

—Logical modifications and stress are mediated through a grammatically complex sentence construction, especially through the use of a range of conjunctions and subordinate clauses.

—Frequent use of prepositions which indicate logical relationships, as well as prepositions that indicate temporal and spatial contiguity.

—Frequent use of the personal pronoun ''I.''

—A discriminative selection from a range of adjectives and adverbs.

—Individual qualification is verbally mediated through the structure and relationships within and between sentences.

—Expressive symbolism discriminates between meanings within speech sequences rather than reinforcing dominant words or phrases, or accompanying the sequence in a diffuse, generalized manner.

—A language use which points to the possibilities inherent in a complex conceptual hierarchy for the organizing of experience.

(From ''Who Are the Socially Disadvantaged?'' by R. J. Havighurst, *The Journal of Negro Education*, 1964, as quoted in Frost and Hawkes, 1966, pp. 18–19.)

The child who has been the product of a restricted language system at home may be at a high risk for academic and related school problems. It becomes clear that many preschool disadvantaged children are products of families using restricted language, and these preschoolers' lack of language experiences at home takes its toll very early in their school life.

Lack of Parent-Child Interaction

In the very first year of his life the child is an active processor of information and is beginning to develop his own structure of language and verbal exchange. While the mother and her child should be active partners in developing language in early infancy, the disadvantaged child may not have these types of experiences. In many instances parents of disadvantaged children are not always at home and there are no reliable parent surrogates to provide this type of involvement. While close nurturing of an infant during these early stages does not necessarily ensure successful language development, many studies suggest that young children who have limited maternal interaction may be at a disadvantage in developing a sophisticated language system.

Lack of Teacher Preparation

Of equal importance is the fact that, while many teachers have been trained to work in the area of early childhood or special education, few teacher-training programs have directly addressed the language deficiences of the disadvantaged child. The authors feel it is imperative that the teacher have some basic understanding of how children develop language if she is to successfully provide compensatory techniques for children who are delayed in this area. For example, by the time the child is two years of age he often understands the basic structure, content, and function of his own language. Many children at this age know how and when to use their limited repertoire of language. While most of these youngsters understand language in broad categories, such as food, play, and sleep, they are constantly learning, refining, and assimilating the information they hear from a variety of sources.

Furthermore, many children who enter the preschool come from environments that are in stark contrast to the environment of the white middle class children to whom they are being compared. This is especially evident in the area of speech and language where inexperienced teachers fail to understand the geographic or cultural dialects of the children they teach and quickly assume they are not receiving correct responses to their questions.

COMPONENTS OF AN EFFECTIVE LANGUAGE ARTS PROGRAM

It is reasonable to assume that programs for disadvantaged preschool children should be built upon a strong foundation in the language arts area where freedom to listen and express one's self is allowed. This assumption advocates prescribing the content of a language arts program in terms of what is necessary for the students to be successful in society rather than basing content structure on what might be expected to be accomplished in traditional language arts programs. Bereiter (1972) has also defined "a minimum teaching language," which consists of two major phases, one of which includes examples of the concept being presented to the young child, while the second phase is a feedback stage through which the child is provided information on how he was doing. A "minimum teaching language," whether it involves signs, nonverbal symbols, or English or another spoken language, must meet the following two requirements:

1. Have the capability of presenting reality, of pointing out or naming things, and, if the language is to be a full-fledged communication system, of creating the symbolic equivalent of what is observable in physical reality
2. Provide the means for indicating truth and falsity in a relatively unambiguous way

Another element suggested by educators as being common to effective language arts programs is the sharing of language by both the teacher and the child. The child must be offered the opportunity to continually ask questions. It becomes obvious that the preschool disadvantaged child will be unable to sort reality from nonrealistic situations if information is not presented in a way that allows for questions, answers, and immediate feedback.

Allowance for Questioning

Young children initially learn to identify the things in their world and to ask questions through their everyday experiences. These experiences allow for comparisons of objects as well as the recalling of past information. The child eventually progresses to a more sophisticated level of language where his comparisons become more complex and the ability to group together ideas and objects based on his conceptions emerges. An awareness of positioning of everyday materials and objects in the student's environment as well as a realization of other attributes, such as colors and shapes, begins to develop at this very early stage. Concurrently, the student begins to ask himself questions and proceeds to investigate the answers on the basis of his past experiences. This stage then tends to lead into the perceptual framework of logical thought as well as those conventions that make logical thinking difficult. For example, the young preschool disadvantaged child might be presented with a problem such as how to lock a door. If he has been able to view or observe this operation before, he may very well mechanically and methodically solve this problem. However, for the student who has not been previously exposed to this experience, a period of questions to seek answers may be required in order to solve this particular problem.

Provision of Feedback

It is important at this very early and critical stage of language development that a student receive feedback on how accurate his responses are to specific situations. In addition, there are certain minimum goals that must be established in terms of ascertaining whether or not a student is fully comprehending what is being told or required of him. Often, the disadvantaged child is able to interact and communicate with the peers in his home and environment, but fails to communicate in his school program where the information to which he is being requested to respond is norm based rather than based on the language the child needs to learn at that particular point in time.

CURRICULAR OBJECTIVES AND ACTIVITIES

There are countless activities that will help the preschool disadvantaged student gain exposure and proficiency in the area of language. The objectives and activities that follow are intended to be a sample of those that have been successfully used in preschool programs for this population of students as well as for those students who are not considered to be disadvantaged. The teacher will find many opportunities to introduce additional objectives and activities since there are limitless areas of learning in this domain. It is important that the teacher be the key individual in developing these activities and not relinquish her responsibility to teach language development to other professionals who may have traditionally performed this role. Use should be made of the talents of speech therapists and pathologists to provide consultations concerning appropriate activities, and their expertise should be called upon when the child presents a unique or difficult language problem with which the teacher feels she is unable to effectively work. Taking children out of the room to work on language skills is not advocated by the authors; its benefits are often offset by the adverse social effect of being singled out for special treatment.

Curriculum Area: Language Skills		
Behavioral Objective: The child states his name.		
Activity	Adaptations/Modifications	Materials
As part of the daily routine, play an introduction game. Say to the child, "Hello, my name is _____. What's your name"? The child should respond by saying, "My name is _____." Praise the child's efforts. Once the child knows his name and is able to say it, encourage the children to introduce themselves to each other.	*(decrease → / ← increase — degree of difficulty)* Role play visiting friends and meeting new people. Encourage the child to introduce himself to these new people by saying "Hello, my name is _____." Stress safety rules: don't talk to strangers, don't get into cars with strangers, don't take candy or gifts from strangers. Collect objects that belong to the child and his peers. Hold up each item, and say, "John's hat," "Stephen's truck." As you hold up the child's belongings, encourage him to say "Stephen's toy." Cut out pictures of peoples' faces from magazines, and paste them on small squares of oaktag. Do the same with the child's picture. Give the child the package of pictures and ask him to find his picture. When he does, he should say his name. As part of the morning class routine, do a roll call. Call each child by name. When he hears his name, the child should raise his hand and repeat his name.	Magazines Scissors Glue Oaktag Pictures of the child Child's belongings

117

Curriculum Area: Language Skills		
Behavioral Objective: The child says his age and the date of his birth.		
Activity	Adaptations/Modifications	Materials
Make a list of the children's birthdays. Construct a large wall calendar for each month of the year. Using colored magic markers, mark the children's birthdays on the calendar. At the beginning of each month, talk about the birthdays that fall within that month. Say the child's birthdate and ask him to repeat it. Periodically review the birthdates of the children in the class, pointing out on the calendar where the birthdays are.	degree of difficulty — decrease → — increase ←	Oaktag Magic markers Chart paper
	Assign the children roles (mother, father, teacher, policeman), and role play situations. As part of the dialogue, ask the child to state his age and birthdate.	
	Write a story about each child on a chart paper. Ask him to supply the pertinent information, including age and birth date.	
	Have a monthly birthday party to honor the people whose birthdays fall during the month. As part of the festivities, have the children who have birthdays during the month stand up and say their birthdate and age.	
	During conversations with the child, tell him your name and birthdate and ask him to say his. Praise the child for giving the correct information.	
	Tell the child his birthdate and ask him to repeat it. Praise his efforts.	
	Sing the song "How old are you now?" and let the child sing or say how old he is.	

Curriculum Area: Language Skills		
Behavioral Objective: The child carries out one-part commands containing prepositions.		
Activity	Adaptations/Modifications	Materials

Activity	Adaptations/Modifications	Materials
Seat the child at a table or desk. Place a small object on the table. Demonstrate placing an object in various positions relative to a stationary point. As you are positioning the object, tell the child what you are doing. Say, "I am putting the car *on* the desk, *in* the desk, *beside* the desk, etc.)." Ask the child to place the object in a variety of positions relative to a stationary point (for example, *on* the chair, *under* the chair, *beside* the chair). Repeat the activity often, introducing new prepositions.	Stand the children in a line. Ask the children to stand in order by saying, "Stephen, stand in front of Joseph." "Joseph you are behind Stephen." Praise the child if he stands in front of or behind the person you ask him to. Give the child four toys; take two and place them side by side. Say, "the car is next to the truck." Ask the child to put the cars and trucks next to each other in different order. Ask the child to put his papers *on* your desk, his toys *on* the shelf. Ask the child to put *on* his hat, put *on* his mittens, put *on* his jacket. Ask the child to step *over* a pile of blocks, to hop *over* a line, to place his hands *over* his eyes, to jump *over* a rope. Ask the child to put an object *in* his desk, *in* his pocket, *in* his locker, *in* a box, *in* the waste basket. As part of a small group activity, introduce the preposition *to*. Demonstrate *to* by handing objects to children, saying, "I'm giving this toy *to* Stephen." Ask the child to choose an object and give it *to* another child. Encourage him to say "I'm giving this *to* Mark."	Table or desk Chair Small toys and objects Blocks Box Waste basket Rope Hat Mittens } (the child's) Jacket

degree of difficulty ← increase   decrease →

119

Curriculum Area: Language Skills		
Behavioral Objective: The child carries out one part commands containing pronouns.		
Activity	Adaptations/Modifications	Materials
Seat the child at a table with his peers, girls and boys. Give each child a toy or object. Say, "I am giving a block to Stephen. I am giving it to him." Then say, "I am giving a ball to Amy. I am giving it to her." Give each child an object, stressing the use of *him* and *her*. Point to each boy and say *him* and to each girl and say *her*. Collect the toys or objects. Ask the child to give the objects to the children; say, "Give a car to Matthew." The child should say, "I'm giving it to *him*." Say, "Give a toy to Sherrie." The child should say, "I'm giving it to *her*." Praise the child for using pronouns correctly.	Repeat the activities, using different pronouns. Show the child something belonging to a male classmate; say, "This is Stephen's back pack. It is his back pack. Give Stephen his back pack." Practice, using articles belonging to the other boys. Show the child something belonging to a female classmate; say, "This is Ann's sweater. It is her sweater. Give Ann her sweater." Practice, using articles belonging to the other girls. Show the child a possession of yours; say, "This is Miss ____ glove. It is my glove." Put the glove down and say to the child, "Please give me my glove." Repeat the activity using different objects. Show the child a collection of belongings, some of which are hers or his. Pick up his or her hat, mitten, etc. Say, "This is your hat, mitten." Put the items back among the others, and say, "Pick up your hat." Praise the child if he does so, repeat the activity if he does not. Place an object, such as a car or a cracker, in front of the child. Point to yourself and say "me." Ask the child to "Give the car to me." Praise the child for obeying your command or repeat the activity until he is able to do so.	Children's belongings Your belongings Small toys Blocks Table Chairs

degree of difficulty ← increase decrease →

120

Curriculum Area: Language Skills

Behavioral Objective: The child carries out commands having two or more parts.

Activity	Adaptations/Modifications	Materials
As part of the daily classroom activities, designate one child to be the "Teacher's Helper." Give the child two or more commands involving classroom duties (for example, "Pick up the blocks and pile them on the shelf," or "Clean up the Play Doh, put it on the shelf, and throw away the newspaper from the work table"). After the child performs the assigned tasks, thank him for being a good helper. Increase the number and difficulty of the commands as the child becomes proficient in carrying out assigned tasks.	Prepare recipes that require three or four steps. Read the instructions and see if the child can follow them. Offer assistance when necessary. Practice. Play a memory game. Give the child three or four things to do (for example, say, "Angela, touch the door, draw a circle on the board, shake hands with me, and return to your seat"). Praise the child's efforts. Do art projects that require two or more steps. Give the child instructions (for example, "Trace the shape, outline it with black, paint it, and cut it out"). Offer assistance. During motor or physical education activities, give two-, three-, and four-part commands (for example, "Stand on one foot, clap your hands, touch your toes, and turn around"). Play "Simon Says," using two-part commands, then three-and four-part commands. Sing "Put Your Finger in the Air." Make up verses that include two- and three-part commands. Review and practice following one-part commands.	Materials for art project Toys Materials for cooking project Song, "Put Your Finger in the Air" (in *Music Activities for Retarded Children*, D. R. Ginglend and W. E. Stiles, Abingdon Press, Nashville, Tenn., 1965.)

(Vertical scale between columns: ← increase / decrease → degree of difficulty)

121

Curriculum Area: Language Skills		
Behavioral Objective: The child uses language courtesies.		
Activity	Adaptations/Modifications	Materials
As part of daily classroom activities, use language courtesies in conversational patterns. For example, as the child enters the room in the morning, say, "Good morning, John. How are you today?" At play time, say, "I see you are building with the blocks. Are you having a nice time?" Encourage the child to respond to these questions and ask conversational questions of his own.	decrease ← degree of difficulty → increase Read the story *The Grouchy Ladybug*. Ask the children to discuss what happens when the ladybug is grouchy versus when he responds in a polite way. Read the story *What Do You Say, Dear?* See if the children can guess the responses to "What do you say, dear?" Role play situations in which the participants engage in conversations using language courtesies. Practice greetings and farewells using hand puppets. Remind the child to use language courtesies such as "Hello," "How are you," "I'm fine, thank you," "Good-bye," "Good morning," and "Nice to see you." During daily activities, say "please," "thank you," and "you're welcome." Encourage the child to include these language courtesies as part of his language repertoire, and praise him when he does so.	Hand puppets Stories *What Do You Say, Dear?* *The Grouchy Ladybug*

122

Curriculum Area: Language Skills		
Behavioral Objective: The child responds appropriately to questions, asking *who, what, when, where, whose, how,* and *how many.*		
Activity	Adaptations/Modifications	Materials
Play a game of "Do You Know the Answer?" Seat the children in a circle. Go around the circle asking questions; ask questions that will serve to review previously developed language skills, such as "What is your name?" "How old are you?" "When is your birthday?" "How many fingers do you have?" "Where is the red ball?" and "Whose picture is this?" Praise the child's efforts to answer the questions.	⟵ increase degree of difficulty decrease ⟶ Encourage the children to ask questions and to answer each other as they play or work together. Read the child stories. As you read, stop and ask the child "What do you think is going to happen?" "How do you feel about what happened?" "How many people are in the picture on this page?" etc. Play "Do You Know the Answer?" letting the children take turns asking the questions. Comment on the good questions the child is asking. As the child works and plays, ask him questions about himself (for example, "What are you playing with?" "How old are you?" and "Whose toy is this?"). Praise his efforts to answer your questions. Ask the child questions about himself that he can respond to easily (for example, "How are you?" "What is your name?" "Where is your coat?" and "What would you like to play with?").	Storybooks

Curriculum Area: Language Skills		
Behavioral Objective: The child engages in simple conversations with another person.		
Activity	**Adaptations/Modifications**	**Materials**
As part of daily classroom activities, establish conversational patterns that are appropriate for specific situations: morning greetings, greetings after a weekend, good-bye statements, greeting for birthdays, holiday greetings, etc. Encourage the child to participate in these conversations and to initiate them with family and friends.	*degree of difficulty* — decrease → ← increase Using a play phone or tele-trainer, practice conversations such as calling the operator for information, calling a friend, or calling grandmother to say hello. Praise the child's efforts at conversation. Ask the child to watch TV specials at home ("Charlie Brown," "Frosty the Snowman"). The next day at school, engage the child in conversation about the program. Encourage the children to talk together about the program. Watch a filmstrip or movie with the child. After the film, encourage the child to discuss it with you. Ask questions to encourage his participation if necessary. Take a walk in the community. Return to class and discuss the walk with the child. Develop a language experience story, based on the child's conversation.	Chart paper Magic marker Filmstrip Movie Filmstrip/movie projector Play phone or tele-trainer

Curriculum Area: Language Skills

Behavioral Objective: The child uses prepositions to describe the positions of people and things.

Activity	Adaptations/Modifications	Materials
Seat the child at a desk or table. Show him pictures that show people, animals, and common objects in different places and positions (for example, a fish in a fish bowl, a boy sitting on a fence, a cat sleeping under a tree, etc.). Ask the child to describe the pictures (for example, the fish is swimming in a bowl). Praise the child's efforts at description using prepositions. If the child has difficulty describing the pictures, ask leading questions such as "Where is the boy?" or "Where is the cat?"	Make up a story in which a common object is placed in various positions: on, under, over, in, behind, beside, in front of. Give the child the object discussed in the story. As you read, ask the child to place the objects in the positions you describe. Place objects in various positions relative to a stationary object, and ask the child to describe what you are doing (putting the car on the shelf, under the shelf, next to the shelf, etc.). Seat the child at a table or desk. Give him an object (book, pencil, toy car), and ask him to move the object into positions relative to a stationary object (on the table, under the table, next to the table, etc.). Stand the child next to a chair. Ask him to stand next to the chair, in front of the chair, behind the chair, and to sit on the chair. Ask him to do these positions independently and describe his position. Using masking tape, mark out a square on the floor. Stand in the square, beside the square, on the line and tell the child what your position is. Ask him to imitate your actions, describing his position in relation to the box as he does so. Praise his efforts.	Desk or table Chair Pictures Masking tape Toys Cars Book Pencil

degree of difficulty ← increase   decrease →

Curriculum Area: Language Skills		
Behavioral Objective: The child identifies colors, names them, and identifies the colors of objects.		
Activity	Adaptations/Modifications	Materials
Place objects of various colors on a table in front of the child. Ask the child to "Hand me the red car," "Give me the green ball," etc. Once you have all the objects, tell the child he can have them back if he asks for them by color (for example, "May I have the orange block?"). Add more objects of varying shades of colors as the child begins to identify all the colors.	Make color charts. Print the color word at the top of a large piece of oaktag and place a block of the color next to the word. Ask the child to cut pictures from magazines and paste them on the corresponding color chart. Bring fruits and vegetables into the classroom. Ask the student to identify them by name and color: a red apple, an orange carrot, etc. Put water in clear jars. As the child watches, drop food coloring into each jar and stir. Ask the children to tell you what color the water has turned. Use the jars as decorations for the classroom. Give the child beads, pegs, or blocks that are different colors. Ask the child to put all the red together, the blue, green, etc. After he has done this, ask him to tell you the color of each pile of objects. Each day, comment on the child's clothes, specifying the color (for example, "Carol, I like your red coat," or "Tom, I like your blue pants"). Ask the child to describe his clothes, designating their colors. Praise his efforts. Introduce each color. Show the child all red objects. Once he identifies red, introduce yellow, then blue. Designate objects by their color: the red car, the blue block, etc., and ask the child to designate objects by their color.	Table Colored objects Child's clothing Colored beads, blocks, and pegs Clear jars Water Food coloring Magazines Paste Scissors Oaktag Magic markers Fruits Vegetables

degree of difficulty
← decrease   increase →

Chapter 11
Music

Unfortunately, most music education programs are relegated to the position of an extracurricular activity and often are not highly integrated into other curricular areas. In the preschool program, however, music can be an adjunct to the teaching of preacademic skills as well as an aid in the development of a strong language program. As has been mentioned previously, culturally deprived or disadvantaged children often encounter difficulty in the language area. Music, therefore, can serve as a medium for introducing critical and functional language development activities.

STRENGTHENING LANGUAGE AND COGNITIVE DEVELOPMENT

Music can be used to translate the actions that may be incorporated in daily lessons into words. An example is the song "Put Your Finger In The Air." The song asks the child to put his finger in the air, and the continuation of verses allows the child to place various parts of his body in different positions, to touch different parts of his body, or to place his body in contact with other objects. The ability of music activities to incorporate knowledge of body parts and objects is especially important for the child with a poor body awareness or inadequate understanding of how his body fits into the world around him. In the song mentioned above, the student can stamp his foot on the floor, place his hand on his head, or put his hand on the desk. Songs of this type provide the student with opportunities to come in contact with objects in a musical way that is fun and is simple and repetitive enough to encourage the student to sing the song at home. While teaching the verses of certain songs, you can also include discrimination between singular and plural forms, such as asking the child to put his hands on his knee or on his shoulder. Left and right discrimination also can be focused upon by asking the child to put his right hand on a part of his body followed by placing his left hand somewhere on his body. Specific songs that emphasize the teaching of concepts are suggested in the curriculum activities at the end of this chapter. It is suggested that the teacher or the individual review this information carefully with the idea of incorporating it into her educational program.

TEACHING PREACADEMIC SKILLS

The medium of music can also do much to teach preacademic and other educational concepts to the culturally deprived preschool child. Songs and verses can teach the young child how to use the past tense and conjunctions as well as how to count and perform counting operations with objects, figures, or materials found around the home or in the school room. The rhyming and blending of words and the ability to recite a series of specific names also can be taught through music and is an approach that allows for individual as well as group participation. A review of the variety of songs that have been developed for nursery school, kindergarten, and prekindergarten programs, as well as those that have been developed for the primary grades, offers the teacher a supporting activity or major activity for nearly every educational concept she may wish to teach. The creativity of the teacher will help her decide when and how to introduce the specific songs in which the child may be interested. It is suggested that the teacher build her lesson around songs that do not introduce major new concepts that are not a part of the child's repertoire.

It is important to note that, while many programs do provide music as a specific activity or as an adjunct to the educational program, few programs select specific songs, poems, or verses that directly relate to the lessons on a day-to-day basis. Music can be utilized to do this and at the same time reinforce concepts that are being taught as part of the daily educational program.

CURRICULAR OBJECTIVES AND ACTIVITIES

Music activities should be presented in a manner that is pleasant for the teacher and enjoyable and highly motivating to the students. The following curricular objectives and activities provide the teacher with a variety of ways to incorporate music into her curriculum.

Curriculum Area: Music

Behavioral Objective: The child participates in musical activities that reinforce the learning of self-care skills.

Activity	Adaptations/Modifications	Materials
Seat the children on the floor. Give each child a face cloth and keep one for yourself. Using the face cloth, pantomime washing your face and hands. Ask the child to imitate your actions. Sing the song "This Is the Way We Wash Our Clothes," changing the verse to "This Is the Way We Wash Our Face" as you and the child pantomime washing your faces. Then sing, "This Is the Way We Wash Our Hands," pantomiming that action. Let the child choose verses to sing ("This Is the Way We Wash Our Feet," "... Knees," "... Legs," etc.).	*(degree of difficulty ← decrease increase →)* Encourage the child's parents to allow the child to wash his hands and face independently at home and to praise his efforts. Following a grooming lesson during which the child has washed his hands and face, combed his hair, tidied up his clothes, stand him in front of a mirror and sing the song "Children Look in the Mirror." Encourage the child to respond to the musical questions "Do you see a nice clean face?" "Do you see hair in place?" Praise the child's appearance. Play the Sesame Street record of "Everybody Wash." Act out the actions the record calls for, and ask the child to do the same. At snack time, require the children to wash their hands and faces. Offer assistance when necessary. Sing "This Is the Way We Wash Our Hands," and practice with the child until he is able to mimic the motion of washing his hands. Praise his efforts.	Songs "This Is the Way We Wash Our Clothes" "Children Look in the Mirror" (in *Music Activities for Retarded Children*, D. R. Ginglend and W. E. Stiles, Abingdon Press, Nashville, Tenn., 1965) Song from the Sesame Street book and record: "Everybody Wash" (Columbia Book and Record Library, New York) Face cloths Mirror

Curriculum Area: Music

Behavioral Objective: The child participates in musical activities involving the identification of body parts.

Activity	Adaptations/Modifications	Materials
Introduce the song "Put Your Finger in the Air." Make up verses to include actions involving the identification of body parts ("Put your finger on your nose," "... eyes," "... ear," "... foot," "... back," etc.). Perform the actions as you sing the verse, and tell the child to do the same. Praise him for following the directions and placing his finger on the appropriate body part. Provide the child with the opportunity to be the leader by choosing the verse and performing the action called for in the verse for the other children to imitate.	⟵ increase decrease ⟶ degree of difficulty Go through magazines and cut out pictures of eyes, noses, mouths, feet, hands. Paste them on tagboard and form collages for each part of the body. Decorate the classroom with the collages. Do art projects involving assembling cutout pieces to form a body or face. For example, paste shapes on paper plates to make funny or sad faces, or make puppets from paper bags and cloth scraps. Construct or purchase a large body puzzle. Work with the child, disassembling the puzzle and then putting it back together. Name the body parts as you do the puzzle. Play "Simon Says," using commands such as "Simon says, touch your toes," and "... clap your hands." Sing the "Body Part Song," and perform the corresponding actions. Sing "Put Your Finger in the Air," changing the verses to include only the parts of the face. Add other body parts as the child is able to identify them.	Songs "Put Your Finger in the Air" (by Woody Guthrie in *Music Activities for Retarded Children*, D. R. Gingland and W. E. Stiles, Abingdon Press, Nashville, Tenn., 1965) "Body Part Song" (by Beleta Griffith in *Music in Development Therapy*, J. Purvis and S. Samet, University Park Press, Baltimore, 1976) Large body puzzle Art materials Magazines Scissors Glue or paste Tagboard

130

Curriculum Area: Music		
Behavioral Objective: The child participates in musical activities involving body movements.		
Activity	Adaptations/Modifications	Materials

Seat the children in a circle on the floor. Sing the song "I Take My Little Hands." Perform the action the song calls for (clap your hands, stamp your feet, nod your head). Ask the child to sing along and follow the directions of the song by performing the action it asks for. Once the child can sing the song, give him the chance to be the leader and choose the activities to be performed.

← decrease   degree of difficulty   increase →

Ask the children to form a circle and hold hands. Sing the "Circle Song," and lead the children in the movements that are called for. After you introduce each new movement, repeat the first verse. Let the child choose movements to include.

Mark out a circle on the floor with masking tape. Ask the children to sit on the floor around the circle. Play the record of "Walk Around the Circle." As the record plays, follow the directions given by the song (running, jumping, walking around the circle). Play the song again, and lead the children through the activities. Play the song another time, and let the children perform the activity independently.

Sing the song "If You're Happy and You Know It." Make up verses to include body movements (touch your toes, pat your tummy, bend your knees, jump up and down, turn around), and act out the actions the verses call for.

Sing "This is the Way We Wash Our Clothes." Make up verses (wash our hands, play the drum, hop on one foot, eat our lunch). Pantomime the actions as you sing.

Repeat the activity, introducing one body movement at a time. Make up verses for the child until he can think of his own verses.

Songs
"I Take My Little Hands" (in *Music Activities for Retarded Children*, D. R. Gingland and W. E. Stiles, Abingdon Press, Nashville, Tenn., 1965)

"This is the Way We Wash Our Clothes"

"If You're Happy and You Know It" (in *Teacher's Guide to the Open Court Kindergarten Music Program*, B. M. Smith, T. C. Harter, and M. M. Walter, Open Court Publishing Co., (*con't*)

Curriculum Area: Music

Behavioral Objective: The child participates in musical activities involving body movements. (con't)

Activity	Adaptations/Modifications	Materials
	degree of difficulty ← increase decrease →	LaSalle, Ill., 1973) "Circle Song" (by Clementine Gigliotti in *Music in Developmental Therapy*, J. Purvis and S. Samet, University Park Press, Baltimore, 1976) Record, "Walk Around the Circle" (in *Learning Basic Skills Through Music Vocabulary*, Hap Palmer, Educational Activities, Inc., Freeport, N.Y., #AR521).

Curriculum Area: Music

Behavioral Objective: The child sings songs, naming animals.

Activity	Adaptations/Modifications	Materials
Seat the children in a circle on the floor. Show the children pictures of a rooster, hen, duck, pig, and donkey. Ask the children to name the animals; name them for the children if they can't. Hold up each picture and make the sound the animal makes. Encourage the children to do the same. Once the children recognize the animals and associates the sound it makes with the animal, sing the song "I Have a Little Rooster." Encourage the children to join you in singing the animal sounds and, eventually, the entire song. Add more animals and animal sounds, once the child knows the original ones. Repeat the activity often.	Play the record "Going to the Zoo." As the record names animals, instruct the child to stand up and imitate that animal through movement and sounds. Encourage the child to sing along with the record. Sing "Old MacDonald Had a Farm." Let the child choose the animals to be included and make the animal sounds as they sing about the animals. Play "The Farmer in the Dell." Include many farm animals, and encourage the child to make the animal sounds as the animals are chosen. Show the children pictures of animals, some that live on farms and some that live in zoos. Have the children decide which are zoo animals and which are farm animals. As they decide, ask them to act out being that animal, with movement and sounds. Sing the "Elephant Song." Demonstrate being an elephant and using your arms as a trunk. Ask the children to pretend to be elephants. Sing the song again and choose one child to be an elephant; then he chooses one, and so on, until all the children are elephants. Show the child pictures of animals, and make the sound the animal makes. Ask the child to imitate your actions and pretend to be animals. *degree of difficulty* — decrease → / ← increase	Pictures of farm animals (rooster, hen, duck, pig, donkey, etc.) and zoo animals Songs "Elephant Song" "I Have a Little Rooster" (in *Music activities for Retarded Children*, D. R. Ginglend and W. E. Stiles, Abingdon Press, Nashville, Tenn., 1965) "The Farmer in the Dell" "Old MacDonald Had a Farm" Record, "Going to the Zoo" (in *Folk Song Carnival*, Hap Palmer, Educational Activities, Inc. Freeport, N.Y., #AR524).

Curriculum Area: Music

Behavioral Objective: The child sings songs that involve counting and numbers.

Activity	Adaptations/Modifications	Materials
Introduce the song "This Old Man." Sing the song for the child. Use your fingers to gesture the numbers 1–10 as you sing the song. Encourage the child to sing along with you, using his fingers to indicate the numbers 1–10. Repeat the song as part of daily activities.	Sing "Take Away Song" to introduce or reinforce the concept of counting backward from 10 to 1. Sing "Ten Little Indians." As the children sing the song, point to children to be the Indians, 1–10. As you sing the backward counting verse of "Ten Little Indians," have the children sit down in response to the verse. Repeat. Sing "Five Little Pumpkins" to introduce counting by first, second, third, fourth, and fifth. Encourage the child to sing along during daily activities (for example, "Stephen is first in line," "Anne is second," etc.). Play the Hap Palmer record of "Number March" to introduce or reinforce counting 1–5. Perform the counting activities along with the record, and encourage the child to do the same.	Songs "This Old Man" "Five Little Pumpkins" "Take Away Song" (in *Music Activities for Retarded Children*, D. R. Gingland and W. E. Stiles, Abingdon Press, Nashville, Tenn., 1965) "Ten Little Indians" Record, Hap Palmer's "Number March" (in *Learning Basic Skills Through Music*, Hap Palmer Record Library, Educational Activities, Inc., Freeport, N.Y. #AR524)

degree of difficulty ← increase   decrease →

Curriculum Area: Music	
Behavioral Objective: The child sings songs, naming the days of the week.	

Activity	Adaptations/Modifications	Materials
Introduce the song "Days of the Week." Sing the song slowly, so the child can understand the words. Discuss the information in the song, and then say the words of the song for the child. Ask the child to repeat the words after you. Sing the song again, and ask the child to sing along with you.	Sing "This Is the Way We Wash Our Clothes." Allow each child to make up a verse for a day of the week (for example, "This is the way we jump up and down so early Monday morning," or "This is the way we play the drum so early Tuesday morning"), and act it out. Repeat the activity. Choose seven children to represent the days of the week. As the verse says what is to be done on Monday, Tuesday, etc., ask the child representing that day to perform the action the verse calls for. Construct a calendar for each month. Each day, say the day and date and have one of the children mark the day on the calendar. Have each child say, for example, "Today is Monday, December 4, 1978." As part of daily activities, talk about the days of the week. Say, "Today is Monday, so yesterday was Sunday," "Tomorrow is Tuesday," etc. ← increase decrease → degree of difficulty	Songs "Days of the Week" (in *Music Activities for Retarded Children*, D. R. Gingland and W. E. Stiles, Abingdon Press, Nashville, Tenn., 1965) "This Is the Way We Wash Our Clothes" Tagboard Magic marker (for calendar)

Curriculum Area: Music		
Behavioral Objective: The child engages in rhythm band activities.		
Activity	Adaptations/Modifications	Materials
Bring a selection of rhythm instruments into the classroom. Seat the child on the floor. Show each instrument to the child, say its name, and demonstrate its use. Pass out the instruments so each child has one. One at a time, ask the children to play their instruments. After each child has played, ask him to exchange instruments with another child. Again, allow each child to play his instrument. Repeat until each child has played each instrument.	← increase decrease → degree of difficulty

Construct your own rhythm instruments. Use dowels to make rhythm sticks; tin cans, beans, jar lids to make shakers; sandpaper and wood to make sandpaper blocks, etc.

Once the student plays rhythm instruments and can keep a beat, introduce more difficult rhythm activities. Develop musical arrangements; play against the beat; have only certain instruments playing at specific times. Practice. Invite parents to watch the children perform.

Form a marching band. Play marching music; pass out rhythm instruments. Once the child establishes the beat of the music with his instrument, encourage him to form a line and march around the room to the music.

Pass out rhythm instruments. Play the record "Yellow Submarine." Demonstrate playing a rhythm instrument to the beat of the music. Ask the child to do the same.

Play the record "Yellow Submarine." Clap out the rhythm for the child. Ask him to join you in clapping out the rhythm; offer assistance when necessary (for example, by physically guiding his hands as he claps the rhythm, or counting as he claps the rhythm). Praise his efforts. | Rhythm band Instruments

Record, "Yellow Submarine" (in *Mod Marches*, Hap Palmer, Educational Activities, Inc., Freeport, N.Y., #AR527)

Records of marching music

Record player

Materials for making rhythm instruments |

Curriculum Area: Music		
Behavioral Objective: The child participates in musical games.		
Activity	Adaptations/Modifications	Materials
Ask the children to form a circle and hold hands. Explain how to play "Ring Around the Rosie." Sing the song once so the child knows what he is expected to do in response to the song. Sing the song and play "Ring Around the Rosie." Encourage the children to play the game at recess, during free-play time, and at play in their neighborhood.	Sing the song "La Raspa." Show the children how to do the Mexican Hat Dance, and ask the child to join you as you dance. Encourage the children to dance at play time and at home. Play "London Bridge Is Falling Down" with the child. Encourage him to play the game at recess, during free-play time, and at play in his neighborhood. Play "The Farmer in the Dell" with the child. Encourage him to play the game during recess and play time and at home. Play "Musical Chairs" with the child. Encourage the child to ask to play the game as part of play time or indoor recess. Sing songs that give directions for body movements (for example, "Put Your Finger in the Air," "Pointing," "This Old Man," "Hokey Pokey," or "Where Is Thumbkin?"). ← increase — degree of difficulty — decrease →	Songs "La Raspa" "Put Your Finger in the Air" "Pointing" "This Old Man" (above four in *Music Activities for Retarded Children*, D. R. Ginglend and W. E. Stiles, Abingdon Press, Nashville, Tenn., 1965) "The Farmer in the Dell" "London Bridge Is Falling Down" "Ring Around the Rosie" Chairs

Curriculum Area: Music		
Behavioral Objective: The child participates in musical activities that involve following directions.		
Activity	Adaptations/Modifications	Materials
Seat the children in a circle on the floor. To the tune of "Put Your Finger in the Air," sing instructions such as "Choose a toy from the shelf, from the shelf," "Stephen, get in line, get in line," "Anne, stand up, stand up," or "Tommy, get your mat, get your mat." Praise the child for following your instructions. As part of daily activities, sing instructions to the child (for example, for getting in line, hanging up outer clothing, or putting toys away).	Dance the folk dance "Czardas." Demonstrate the movements called for by the song, and ask the child to join you as you follow the directions. Do the dance. Sing the song, "Chiapanicas," and demonstrate the actions the song calls for. Encourage the child to follow the directions in the song by exhibiting the requested movement. Sing the song "Pointing." Make up verses that require pointing to body parts, colors, classmates, furniture, and directions (up, down, right, left). Sing "Put Your Finger in the Air." Include directions involving body parts, pieces of furniture, parts of the classroom (floor, wall), and toys in the classroom. Sing the "Hokey Pokey," and praise the child's efforts at responding to the directions in the song. Play "Simon Says," including a variety of instructions (for example, "Simon says, get in a line," "Simon says, look out the window"). ⟵ increase decrease ⟶ ⟺ degree of difficulty	Songs "Czardas" "Chiapanicas" "Pointing" "Put Your Finger in the Air" (above four in *Music Activities for Retarded Children,* D. R. Ginglend and W. E. Stiles, Abingdon Press, Nashville, Tenn., 1965) "Hokey Pokey"

138

Curriculum Area: Music		
Behavioral Objective: The child participates in musical activities that involve discrimination between left and right.		
Activity	Adaptations/Modifications	Materials
Play the "Hokey Pokey." Stand the children in a line. Turn your back to them and sing the "Hokey Pokey." Do the actions as the song calls for them ("Put your right hand in," "Put your left hand in," etc.). Watch the child to see that he is using right and left at the appropriate times. Once the child discriminates between left and right, play the game in the traditional circle formation. Play the game often to reinforce the discrimination between left and right.	Play the record, "Walk Around the Circle." As the record tells the children to walk, run, and jump around the circle, add the direction of "Walk to the left (or right)," "Run to the left (or right)," etc.

Sing "How Do You Do, My Partner?" Change the direction "Will you dance in the circle?" to "Will you circle to the left?" "Will you circle to the right?"

Sing the song "Little Sally More," changing the words from *east* and *west* to turn to the *right* and turn to the *left*. Add movements, such as "Slide to the right," "Slide to the left," "Skip to the right," "Skip to the left," etc.

Sing "Put Your Finger in the Air," changing the verses to say left and right (for example, "Put your left hand on your knee," "Put your right hand in the air"). Provide help when the child needs it.

Play the "Hokey Pokey." Place a red paper bracelet on the child's right arm and leg to remind him that it is his right side and the other side is his left. Remove the bracelet once the child is more sure of right and left.

← decrease   degree of difficulty   increase → | Songs
"Put Your Finger in the Air"
"Little Sally More"
"How Do You Do, My Partner?"
(above three in *Music Activities for Retarded Children*, D. R. Ginglend and W. E. Stiles, Abingdon Press Nashville, Tenn., 1965)
"Hokey Pokey"
Record, "Walk Around the Circle" (in *Learning Basic Skills Through Music Vocabulary*, Hap Palmer, Educational Activities, Inc., Freeport, N.Y., #AR521) |

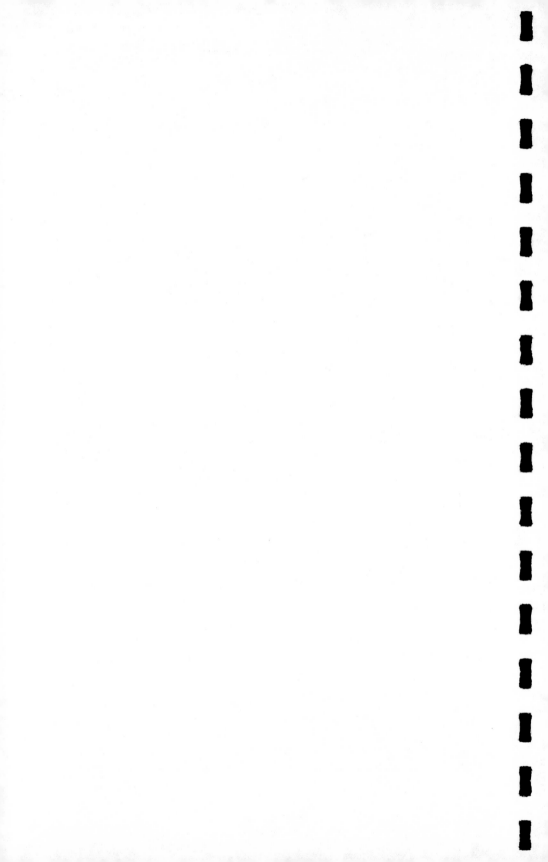

Chapter 12
Art

The inclusion of art activities in the educational program of the preschool child has been advocated by many educators for a myriad of reasons. To list but a few, art:

1. Helps the child become more observant
2. Allows the student to explore different media
3. Helps develop the understanding that objects and individuals take up space
4. Offers experiences in the use of leisure time
5. Helps to develop good feelings
6. Allows for creativity

Art activities have been especially useful in curricula for disadvantaged preschool children because they help to stimulate the child's ability to create and improve the manner in which he expresses himself. It also affords him the opportunities to appreciate art forms and experiences that may not be available within his immediate environment.

It is important that the teacher realize that the earliest efforts of the child to place marks on paper constitute one of the child's first attempts to express ideas or thoughts. While the teacher may be unable to identify the picture that is drawn, it is important that she recognize that the drawing has meaning for the child. Often first attempts at pictures represent a part of the child's environment or fantasy world, or are an effort to recreate an experience or story he has heard.

The planning and preparation of art objectives and activities is of vital importance to the overall effectiveness of the preschool curriculum. It is important that the activities that are selected serve to motivate the children and promote enthusiasm so they want to continue in their exploration of the art area. Art experiences at this preschool level usually encourage the manipulation of objects as well as those materials and tools involved in drawing, painting, constructing, and modeling activities. Sensory experiences can be emphasized in order to satisfy the child's natural interest concerning the look and feel of things in his immediate world. Working with paint, wood, clay, cardboard, paper, and discarded scrap materials offers the child a means through which he may explore the art world as he uses and develops his fine motor skills. In addition, the manipulation of paintbrushes, tools, and other instruments allows the child to experience satisfaction and can provide an outlet for stored up physical energy.

DEVELOPMENTAL STAGES IN ART SKILLS

Art activities have long been recognized for their potential to develop the area of visual perception as well as for reinforcing other classroom learning activities. There are numerous stages the child goes through as he begins to develop skill and expressiveness in the art area. Examples of the characteristics of some of these stages include:

1. Prescribble stage: The child explores any type of material that will mark or smear.
2. Random scribble stage: The child makes marks on a surface with any instrument that is available. There is little if any muscle control over the scribbles.
3. Shape repetition: The child scribbles in line fashion or in a circle.
4. Outlining of shapes: After consistent repetition of shapes, the child can draw crude shapes at will with some degree of muscular control.
5. Naming the scribbles: After scribbling, the child tries to label or explain his work.
6. Pattern development: Lines and shapes are combined to form patterns; this is the beginning of the development of the personal symbols stage.
7. Shape combinations that form symbols: The child attaches meaning to the forms he is developing.
8. Utilization of space around objects: Here the child finishes his artwork by providing borders, base lines, skies, etc., around his symbols.
9. Relating symbols: The child begins to group two symbols together to show their relationship to each other.
10. Completing a picture: The child completes a picture in which all the items appear to be related.
11. Suggesting motion: At this stage, the child indicates movement of the objects and people he has drawn by drawing in lines and shapes in a repeated fashion.

CURRICULAR OBJECTIVES AND ACTIVITIES

The art objectives and activities that follow have proved to be effective and motivating to the preschool disadvantaged child. As additional activities are added by the teacher, notes should be taken as to which were the most effective in achieving the student's educational goals. It is suggested that successful activities be shared with the parents of the children so they may be included in nonschool hour activities. It is also desirable that each child experience a variety of art materials. These experiences should be repeated on a regular basis so the child begins to understand that he can manipulate different types of media and develops a degree of satisfaction in his artwork.

Curriculum Area: Art	
Behavioral Objective: The child molds clay.	

Activity	Adaptations/Modifications	Materials
Cover a table or work area with newspaper or a plastic table cloth. Seat the child at the table. Give the child and yourself a large ball of clay or Play-Doh and a rolling pin. Demonstrate rolling out the clay or Play-Doh until it is in slab form. Use cookie cutters to cut shapes into the clay. Lift out the shapes you have made and show them to the child. Give him the cookie cutters and let him cut shapes. The child may reroll the clay into a ball, roll it out with a rolling pin, and make new shapes using the cookie cutters.	Make plasticene jewelry. Pound clay flat with your hands. Cut out shapes with cookie cutters, bottle caps, or other shapes you desire. Make a hole in the shape so it may be strung to form a pendant. Add details; let dry and string on rawhide or yarn. Demonstrate making pinch pot pottery; use trays, candy dishes, and flower pots. Shape clay or plasticene into a ball. Make a hole in the middle of the ball by inserting your thumb under the hole by punching the clay outward between your fingers and thumb. Add details and let dry (if you use clay, repeat the process and fire in a kiln). Make cooked playdough so each child can have his own supply of playdough with which to work. Recipe: 1 cup flour ½ cup salt 2 tsp. cream of tartar 1 tbsp. cooking oil 1 cup water food coloring In a saucepan, stir ingredients together. Cook until firm. Cool and use. Give the child a large ball of clay or Play-Doh. Demonstrate how to pinch, pull, and pound the clay to form different shapes. Encourage the child to experiment with the clay, imitating the techniques you have demonstrated. ← increase decrease → degree of difficulty	Table or work area Chairs Newspaper or plastic table cloth Clay Play-Doh Plasticene Rolling pin Cookie cutters Flour Salt Cream of tartar Cooking oil Water Food coloring Measuring cup Teaspoon Tablespoon Saucepan Stove or hot plate Large spoon Plastic bags

Curriculum Area: Art

Behavioral Objective: The child molds clay. (con't)

Activity	Adaptations/Modifications	Materials
	Give the child a large ball of clay or Play-Doh. Demonstrate separating the clay into portions and rolling each portion into a ball. Put the balls together to form shapes and objects: snowmen, people, etc. Encourage the child to imitate your actions. Praise his efforts. ← increase / decrease → degree of difficulty	

Curriculum Area: Art

Behavioral Objective: The child colors with crayons.

Activity	Adaptations/Modifications	Materials
Seat the child at a desk or table. Give each child a box of primary crayons and a piece of construction paper. Show the child how to hold the crayon and guide his hand in making marks on the paper. Once he is able to do so independently, encourage the child to draw on his paper. Praise his efforts, whether the child scribbles or draws a recognizable picture. Encourage the child to color, using crayons and paper, during art time, free-time activities, and at home.	← increase decrease → degree of difficulty Give each child a small piece of drawing paper. Using crayons, assist the child in drawing a picture or a design on the paper. Stress pressing down hard with the crayons. Using blue, black, or dark green tempera paint, paint over the picture. Comment on how the picture shows through. Explain that this is called "crayon resist." Encourage the child to do more crayon resist projects. Cut out pages from a coloring book (they should be simple, large pictures to begin with). Ask the child to "color in" the pictures. As the child becomes more proficient at coloring in the pictures, use more difficult pictures (smaller with more detail). Using a black crayon or magic marker, draw simple shapes on paper. Give the child crayons and show him how to color inside the lines. Ask the child to "color in" the shapes. Play music. Give the child paper and crayons and ask him to draw to the music. He may express the music in colors or types of drawing. Praise the child's efforts. Repeat the activity, using only one crayon. Add crayons as the child begins to enjoy using crayons.	Desk or work table Chairs Crayons Paper Tempera paint Large paint brush Paint pans Coloring books Magic marker Records Record player

Curriculum Area: Art

Behavioral Objective: The child paints, using sponges.

Activity	Adaptations/Modifications	Materials
Seat the child at a table or work area. Cover the work area with newspaper. Put tempera paint into paint pans or some other shallow containers, and place them on the table. Place sponges cut into different shapes on the table. Demonstrate dipping the sponge into the paint and pressing the painted sponge onto construction paper to create shapes, designs, or pictures. Give each child a piece of paper and sponges. Encourage the child to sponge paint a picture. Praise the child's efforts. Display the paintings in the classroom.	Let the child sponge paint, using squares of sponge and many colors. When the child is finished, draw in details to form an abstract picture (for example, stems, leaves, and a vase to form flowers; an outline of a boat; a trunk and branches to form a tree). Using sponges cut into holiday shapes and holiday color paints, spong paint large sheets of white paper to use as holiday wrapping paper to wrap gifts made in class (for example, red and green Christmas trees, or red hearts for Valentine's Day). Cut sponges into shapes for holidays: Christmas trees, ghosts, pilgrim hats, shamrocks, hearts, etc. Give the child paper in a holiday color (for example, orange for Halloween), paint in a corresponding color (black) and a sponge cut in a shape (cat). Sponge paint the paper. When it dries, use the painting as holiday cards or place mats. Repeat the activity, using one sponge and one color of paint. Add sponges and colors as the child becomes more adept and interested in sponge painting.	Table or work area Sponges cut into shapes Tempera paints Paint pans or shallow containers Construction paper Magic markers Sheets of white paper

degree of difficulty — increase / decrease

147

Curriculum Area: Art		
Behavioral Objective: The child finger paints.		
Activity	Adaptations/Modifications	Materials

Materials

Finger paints
Finger painting paper
Sponge and water
Construction paper
Scissors
Magic markers or crayons
Paste or glue
Paint shirts or plastic garbage bags
Newspaper
Table or work area

Adaptations/Modifications (degree of difficulty ← increase / decrease →)

Cut shapes from the child's finger paintings. Paste on art paper and draw in details (for example, cut out flower and vase). Cut out different shapes to make pictures.

Do finger painting with the child. Make interesting shapes and textures. Carefully place a piece of paper on top of the painted one; press down and remove. Tell the child he has made a print. When dry, fold the paper; use as a folder or greeting card.

Smear finger paint on the palm and fingers of the child. Press the painted hand onto white or colored paper, and comment on the hand print. Give the child large pieces of paper and help him make hand prints. Print the child's name in between the prints.

Demonstrate the use of the whole hand. Assist the child in using the fingertips, fingernails, palms, knuckles, heel, and side of his hand to create lines, shapes, and patterns.

Start with one color and add colors until a number of colors are being used.

Repeat the activity, using many colors and allowing the child to choose the color combinations he wants to use in his painting.

Repeat the activity, using only one color and guiding the child's hand as he finger paints.

Activity

Cover the table or work area with newspaper. Ask the child to put on a paint shirt (plastic garbage bags with holes cut out for head and arms may be used in place of paint shirts). On the table, place finger painting paper, and two colors of finger paint. With a wet sponge, wet the finger painting paper. Place a blob of paint on the child's paper and yours. Demonstrate using your fingers to paint, and encourage and assist the child in doing the same. Once the child is "into" the painting, let him take a blob of the second color paint, place it on his paper, and finger paint. Praise the child's efforts. Display the paintings in the classroom.

Curriculum Area: Art

Behavioral Objective: The child engages in string-painting activities.

Activity	Adaptations/Modifications	Materials
		Table or work area
		Chairs
		Tempera paint
		String
		Construction paper
		Paint pans
	Repeat the instructions for making folded paper string paintings. Use three or four colors, drying between using each color paint to avoid smudging the colors. Display the paintings.	
	Make folded paper string paintings. Fold a piece of construction paper in half. Unfold it. Dip string into paint and lay it on one half of the paper. Refold the paper. Be sure one end of the string is protruding from the paper. Place your hand on the folded paper. Press down. Grasp the string and pull it out. Open the paper and comment on the "surprise" inside. Ask the child to make a folded string painting. Offer help when necessary. Praise the finished paintings.	
	Repeat the activity, using one color paint and smaller paper.	

degree of difficulty ← increase   decrease →

| Seat the child at a table or work area. Within the child's reach, place paint pans or other shallow containers of different color paints. Give the child and yourself a large piece of construction paper. Place a piece of heavy cord or string into each paint pan (be sure part of the string is not in the paint so it may be grasped with ease). Take a string and snake it around your paper. Put the string back in the paint pan. Choose another color string and do the same. Comment on how pretty your paper looks. Encourage the child to use the strings and create a string painting. Praise the child's paintings. Once the paintings are dry, display them in the classroom. |

Curriculum Area: Art

Behavioral Objective: The child creates inkblot designs, using tempera paints.

Activity	Adaptations/Modifications	Materials
Seat the child at a table or work area. Take a piece of construction paper and fold it in half. Open the paper. On one side of the paper, place a small drop of paint. Refold the paper, rub it with your hand, and open the paper. Comment on the "ink blot" design you formed. Repeat, using different color paints, until you have a pleasing design and combination of colors. Give the child a piece of construction paper. Repeat the demonstrated activity with the child, offering assistance when necessary. Praise the child's efforts. Display the paintings in the classroom before sending them home with the child.	Repeat the activity, using colored inks and different types of paper (rice, onion skin, tissue) to create a variety of effects. Use as wrapping paper. Repeat the activity, using different colors of drawing ink. Encourage the child to make "ink blot" designs. Use the finished pictures as greeting cards or folders for papers, or mat as pictures. Make simulated ink blots. On construction paper, place a drop of paint; take a straw, hold it near the paint, and blow through the straw. Direct the paint across the paper to form designs or abstract pictures. Mat on a contrasting color of paper or tagboard. Display as paintings, and give to parents as gifts. Repeat the activity, using one color paint and making one "ink blot" design. As the child is able to do the activity independently, make more than one ink blot design with one color of paint.	Table or work area Chairs Construction paper Tempera paints Drawing inks Straws Rice paper Onion skin paper Tissue paper

degree of difficulty — decrease / increase

Curriculum Area: Art

Behavioral Objective: The child paints with a brush and paints.

Activity	Adaptations/Modifications	Materials
Cover a table or work area with newspaper or a plastic tablecloth. Place paint (in paint pans), brushes, and paper on the table. Seat the child at the table. Show the student the objects on the table. Name each object, and state its function. Demonstrate picking up a paint brush, dipping the paint brush into the paint, applying the brush to the paper, and painting lines, shapes, or scribbles on the paper. Repeat for each of three colors. Place art materials within the child's reach, and encourage the child to paint. Praise the child's efforts.	*increase ← degree of difficulty → decrease* After field trips or special occasions, develop a language experience story. Ask the children to paint pictures "illustrating" the story. Use story and pictures as a bulletin board. Draw simple pictures on large sheets of paper. Give the child paints and brushes and let him paint the pictures. Trace an outline of the child on large brown or white paper. Give the child paints and brushes and assist him in drawing in details and painting in clothing, hair, facial features, etc. Display in the classroom. Set up a painting area with paints, brushes, paper, paint shirts, and easels. Put a brush in each color paint to avoid the need for water. Encourage the child to paint during free time. Play music. Ask the child to paint to the music. Demonstrate. Use paint to express the way the music makes you feel or the beat of the music. Repeat the activity using two colors of paint. Repeat the activity, using one color of paint.	Table or work area Chairs Newspaper or plastic tablecloth Paints Paint pans Brushes Paper Records Record player Easels Paint shirts Magic markers Chart paper

151

Curriculum Area: Art

Behavioral Objective: The child cuts and pastes as part of art activities.

Activity	Adaptations/Modifications	Materials
Seat the child at a table or work area. Place paper plates, paste or glue, scissors, and construction paper on the table. From different colors of paper, cut out eyes, nose, mouth, ears, and hair. Place a small amount of glue or paste on a tongue depressor, popsicle stick, Q-tip, or your finger. Transfer glue or paste to the back of the eyes, nose, etc. Paste the cutouts onto the paper plate to form a face. Draw in extra details (freckles, eyelashes). Give the child a paper with predrawn facial features. Help him cut out the pieces, paste them on a plate, and draw in the details. Praise his efforts, and display the faces.	Make a mosaic. Give the child scissors and different colors of paper or pictures from magazines. Tell the child to cut the paper or pictures into small pieces. Give the child a piece of construction paper or tagboard with an outline drawn on it (a car, a butterfly, a dog, fruit, etc.). Demonstrate filling in the picture by pasting cutout papers within the outline. Encourage the child to do the same. Be sure to overlap, and use many colors to create a mosaic effect. Cut out completed mosaics and use as Christmas tree decorations or room decorations. Make a collage. Hand cut tagboard colored paper, and cloth scraps. Cut the scraps and paper into different shapes and sizes. Encourage the child to cut along with you. Demonstrate gluing the pieces onto the tagboard, overlapping different colors and textures. Ask the child to do the same. Praise the child's efforts. Display the collages. Make paper-bag puppets. Give each child a lunch-size paper bag and small pieces of different colors of construction paper. Demonstrate cutting out eyes, ears, nose, and mouth and pasting them on the bag to make an animal puppet. Ask the child to make a puppet of his own. Be sure to use the fold of the bag to form the puppet's mouth so the child can put his hand into the bag and move the puppet's mouth. Repeat the activity, precutting the features and helping the child paste them on a plate. Repeat the activity, precutting the features, applying the paste to them, and assisting the child in placing them on the plate to form a face.	Table or work area Chairs Paper plates Glue or paste Colored paper Tongue depressor Popsicle stick Q-tips Magic markers Crayons Scissors Paper bags Tagboard Cloth scraps Magazines

degree of difficulty: ← increase / decrease →

152

Curriculum Area: Art

Behavioral Objective: The child makes jewelry from pasta.

Activity	Adaptations/Modifications	Materials
Bring different shapes of pasta into the classroom. Using food dyes, dye the pasta a variety of colors. Let dry. Show the child how to string the pasta, using a plastic needle and string, heavy thread, or embroidery cotton, to form a single-strand pasta bracelet. Give the child colored pasta, plastic needle, and thread, and assist him in stringing the pasta. Tie the ends together and let the child wear the bracelet, or wrap it up for the child to take home as a gift.	Make double-strand necklaces and bracelets by tying single-strand necklaces and bracelets together.	Pasta (different shapes)
	Set out materials for making pasta jewelry. Encourage the child to make jewelry for himself and as gifts during art or free-time activities.	Food dyes
	Make a single-strand necklace or bracelet, using different shapes and colors to form a definite design. Ask the child to copy the pattern, offering assistance when necessary. Encourage the child to also create his own designs and patterns.	Plastic needles
	Make a single-strand necklace or bracelet, alternating shapes of pasta to form a definite pattern. Ask the child to make a necklace or bracelet, copying your pattern. Praise the child's efforts.	String, Heavy thread, Embroidery cotton
	Make a single-strand necklace or bracelet, alternating colors of pasta to form a definite pattern. Ask the child to make a necklace or bracelet, copying your pattern. Praise the child's efforts.	Yarn, Margarine tub covers
	Make Christmas decorations using pasta. Punch a hole in and spray paint the covers of margarine tubs. When dry, string yarn through the hole so the cover can be hung on a tree. Assist the child in gluing different colors and shapes of pasta onto the cover. Use matching or contrasting colors. When dry, wrap and send home as Christmas gifts.	Spray paint, Hole punch, Glue
	Let the child choose the pasta he wants to use to make his bracelet. Assist him in stringing the pasta. Practice until he is able to string the pasta independently.	

degree of difficulty — increase / decrease

Curriculum Area: Art		
Behavioral Objective: The child makes puppets.		
Activity	Adaptations/Modifications	Materials

Activity	Adaptations/Modifications	Materials
Precut simple shapes from felt; cut them in pairs. Examples of shapes might be a snowman, a dog, a person, or a Christmas tree. On a sewing machine or by hand, stitch the two pieces together around the edges, leaving the bottom open so the child can slide his hand in. Precut details from felt; for a snowman, cut eyes, nose, mouth, scarf, and hat. Seat the child at a desk or work area. Place cutouts, details, and glue on the table. Give him the cutout of the snowman and show him a completed one. Put the completed one on his hand and let him play with it for a minute. Take the completed puppet back. Show the child the precut features, and tell him to glue them onto his puppet. Offer help when necessary. Praise the child's efforts. Encourage the child to play with the puppet by using puppets in language activities.	Make a puppet on a string. Precut shapes: a circle for the face, ovals for the ears, rectangle for the body, elongated rectangles for arms and legs, a small rectangle for a neck. Punch holes where the body parts connect to each other, attach with paper fasteners. Cut out features: eyes, nose, mouth, and hair from scraps of colored paper. Glue onto puppet's face. Punch a hole in the top of the head and tie a string through it. Bend arms at wrist and elbow, legs at knee and ankle. Hold puppet by the string and make him "dance." Assist the child in making his own puppet. Make sock puppets. Make up one sock puppet, using the sock as a body and adding features: buttons for eyes, bottle caps for noses, yarn for hair, felt scraps for mouth, ears, etc. Show the child the puppet. Demonstrate making one. Give the child the necessary materials and assist him in creating an original puppet. Give as gifts, or use in class as part of language activities. Make stick puppets. Precut simple shapes: flowers, animals, people, from construction paper. Ask the child to color in the details. Glue onto oaktag. When dry attach (glue or staple) the cutout to a stick or dowel. Use in puppet shows or to act out simple stories. Make paper bag puppets. Pass out lunch-size bags and precut features. A rabbit makes a good puppet: include long ears, a nose, a mouth, eyes, and whiskers. Assist the child as he glues the features onto the bag, placing the mouth at the fold of the bag so the child can make the mouth move. Have conversations with the child and his puppet. Use in language activities.	Desk or work area Chairs Felt Construction paper Oaktag Glue Needle and thread or sewing machine Paper lunch bags Dowels or sticks Socks Buttons Bottle caps Yarn Felt scraps String Paper fasteners

degree of difficulty — increase ← / decrease →

Chapter 13
Industrial Arts

Although few programs including industrial arts activities for elementary-age children currently exist, this chapter addresses the area of industrial arts as an important component of the preschool curriculum. It is hoped that the need for these types of activities will be realized as the teacher begins to work with her children in this area.

What is *industrial arts*? What areas does it encompass, and why include it in a program for the preschool disadvantaged student? In an attempt to answer these questions, the authors have reviewed the few existing programs that do incorporate industrial arts activities in the preschool curriculum. Perhaps most prominent are those designated as Montessori programs, which have long included teaching the world of work.

BENEFITS OF AN INDUSTRIAL ARTS PROGRAM

Traditionally, industrial arts has been defined as the study of industry and technology and the tools, processes, and materials that relate to understanding these areas. Contemporary industrial arts, especially for the disadvantaged preschool student, is much more comprehensive. Specifically, it can provide the opportunity for the very young child to explore and challenge his environment. Its diversity of content allows each student to develop his creativity, be it through building a simple woodworking project, or taking part in a class or group undertaking that encourages the students to work together, each performing different jobs. It has long been advocated that industrial arts activities offer opportunities for accomplishment and success for students at all levels of ability because it develops concrete educational experiences resulting from realistic and functional work-type situations. Perhaps one of the overwhelming attributes of utilizing industrial arts experiences is its ability to incorporate numerous learning theories, specifically those involving motivation, reinforcement, individualization of instruction, self-corrective feedback, and multisensory involvement. The disadvantaged preschool child can benefit greatly from these avenues of learning in addition to being exposed to systems of learning that incorporate the verbal, motor, visual, and kinesthetic domains.

While industrial arts activities are slowly being integrated into some elementary curricula, few programs at the preschool level have been developed that capitalize upon this significant teaching area. It is only recently that industrial arts teachers began working with disadvantaged children as a means of providing them with a relevant curriculum that would motivate them to stay in school.

The older disadvantaged child often has viewed school as an evil trap that ultimately becomes frustrating and provides little immediate reinforcement. In many instances, he views completing a grade as something he must do rather than utilizing it as a learning situation. Often the student is exposed to his first industrial arts activities at the junior high level, when he has lost much of his motivation for school and his frustration level is at its peak.

Industrial arts activities can help the young child learn about different facets of American life and the world of industry. He soon learns that its people are working in all types of occupations and that the majority of these jobs require specific training programs. It is not too early for the preschool child to be taught that obtaining a job where he can earn money may not be an easy task. He also needs to know that the content of industrial arts activities are typically modeled after realistic experiences found in industry. The disadvantaged preschooler soon realizes that industrial arts activities allow him to explore other avenues of learning, specifically those involving the tools, materials, and resources of industry.

By their very nature, industrial arts activities require the teacher to closely monitor the progress of the child, and often a close personal relationship develops. The close teacher-student relationship demanded by industrial arts activities results in the teacher knowing her student better and being better able to plan for him. It is well documented that the teacher has a great influence on the preschool child's attitude about school and eventually how the child views the world of work. It was the intent of the authors to purposely include industrial arts in this curriculum because of its ability to provide the framework for appreciating the world of work into which so many of these students have difficulty entering. Heggen (1970) listed several suggestions that he felt the teacher who is considering teaching industrial arts to her students should be aware of:

> ... (1) recognize what can and cannot be accomplished within the educational framework, (2) develop an understanding of the emotional make-up of disadvantaged children in your class, (3) realize your importance to these children as they relate to you in their learning experiences, (4) accept failure and be able to accept success and reward it properly and (5) be sensitive to the individual student's needs. Patience, sincerity, flexibility, and a sense of humor are, of course, personal characteristics needed by all teachers regardless of their assignments (pp. 88-89).

LINE PRODUCTION

While there are numerous methods and activities that can be incorporated into an industrial arts program, the authors have selected one representative method that can be used in a preschool setting and that best illustrates the way in which many educational goals can be accomplished by using the world of work as a basic foundation.

This method, which appears to be quite appropriate for this population, has gone under a myriad of names—mass production, line production, assembly line, etc.—but the basic concepts are similar. It is important to note that the line production method is one that may be used as part of a total school program and accomplished in or out of an industrial arts setting. It can utilize various forms of media (paper, wood, paint) to help achieve its goals. The ability to work with concrete materials and to perform functional motor tasks and the development of work habits are unique by-products of a line production. The process results in a finished article, which provides reinforcement and a sense of accomplishment for the student as well as for his parents.

Definition

Line production, in this context, is the accomplishment of a joint endeavor through an organization of individuals. The students are seated near each other (put on a line) where each works on one part of a project and then passes it to the next student. The student's actions, emotions, and interactions that occur during this process are observed and form the basis of his evaluation.

Implementation

In implementing a line production, it is advisable to discuss with the students the importance of working with others. You might want to develop interest by discussing the occupations of the students' parents at a level commensurate with the students' level of comprehension. It is advisable to take a field trip to an industry to observe a line production; areas of emphasis during these trips should include observing socially acceptable work habits and cooperative work efforts.

Before implementing the line production it is always advisable to conduct a "dry run." This should occur after a task analysis of the item has been performed in addition to a cost analysis. It is important to remember that a project with too many steps may be confusing to the preschool student, who requires closure or who needs the reinforcement of seeing how his effort fits into the overall project.

Motivation

Student motivation is critical if the line production is to be successful. It is suggested that you show the students a variety of completed line production projects and encourage them to look at and feel them and discuss how they

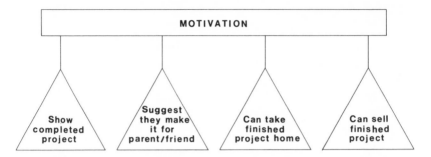

Figure 1. Motivation considerations.

might have been made. The projects you suggest should be carefully researched for feasibility in terms of the population with which you are working and their ability to be completed in a specific length of time. It is extremely important that each student be reminded that he will be able to take home a finished product to give as a gift, etc., thereby providing him with an incentive for continuing to work on the line. (See Figure 1.)

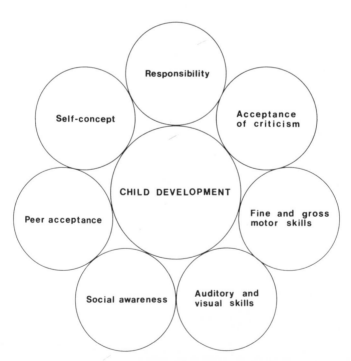

Figure 2. Development of skill and behavioral areas.

Child Development

The many skill and behavioral areas that may be developed as a result of participating in a line production are demonstrated in Figure 2.

The uniqueness of running a line production can be attested to by the opportunities it provides the student in areas that traditionally have not been emphasized in the regular education preschool curriculum. For example, the student will be able to develop an understanding of work habits as he interacts with his peers. The line production experience will also provide an opportunity for the student to learn safety practices, to accept criticism, and to work within time limits. Additionally, dependent upon the project, he will be exposed to a variety of media, materials, and tools as he develops important prerequisite work skills. The performance of repetitive tasks is especially valuable for this population of students because it provides a realistic work experience which other curricular areas do not usually include. The opportunity to be a member of a work team, in addition to receiving social acceptance and praise, makes the line production self-reinforcing.

Project Criteria

The following list offers possible criteria for project selection. It is important that these criteria be adhered to strictly if the line production is to be conducted successfully.

1. Select inexpensive materials.
2. The project should lend itself to a breakdown of parts (task analysis).
3. The project should require jigs and fixtures (templates and holding devices).
4. The project should have some commercial appeal and definitely have student appeal.
5. The production time should be geared to the size and abilities of the class.
6. The project should have the ability to be stored until completed.

Class Organization

The line production can incorporate as few as three or four preschool students or be expanded to include a large number of students. Initially, it is suggested that the line be set up as pictured in Figure 3. At a later time additional students, such as a quality control person and a public relations person, may be added. Each of these positions should be explained to the student in terms that are understandable to them. Wages may be paid if the production results in a marketable item.

The role of the supervisor is to oversee the line production and to help out whenever bottlenecks occur. He is ultimately responsible, under supervision of the teacher, for making sure that the line runs smoothly. The safety person continually monitors the progress of the project and is constantly checking

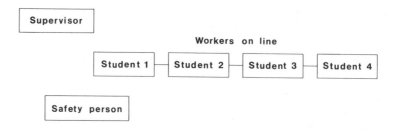

Figure 3. Line production organization.

that tools and materials are being used safely. The quality control person not only checks the finished project to make sure it has been built according to plans or specification, but also checks at intervals along the line to make sure each worker is performing his job accurately. The public relations position should be a rotating job, which allows each student to explain the project to people who are visiting the class. This can be especially important for the preschool student who needs to feel he is part of a group and requires constant reinforcement. The supply person provides the materials and tools and is continually checking to make sure that no specific phase of the project runs out of materials. This person's responsibilities also include having materials continually available and arranging for any special tools that might be required for the day's work, replacing broken tools or those requiring adjustment, and supplying appropriate jigs and fixtures to the line when they are necessary.

An example of a simple line production lesson is outlined below:

Sample Line Production

Pencil or Crayon Holder

Materials required: Small or medium-size cardboard juice containers (such as those obtained from frozen juices), white glue, paper or burlap, scissors, artist brushes, and rubber bands.

Arrangement: A long table, series of desks, or workbenches, arranged in a long line.

Procedure: The line can be set up in many ways, depending upon the abilities of the children involved. One or two students can work at the same job.

Suggested work stations:

Station 1: Student obtains required colored paper or burlap and places a template (cardboard or wooden) over paper. He outlines it and cuts to size with scissors. Christmas paper is very attractive for a seasonal project. The teacher should determine if the child at this station is capable of using scissors. This activity is especially good for promoting finger dexterity and eye-hand coordination.

Student(s) then passes the completed job to station 3 and repeats what he has been doing.

Station 2: Student completely paints container with white glue. He then smooths out the glue with his finger or a stick and passes it to station 3. He then repeats what he has been doing.

Station 3: Student wraps paper around container with glue, making sure glue is evenly spread under paper. He may want to roll container between hands. He then passes it to final station 4.

Station 4: Last student(s) on line places 3 rubber bands around each container and sets them aside to dry.

Expanding the Line

The line can be expanded in many ways. The easiest way is to create more work stations, such as including a station for packaging the product. In the sample above, the pencil holder may be placed in a plastic bag and tied with a metal tie. The line can also be expanded by choosing a product that requires more steps for its completion.

Role of Supervisor

The basic role of the supervisor is to make sure the materials pass from one station to the next. In case of tie-ups the teacher and supervisor should be aware of which students can have their positions changed in order to keep the line flowing. (Industrial titles may also be used, depending upon the level of the class. Name tags or name plates usually add incentive for succeeding on the line.)

CURRICULAR OBJECTIVES AND ACTIVITIES

It is important to remember that three of the most quoted reasons as to why disadvantaged children eventually drop out of school are: 1) disinterest in school, 2) no relationship between school and the world outside, and 3) poor achievement in regular school work. It appears that if the dropout cycle is to be interrupted, it must involve teaching the child at as young an age as possible about the world of work and how it can directly relate to the learning of academic subjects.

Industrial arts provides a learning by doing approach, which includes concrete experiences and a variety of activities involving a multiplicity of media. There is always a strong degree of physical involvement through which the child is encouraged to handle tools and materials as he begins to explore the working environment. Group activities are also stressed and children learn to work cooperatively on a project according to a schedule that employs good work habits and the safe use of tools and materials.

It has been suggested that industrial arts allows the preschool disadvantaged child to become a participant rather than an observer of activities. It takes him out of the realm of hypothesis into the realm of happening. In essence, there becomes a purpose for learning that can be quickly reinforced.

The following curricular objectives and activities are provided for the teacher's consideration as she develops an industrial arts program, suited to the needs of her students.

Curriculum Area: Industrial Arts		
Behavioral Objective: The child identifies tools.		
Activity	Adaptations/Modifications	Materials
Bring a selection of hand tools into the classroom (for example, hammer, pliers, screwdriver, and wrench). Place the tools on a table or workbench. Hold up each tool, say its name, and demonstrate its use. As you name each tool, ask the child to repeat its name. Review the tools, their names, and their uses with the child until he is able to identify each one.	As part of industrial arts projects, ask the child to select the tools he needs to do each task in the project. Give the child pictures of tools and non-tools. Ask the child to sort the pictures into categories: non-tools and tools, and then the tools into hammers, pliers, screwdrivers, wrenches, etc. Give the child catalogs with tool sections. Ask the child to cut out pictures of tools; glue the pictures on construction paper or oaktag to form collages of tools. Construct a tool pegboard. Draw the outlines of the tools as they hang from hooks on the pegboard. Remove the tools, and ask the child to tell you where each tool belongs by looking at the outlines on the board. Praise his efforts. Bring a selection of tools into the classroom. One at a time, hold up the tool, name it, and identify its use. Once the child identifies one tool, introduce another. Continue until each of the tools has been introduced to the child.	Hand tools Table or workbench Pictures of tools Pictures of non-tools Catalogs Glue Oaktag or construction paper Scissors Pegboard Hooks Magic markers

degree of difficulty
← increase   decrease →

163

Curriculum Area: Industrial Arts

Behavioral Objective: The child identifies materials (wood, nails, sandpaper, nuts, bolts).

Activity	Adaptations/Modifications	Materials
Bring into the classroom a selection of materials used in industrial arts projects (for example, wood, nails, sandpaper, nuts, and bolts). Place the materials on a table or workbench. Hold up each material, name it, and demonstrate its use. As you name each material, ask the child to repeat its name. Review the materials, their names, and their uses with the child until he is able to identify each one.	*(degree of difficulty: increase ← / → decrease)* As part of an industrial arts project, ask the child to select the materials he needs. Give the child a catalog that has a hardware section, and ask the child to find pictures of materials used in industrial arts projects. Glue the pictures on construction paper and make collages of industrial arts materials. Allot a specific area as a storage area for industrial arts materials. Put a sample of the material above the space provided to store that material. Give the child an assortment of materials, and ask him to sort them and place them in the appropriate storage areas. Bring a selection of materials into the classroom. One at a time, hold up each material, name it, and demonstrate its use. Once the child is able to name one material, introduce another, and another, until the child is able to identify all the materials presented.	Wood Nails Sandpaper Nuts Bolts Table or workbench Glue Construction paper Storage area Catalogs Scissors

Curriculum Area: Industrial Arts

Behavioral Objective: The child sorts objects by size, shape, and color.

Activity	Adaptations/Modifications	Materials
Give the child a selection of small, medium, and large juice containers. Explain that the containers are small, medium, and large and that you would like all the small ones in one pile, the medium ones in a second pile, and the large ones in a third pile. Assist the child if necessary. Praise his efforts and correct any mistakes.	*(degree of difficulty: increase ↔ decrease)* Give the child a selection of different shapes of pasta. Ask the child to sort the pasta according to shape. Give the child two large packages of assorted colors of construction paper. Tell him to put the paper into piles according to color. Give the child one pound each of six, eight, ten, and twelve penny nails. Mix them together and ask the child to sort them and place them by size in boxes or containers. Give the child poker chips of assorted colors. Place four boxes in front of the child, and place one color chip in each box. Tell the child you want all the chips of one color in one box and that there is one box for each color. Encourage the child to sort until all the chips are in containers according to color. Give the child a Playskool Mailbox. Mix up the shapes that come with the mailbox. Tell the child to sort through the objects and insert each one into the corresponding opening in the mailbox.	Small, medium, and large juice containers Different shapes of pasta Construction paper One pound each of six, eight, ten, and twelve penny nails Boxes or containers Poker chips Playskool Mailbox

Curriculum Area: Industrial Arts		
Behavioral Objective: The child picks up and holds simple tools.		
Activity	Adaptations/Modifications	Materials
Set up an industrial arts area within the classroom. On a work table or workbench, place a hammer, screwdriver, and a pair of pliers. Demonstrate the proper way of picking up and holding each tool, naming the tool as you do so. Invite the child to pick up and hold each tool, being sure he does so in the proper way. Practice picking up and holding the tools. Supervise closely.	As part of the classroom routine, include time for industrial arts activities. Set up tools and materials in a specific area of the classroom, and, with supervision, encourage the child to use the tools and materials. Use a pair of pliers to tighten nuts onto bolts. As you choose the nuts and bolts, ask the child to hold the pliers for you. Praise the child for holding the pliers correctly. Correct any errors or unsafe practices. Do an industrial arts project that requires using a screwdriver to turn screws into wood. As you set up the screws, ask the child to hold the screwdriver for you. Praise him for holding it correctly. Correct any errors or unsafe practices. Do an industrial arts project which requires hammering a nail into a piece of wood. When you are setting up the wood or lining up the nail, ask the child to hold the hammer for you. Praise him for holding it correctly. Correct any errors or unsafe practices. Introduce hammer, screwdriver, and pliers to the child one at a time. Once the child is able to pick up and hold one tool, introduce the next, etc. ← increase decrease → degree of difficulty	Workbench or work table Hammers Screwdrivers Pliers Wood Screws Nails Nuts Bolts

166

Curriculum Area: Industrial Arts		
Behavioral Objective: The child uses sandpaper to sand wood.		
Activity	Adaptations/Modifications	Materials
Place a large piece of wood on a table or workbench. Give the child a piece of medium-weight sandpaper about 3″ × 4″. Tell him to feel both sides of the sandpaper and to place it on the piece of wood, rough side down. Take the child's hand and place it on the top of the sandpaper. Using a back and forth motion, guide the child's hand so he sands the wood. As the wood dust begins to appear, point it out to the child saying, "See what the sandpaper does to the wood." Let the child feel the wood dust. Encourage him to continue sanding the wood.	Develop industrial arts projects that require sanding wood. Encourage the child to sand wood until it is smooth as part of wood sculpture or constructions. Cover one wide side of a piece of wood 1 inch wide by 4 inches long with white glue. Glue a piece of sandpaper on the board. Let dry and use as a sanding block. Bring sand into the classroom. Cut large squares from oaktag or heavy cardboard. Cover the squares with white glue and sprinkle the sand over it until the entire surface is covered with sand. Let dry and use to sand soft wood. Bring into the classroom a selection of different weights of sandpaper. Encourage the child to feel the sandpaper. Comment on its roughness.	Wood Workbench Sandpaper Sand Glue Oaktag or heavy cardboard

degree of difficulty

← increase   decrease →

Curriculum Area: Industrial Arts

Behavioral Objective: The child uses a hammer.

Activity	Adaptations/Modifications	Materials
Demonstrate to the student how to hold a hammer. Place your hand at the end of the hammer handle and grasp it tightly. Give the child a hammer and ask him to imitate holding the hammer. Using a board of soft wood, demonstrate hammering on the board. Ask the child to imitate your actions. Practice using hammers in a hammering motion. Supervise closely.	*(degree of difficulty: decrease → / ← increase)* Provide different sizes and shapes of wood, nails, and hammers. Demonstrate nailing wood together to form wood sculptures. Supervise closely, and encourage the child to create wood sculptures. Bring a section of an old tree stump into the classroom. Allow the child to hammer nails into the stump. Supervise closely. Provide time for hammering activities. Start nails in blocks of soft pine wood. Demonstrate hammering the nails. Ask the child to imitate your actions, and hammer the nails into the wood. Supervise closely, and provide time for practicing hammering. Use a hammering bench to hammer pegs through the bench. Turn the bench over and hammer the pegs back through the bench again. Practice hammering. Sing the song "If I Had a Hammer." Practice the hammering motion, using imaginary hammers, as you sing.	Hammers Board Song, "If I Had a Hammer," Nails Blocks of soft pine wood Tree stump Wood scraps

Curriculum Area: Industrial Arts		
Behavioral Objective: The child uses a screwdriver.		
Activity	Adaptations/Modifications	Materials
Demonstrate the use of a screwdriver by placing the screwdriver blade in a screw that has been partially started in a piece of wood. Turn the screw, using the screwdriver. Hand the child the screwdriver, and ask him to imitate your actions. Praise the child's efforts, and correct any errors or unsafe practices. Provide opportunities for practicing using a screwdriver. Supervise closely.	← increase degree of difficulty decrease → Provide screws, screwdrivers, and soft wood. Encourage the child to start screws and turn them into the wood. Form faces or patterns in the wood with the screws. Supervise closely. Start large screws in a soft pine board. Give the child a screwdriver, and ask him to turn the screws into the wood. Practice often, and supervise closely. Praise the child's efforts. Start a large headed screw in a piece of balsa wood. Give the child a screwdriver, and ask him to turn the screw into the wood. Practice. Supervise closely. Using plastic screwdrivers and screws, allow the child time to practice using screws and screwdrivers. Using an imaginary screwdriver and screws, practice the actions used in turning a screw with a screwdriver.	Screwdrivers Screws Balsa wood Pine wood Plastic screws and screwdrivers

Curriculum Area: Industrial Arts		
Behavioral Objective: The child uses pliers.		
Activity	Adaptations/Modifications	Materials
Demonstrate the use of a pair of slip joint pliers. Show the child that the pliers are adjustable according to the way they are held and the way the slip joint opens. Demonstrate tightening a nut on a bolt with the pliers. Hand the child the pliers, and ask him to imitate your actions and tighten and untighten a nut on a bolt. Supervise closely.	Provide an assortment of nuts, bolts, and pliers. Provide time for the child to practice using pliers to tighten and loosen nuts on bolts. Supervise closely. Construct a bolt board, using different sizes of nuts and bolts. Give the child the bolt board and an assortment of pliers. Assist him as he chooses which pliers fit which nuts and bolts. Practice using the bolt board. Supervise closely. Put two bolts through a piece of wood 2 × 6 × 1 inches. The bolts must be longer than 1¼ inches, be threaded on both ends, and protrude from the wood on both sides. Give the child two nuts and assist him in threading one onto each end of the bolt. Tell him to use the pliers to tighten the nuts. Practice. Supervise closely. Using an imaginary pair of pliers, practice the motions used in tightening and untightening a bolt.	Pliers Nuts Bolts Wood

degree of difficulty

← increase   decrease →

170

Curriculum Area: Industrial Arts	
Behavioral Objective: The child builds, using hammer, nails, wood, and other materials.	
Activity	Adaptations/Modifications	Materials

Activity	Adaptations/Modifications	Materials
Collect scraps of wood, wheels, propellors, and other parts of old toys. As a project, show the child how toys and wood sculptures can be made by attaching the parts to each other, using hammer and nails. Encourage the child to create his own toys and sculptures. Supervise closely.	↑ increase / ↓ decrease — degree of difficulty Make wooden trucks, trains, and other toys. Precut wooden blocks and wheels. Demonstrate attaching the wheels to the block, using hammer and nails. Once the child constructs his toy, give him paints and brushes to paint his toy. Using discarded wooden items and pieces of "junk" (wooden spools, felt scraps, rick-rack, sandpaper, wood scraps, popsicle sticks, old blocks), create junk sculpture by joining the items together. Collect scraps of wood. Tell the child to nail the pieces together forming a wood sculpture. Give the child felt scraps and white glue. Encourage the child to add colorful details to his wood sculpture. Use as paper weights, room decorations, etc. Give the child wood, hammer, and nails. Encourage him to hammer the nails into the wood to create patterns, designs, or pictures. Supervise closely.	Scraps of wood Parts of old toys Hammer Nails Glue Wooden blocks Wooden wheels Wooden items (spools, old blocks, popsicle sticks) Rick-rack Sandpaper Felt scraps

171

	Activity	Adaptations/Modifications	Materials

Curriculum Area: Industrial Arts

Behavioral Objective: The child participates in a line production project.

Activity	Adaptations/Modifications	Materials
Construct a pencil or crayon holder using a line production approach. Arrange tables, desks, or workbenches in a long line. Set up work stations. *Station 1*: Child places a template on burlap, felt, or heavy construction paper, outlines the template, cuts on the line, and passes the finished product to station 3. *Station 2*: Child paints the outside of a juice container with white glue and passes container and burlap or paper cutout to station 3. *Station 3*: Child wraps paper or burlap around container, smooths material, and passes it out. *Station 4*: Last child places three rubber bands around each container and sets it aside to dry. Each station repeats its task until all projects are completed. The teacher watches to be sure the materials are passed from station to station.	degree of difficulty — decrease → / ← increase Do more difficult projects, requiring seven or eight stations to complete the steps involved. Do cooking activities, using the line production format. For example, make sandwiches: one person chooses two slices of bread, the next one spreads peanut butter, the next one spreads jelly, the next puts it on a plate, and the last cuts the sandwich. Repeat the activity, assigning two children to each station to work together. Repeat the activity, using a simpler project with less steps (for example, only two work stations).	Tables or workbenches Small juice containers White glue Burlap, felt, or heavy paper Scissors Paint brushes Rubber bands Bread Knives Peanut butter Jelly Paper plates

Chapter 14
Preacademic Skills

There has been considerable controversy over whether or not academic or preacademic skills should be taught at the preschool level. Many preschool programs have formulated their philosophy upon the basis of introducing few, if any, preacademic skills with the rationale that the preschool child is not developmentally ready to participate in academically oriented tasks. Many of the activities included in traditional preschool programs emphasize free play, the building of positive self-concepts, and the socialization of the young child. Yet the absence of preacademic skills in the child's repertoire eventually restricts the progress of the disadvantaged child during the kindergarten and primary school years. It now seems imperative that preacademic skills be carefully selected for use with each individual child. The necessity of including these skills in educational programming appears to be warranted if a preschool education is to accomplish the task of bringing the disadvantaged child up to the level of his peers and provide the foundation for successful future school experiences.

The preacademic skills selected for presentation in this section involve the areas of arithmetic and reading. It is these very areas that have traditionally been excluded from many preschool programs on the basis that children of preschool age are not developmentally ready for them. While there is some evidence to support this theory, activities are being provided in these areas with the suggestion that the teacher incorporate them as soon as she feels her preschool student can benefit from these experiences. Activities stressing the development of math and reading readiness activities will aid the disadvantaged child as he moves through the primary grades. Conversely, the preschool disadvantaged child who has not been exposed to these readiness activities as part of an initial development of readiness skills, often has difficulty with academic skills as he is advanced into the primary grades.

ARITHMETIC

It has often been quoted that the language of arithmetic and everyday language are quite similar because both employ statements that are made up of specific parts that imply questions and require answers. The child who is having difficulty in the language area may also have trouble in the arithmetic area. He may not understand what is required of him and may also be relatively weak in solving problems that depend highly on arithmetical prerequisite skills. The ability to question often helps the young child develop an arithmetic repertoire, and when this does not exist the child has little opportunity to judge whether he is right or wrong. While many disadvantaged preschool children have difficulty repeating simple statements or remembering certain rote facts, they do, however, after slow starts, progress more rapidly in basic arithmetic operations than they do in the areas of reading and the other language arts.

Typically, preschool children who have been described as disadvantaged have entered kindergarten programs with a discrepancy in their ability to handle arithmetic comprehension. An example of this is the child who enters the preschool with the ability to count to 10 but has no understanding or comprehension of the one-to-one correspondence the numbers imply.

Many preschool disadvantaged children can count by rote, which may be compared to memorizing the lines of a song, verse, or a poem. However, when the student is asked to count out objects, he is often unable to because this is a much more difficult task, requiring prerequisite skills such as pointing to the objects while at the same time considering each of the objects to be counted once and only once. Preschool children must also be taught that once they recite the specified numbers they are to stop counting. For example, the student who is counting or pointing to objects must recognize that when he reaches the last object, that specific task is concluded. Too often we find children who become perseverative in their counting behavior; that is, after they have counted the last object, they continue to count, although no additional objects may be present. The concept of final number, which refers to all of the objects in the counting operation and not the last object counted, is also a difficult task which must be specifically taught to the disadvantaged preschool child.

In the beginning of any arithmetic program, it is advisable that some specific time be set aside for symbol recognition. This information should be presented as part of each lesson until the child can recognize the symbols for the numbers that are being taught. This may also be a time to introduce the process signs of plus, minus, and equals.

It becomes clear that any arithmetic program for the disadvantaged preschool child must provide a basic understanding of the arithmetic process in terms of the process of counting. Counting, then, becomes the foundation upon which arithmetic is based and constitutes components of many future prerequisite skills that the child will need if he is to experience success as he advances through the primary grades.

While the same criticisms that are associated with teaching reading at too early a time are also leveled at teaching math prematurely, the authors believe that many math readiness skills should be taught in the preschool program. Recognition of numbers, one-to-one correspondence, and simple concepts involving money are all skills most children from nondisadvantaged environments bring with them to the preschool setting. Much of this critical information can be introduced through music and art activities and integrated into numerous units or projects that involve the holidays or special times of the year. Games and physical education activities can also be used as a medium for introducing basic skills in the math area.

READING

It is becoming increasingly clear that success in reading during the early school years enhances the chances of success in all other academic areas. It therefore becomes essential that any program for preschool disadvantaged children include the basics of a sound reading program, presenting the necessary prereading or reading readiness skills and activities that lay the foundation for successful reading experiences.

Compared to other children whose families provide average or better advantages for getting started in modern society, the disadvantaged preschool child typically lacks: 1) a family environment that sets an example of reading, 2) parents who read a great amount, and 3) parents who read to him.

Many children enter reading instruction with a preconceived idea of what reading is all about. They typically know many letters of the alphabet and may even know a few common sight words they have observed in their environment. These children tend to be successful in learning to read, using any method of instruction, and often progress quite rapidly. In contrast, the disadvantaged preschooler often has little understanding as to what reading constitutes and lacks even basic reading readiness skills.

There are many components to a strong reading and reading readiness program and it is imperative that each be treated seriously, and not merely as an opportunity for drill exercises. While there are diverse and conflicting views concerning when a child may be ready to undertake a comprehensive reading program, it is generally accepted that, for the preschool disadvantaged child to be successful in the area of reading, he must be exposed to reading basics during his tenure in the preschool program. These may include alphabet skills, recognizing one's name, and identifying other sight words. In addition, tasks such as selecting or presenting words that rhyme and the continual reading of stories to the children should be included in daily activities. The majority, if not all, of the children's work in reading at the preschool level is verbally oriented since many of the children have not mastered the necessary prerequisite or fundamental fine motor skills to perform writing tasks. When the preschool child exhibits an ability to perform writing tasks, it is highly recommended that the printed word, or whatever form the printing takes, be closely coordinated with any new words the child is being taught as part of his daily reading program.

Many tasks have been suggested for inclusion in reading programs for the preschool child, including tasks that incorporate the ability for the child to distinguish printed words from pictures and activities that focus on the ability to rhyme in some specific fashion or produce a word that rhymes with a given word. Providing experiences in the ability to identify when a word does or does not rhyme is a skill that proves useful in the further development of the reading program. Developing a sight-reading vocabulary of at least three or four words as well as the proper names or family names that the student recognizes is highly recommended. These words should also be correlated with the printed words so that the student begins to see the relationship between the printed words and the vocabulary words he is verbalizing.

This subsection on reading is not intended to suggest any one method of reading or reading readiness activities over another. There remains too much controversy over which methods are most appropriate for the nondisadvantaged child to even attempt to indicate which methodology would be appropriate for the disadvantaged child. It is the responsibility of the teacher to decide in what skill areas her students seem to be weak and strong and to then develop a formalized reading program on the basis of this diagnostic information.

CURRICULAR OBJECTIVES AND ACTIVITIES

It is important to stress that the following curricular objectives and activities designed to encourage the acquisition of preacademic skills are only samples of what can be done in developing math and reading readiness activities. The level of difficulty and time of introduction must be decided by the teacher in accordance with the developmental readiness of her students.

Curriculum Area: Arithmetic		
Behavioral Objective: The child matches objects to objects (one-to-one correspondence).		
Activity	Adaptations/Modifications	Materials
Seat the child at a desk or table. Place a pile of wooden cubes in front of yourself and a pile in front of the child. Take two cubes from the pile and place them in front of you and separate from the other cubes. As you do it, tell the student what you are doing. Ask him to imitate your actions, using cubes from his pile. Offer assistance when necessary and praise the child's correct performance of the activity. Repeat the activity, taking different numbers of cubes from the pile.	Using a placemat, dishes, silverware, and glasses, set a place at the table. Give the child the materials needed to duplicate the place setting, and tell him to set a place for himself. Once he has done so, serve lunch or a snack. On oaktag cards, glue groups of objects: plastic spoons, straws, blocks, pegs, buttons. Give the child an assortment of objects corresponding to those on the cards. As you show the child each card, ask him to duplicate the grouping. Repeat for each card. On two large sheets of oaktag, glue duplicate groupings of small articles, such as buttons, paper clips, straws, pasta, or toothpicks. Give the child both sheets of objects and pieces of yarn, and ask the child to place the yarn between the two matching groups. Give the child a selection of objects, and tell him to choose just one. Praise his efforts. Give the student clothes that come in pairs (for example, mittens, socks, shoes, and gloves), and ask him to match them. Set up a flannel board. Place one flannel cutout on the flannel board. Give the child an assortment of flannel cutouts from which to choose. Tell him to look at the one on the flannel board and to choose one just like it. If he chooses correctly, let him place it on the flannel board next to the other cutout. If he chooses incorrectly, assist him in making a correct choice.	Desk or table Chairs Wooden cubes Flannel board Flannel cutouts Clothing that comes in pairs Oaktag Glue Small objects Placemats Silverware Dishes Yarn

degree of difficulty

decrease →

← increase

Curriculum Area: Arithmetic		
Behavioral Objective: The child counts with meaning.		
Activity	Adaptations/Modifications	Materials

Activity	Adaptations/Modifications	Materials
Seat the child at a table or desk. Place a container of pennies on the table. Tell the child he needs six pennies for milk, three pennies for candy, one penny for a gumball machine, etc. Ask the child to count out the correct number of pennies for a specific item, for example, three pennies for candy. If he counts out the correct number, praise him. Assist him if he is unable to do so independently. Gradually increase the number of pennies the child must count out.	Play board games (simple ones), using dice. Ask the child to count the dots on the dice as he plays the games.	Table or desk
		Chairs
	Place a number (1–10) on the flannel board. Give the child flannel cutouts, and ask him to place the corresponding number of objects under the number.	Pennies
		Magazine pictures
		Counting box
	As part of taking daily attendance, count the children in the classroom. Encourage the children to count with you.	Items for counting
		Flannel board
	Prepare a "Counting Box": Each day place a different number of interesting objects into a brightly decorated box. Each day ask one or more children to count the items in the box.	Flannel numbers
		Flannel cutouts
		Board games with dice
	Sing songs such as "This Old Man," "Ten Little Indians," "Angel Band," and "One, Two, Buckle My Shoe" for practice in counting from 1 to 10.	Songs
		"Angel Band"
		"This Old Man"
	Use Hap Palmer's "Number March" for practice in counting from 1 to 5.	(above two in *Music Activities for Retarded Children*, D. A. Ginglend and W. E. Stiles, Abingdon Press, Nashville, Tenn., 1965)
	Cut pictures of scenes or objects from magazines. Ask the child to count the number of kittens, dogs, people, dishes, etc., in the pictures.	"One, Two, Buckle My Shoe"

degree of difficulty ← increase   decrease →

Behavioral Objective: The child counts with meaning. (con't)

Activity	Adaptations/Modifications	Materials
	← increase decrease → degree of difficulty	"Ten Little Indians" Record, "Number March," (in *Learning Basic Skills Through Music,* Hap Palmer Record Library, Educational Activities, Inc., Box 392, Freeport, N.Y., #AR514)

Curriculum Area: Arithmetic		
Behavioral Objective: The child counts out a requested number of objects.		
Activity	Adaptations/Modifications	Materials
Plan a ''crunch'' party for the children. Use crunchy foods such as celery, carrots, green pepper, apples, and granola. Seat the children at tables. With the child, count how many children there are. Once the number has been counted, ask different children to count out the necessary number of napkins and paper plates and place one of each in front of each child. Give the child the crunchy foods to pass out, being sure he counts out the number needed before he begins to pass out the food. Once all the foods have been passed out, encourage the child to taste each food and eat the ones he likes.	Plan a woodworking project that uses nails (large, 16-penny nails are best). Tell the child how many nails he needs for the project. Give him a box of nails, and let him count out the number of nails. Plan a baking activity with the child, such as cookies or cupcakes. Print the recipe on chart paper, underlining the number of eggs needed. Point this out to the child, and ask him to bring you the correct number of eggs. Plan an art activity, such as collage, mosaic, or stringing pasta, that requires a variety of materials. Ask the child to count the number of children, count out corresponding numbers of materials, and give one to each child. At snack time, ask the child to count the number of children and to pass out one napkin and one snack to each child. Praise his efforts. During snack or art time, tell the child to take ''just one.'' Praise him for doing so. <div align="right">increase ← decrease → degree of difficulty</div>	Crunchy foods Tables Chairs Napkins Paper plates Snack foods Eggs Baking ingredients Cooking facilities Cooking utensils Chart paper Magic markers Art materials Woodworking materials Nails

Curriculum Area: Arithmetic		
Behavioral Objective: The child recognizes number symbols.		
Activity	Adaptations/Modifications	Materials
Discuss television programs with the child. Ask him to tell you his favorite show. With the aid of a *TV Guide*, locate the channels and times of the shows. On a large piece of oaktag, write the times and channels of the programs. Next to the time and channel, paste a picture that represents the program. "Read" the chart to the child, encouraging him to read the channel numbers and the time along with you. Praise the child for recognizing the channel and time numbers.	degree of difficulty ⟵ decrease increase ⟶ As you read books to the child, point out the page numbers and ask the child to identify them. Print simple recipes on chart paper, and underline the numbers in the recipe. Ask the child to read the numbers. Prepare the recipe with the children, and let them eat what they prepared. Print large numbers on oaktag cards (1-foot square). Place the number cards on the floor in various areas of the classroom. Tell the child, "Stand on the card that says '1,' ('3,' '7,' etc.)." Help the child find the number, if necessary. Construct a calendar for each month. Each day, say the date and have the child repeat it. Beginning with day one, count 1, 2, 3, etc., pointing to each number as you say it, until you reach the day's date. Make number cards (1–10) from oaktag. Show them to the child and say their names: "This is a 3," etc. Ask the child to repeat, "This is a 3." Show the cards again and see if the child recognizes the number. Repeat the activity for each number until the child recognizes 0–10.	*TV Guide* Oaktag Magic markers Pictures of TV characters Recipes Storybooks

Curriculum Area: Arithmetic

Behavioral Objective: The child matches numerals.

Activity	Adaptations/Modifications	Materials
Bring a flannel board and flannel board numbers into the classroom. Seat the children in the classroom. Seat the children in front of the flannel board. Place flannel numbers 0–10 on the flannel board. Give the child a selection of flannel numbers. Ask him to match the numbers by placing the number from his pile next to the matching one on the flannel board. Praise the child's efforts, correcting any mistakes he makes.	Play the game "Missing Match-Ups" with the child, using the number card. Play "Number Lotto" with the child. Construct a number Bingo game. Give each child a Bingo card and markers with numbers printed on them. Call out numbers, and ask the child to match his number markers to the numbers on his card. Draw several large ovals or circles; cut them in half (in a jagged or wiggly line) so that the halves of each oval or circle can be put together to form a two-piece puzzle. On each of the puzzles, write the same number. Ask the child to match the numbers and put the puzzles together. Repeat the activity, beginning with 1, 2, 3 and 0 and adding the others one at a time.	Flannel board Flannel board numbers Oaktag Scissors Magic markers Games "Number Lotto" "Missing Match-Ups" (Milton Bradley)

degree of difficulty — increase / decrease

Curriculum Area: Arithmetic

Behavioral Objective: The child identifies and names coins.

Activity	Adaptations/Modifications	Materials
Show the child a penny, nickel, dime, and quarter. Pick up each one and tell the child what it is called. Encourage the child to pick up the coins and feel them. Point out the characteristics of each one—size, color—and compare them to each other. Repeat the activity until the child can identify each coin.	Play "Musical Money." Stand the children in a circle. Tape coins at various places around the circle. Play a record and stop it. When the music stops, the child must stand on a coin. Go to each child and ask the child to name the coin he is on and remove a coin each time you play the music until only one child is left. Play a Bingo game using pennies, nickels, dimes, and quarters. Draw or paste pictures of coins on the Bingo cards. Give the child coins as markers. Call out dime, nickel, etc., and tell the child to match his coin markers to the coin pictures on the Bingo card. Get small boxes or milk cartons, and cut slots into the top of each box to form banks. Glue one coin on each box. Give the child a selection of coins, and ask him to put each coin into the bank that has a matching coin. Say the name of the coin as the child inserts it into the coin box. Repeat the activity, introducing the coins one at a time. ← increase　　　decrease → degree of difficulty	Pennies Nickels Dimes Quarters Milk cartons or small boxes Scissors Glue Oaktag Magic markers Tape

183

Curriculum Area: Arithmetic

Behavioral Objective: The child recognizes and names the money sumbols of cent sign, dollar sign, and decimal point.

Activity	Adaptations/Modifications	Materials
Print the cent sign, dollar sign, and decimal point on cards. Use as flash cards and show the cards to the child. As you display each card, name the symbol that is on it. Ask the child to look at the card and repeat the name of the symbol after you say it. Practice using the flash cards with the child until he is able to identify each of the symbols.	*← increase degree of difficulty decrease →* Go to a grocery store. Encourage the child to read price tags and identify money symbols. Cut out pictures of clothing and household appliances from catalogs. Paste each picture on an oaktag card and print its price below the picture. Ask the child to read the price on each card. If he can't read the numbers, ask him to point out and identify the money symbol. Bring in washed, empty food cans and boxes. On each item, print a price, using money symbols. Ask the child to tell you the price of each item as you point to it. Praise his efforts and correct any mistakes. Make price tags on oaktag: 39¢, $1, $2.50. Read the price tags to the child and ask him to do the same. If he can't read the numbers, ask him to find and identify the money symbols. Repeat the activity. Introduce one sign at a time. Once the child recognizes the one money symbol, introduce the others, one at a time, until the child identifies each symbol.	Oaktag Scissors Catalogs Empty food cans and boxes Magic markers

184

Curriculum Area: Arithmetic

Behavioral Objective: The child uses measuring cups and spoons in functional situations.

Activity	Adaptations/Modifications	Materials
Plan a cooking or baking activity (cookies, cake, muffins) that requires the use of measuring cups and spoons. Show the child the measuring cups and spoons and name them. Print the recipe you are using on chart paper. When the recipe calls for cups or spoons of ingredients, draw in pictures of the items to create a rebus as well as printing in the words. Assist the child in "reading" the recipe, encouraging him to match the appropriate measuring device to what the recipe calls for. Prepare the recipe and let the children eat what they have baked or cooked.	← increase decrease → degree of difficulty Encourage the parents to include the child in cooking and baking activities, allowing the child to use measuring cups and spoons in cooking. Bring in boxes and containers of powdered and liquid laundry detergent. Read the directions, stating how much detergent to use. From a selection of measuring cups, ask the child to choose the one matching the amount called for on the box. On chart paper, copy simple recipes, using rebus symbols to represent measuring cups and spoons. Read the recipes with the child, and, as you come to rebus symbols for measuring devices, ask him to identify each one and choose the corresponding measuring cup or spoon from a selection of measuring devices you have given him. Introduce measuring cups and spoons one at a time. As the child recognizes and labels one, introduce the next one. Continue this until the child is able to identify each measuring cup and spoon.	Measuring cups Measuring spoons Baking ingredients Recipes Magic markers Chart paper Boxes of powdered laundry detergent Containers of liquid laundry detergent

Curriculum Area: Arithmetic

Behavioral Objective: The child identifies the signs $+$, $-$, and $=$.

Activity	Adaptations/Modifications	Materials
Make flash cards of the process signs $+$, $-$, and $=$. Show each sign to the child and name it. Ask the child to repeat the name after you say it, and point to the sign as he says it. Practice until the child is able to identify each sign.	Print arithmetic examples on chart paper. Ask the child to point out and identify all the $+$, $-$, and $=$ signs he can find.	Oaktag
		Magic markers
	On sheets of drawing paper, print numbers and the signs $+$, $-$, and $=$, ask the child to circle all the $+$, $-$, and $=$ signs he can find. If he can't circle them, sit with him as he points them out and names them for you.	Flannel board
		Flannel
	Make flannel cutouts of the signs $+$, $-$, and $=$. Place them on a flannel board. Give the child corresponding cutouts and ask him to match them to those on the flannel board, naming them as he places them on the flannel board.	Scissors
		Drawing paper
	Repeat the activity, introducing one sign at a time and adding a new sign once the child is able to identify the original sign.	Chart paper

degree of difficulty

← increase

decrease →

186

Curriculum Area: Arithmetic		
Behavioral Objective: The child performs simple addition and subtraction in functional situations.		
Activity	Adaptations/Modifications	Materials

Activity

On a flannel board, place cutout numbers and signs to form an addition problem, e.g., $3 + 1 =$. Under each number to be added, place the corresponding number of flannel cutouts. Show the child how to count the 3 plus 1 more to $= 4$. Repeat for subtraction. Practice until the child understands the processes of addition and subtraction.

Adaptations/Modifications

Go to a store. Purchase inexpensive items. Show the child how to list how much money you gave the cashier, 10¢, how much the item cost, 7¢, and how much change you should get 3¢. Write this as $10 - 7 = 3$. Use pennies as a concrete way of showing how subtraction works.

Play games that require the child to add numbers to find the score.

Using children as concrete items, set up addition and subtraction examples: 4 girls − 2 girls = 2 girls. Write as a number problem, $4 - 2 = 2$, after the child computes the answer.

Print the child's name on a card. Ask him his age and print it beneath his name. Tell him that on his next birthday he will be 1 year older. Print a + and a 1 beneath his age. Ask him to add the numbers to find out how old he'll be at his next birthday.

Cut a large +, −, and = sign from oaktag. Place the + sign on the child's desk. On either side of the sign, place the number of objects to be added, e.g., 2 oranges + 1 orange. Place an = sign at the appropriate place. Once the child has added the oranges, let him place 3 oranges after the = sign. Repeat for subtraction. Practice.

degree of difficulty — decrease → / ← increase

Materials

Flannel board
Flannel cutouts
Pennies
Oaktag
Markers
Scissors

Curriculum Area: Reading		
Behavioral Objective: The child recognizes his name when he sees it printed.		
Activity	Adaptations/Modifications	Materials
Call attendance as part of the daily classroom routine. As you call the child's name, hold up a card on which the child's name has been printed. Tell the child it is his name, and ask him to look at it carefully. Do this on a daily basis, gradually reducing the use of the verbal cue, until the child recognizes his name when he sees it printed.	Give the child a pack of name cards, and ask him to find the cards with his name printed on them. Prepare individualized activity boxes. On the outside of a shoebox, print the child's name. On the inside, place games, toys, or puzzles. At a scheduled activity time, tell the child to find his activity box and play with the contents. At snack time, set the table and put place cards with the children's names at each place setting. Tell the child to find the card with his name on it and to sit at that place. Praise the child's efforts. Offer help when necessary. Ask the child's parents to sew name tags or print the child's name on his outer clothing (boots, hats, mittens, coats). Put the children's books, hats, etc., in a pile, and encourage the child to find his clothes by identifying his name on the clothes. Print the child's name on cards and attach to the child's chair, locker, and cubbyhole. Encourage the child to find his chair, locker, etc., by identifying his name. Place a picture of the child on a bulletin board in the classroom. On a piece of oaktag or a sentence strip, print the child's name. Tape the child's name under his picture. Point to the printed name and the picture and say the child's name. Ask the child to do the same. At various times during the day, ask the child to find his picture and name.	Oaktag cards Sentence strips Magic markers Name tags Shoe boxes Small toys and games Puzzles Name cards

degree of difficulty — decrease → increase

Curriculum Area: Reading

Behavioral Objective: The child identifies the printed names of family members.

Activity	Adaptations/Modifications	Materials
On chart paper, print the names of the people in the child's family. Next to each name, place a photograph of the person (ask the child's parents to send in photographs, invite the family to visit school and take their pictures, or make home visits and take pictures of the child's family). Point out each picture on the chart and the corresponding printed name. As the child begins to recognize the printed names, remove the picture cue by covering the pictures with construction paper.	*degree of difficulty* — *decrease* → ← *increase* Plan a class snack and invite the children's families. Set the tables, making place cards for the children and their families. Ask the child to find the names of his family members on the place cards and to escort them to their places at the tables. At holiday or birthday time, make gifts for family members. Print name tags and ask the child to choose the tags that have the names of his family members printed on them. On pieces of oaktag, paste a picture of a family member and its printed name. Do this for each family member, introducing one family member's picture and name at a time until the child is able to recognize the name of each family member.	Chart paper Magic markers Pictures of family members Oaktag Name tags Food for snack Tables Chairs Paper plates Napkins

Curriculum Area: Reading		
Behavioral Objective: The child identifies written words, labeling objects found within his home and school environment.		
Activity	Adaptations/Modifications	Materials
Develop a chart, listing objects found in the child's learning and home environment, e.g., door, key, ball, table, sink, desk. Draw a picture or cut one from a magazine and glue it next to the word it represents. As part of the daily activities, review the chart. Point to the pictures, ask the child to identify it, and point out the word next to it. Say the word as you point to it. Ask the child to repeat it. Review the chart each day, encouraging the child to bring in different pictures and adding the pictures and words to the chart.	← increase decrease → degree of difficulty Make a large chart, and divide it into two columns. In one column print the names of common objects. In the other, draw or paste pictures of the objects named. Ask the child to match the words to the objects by pointing with his fingers or drawing a line from one to the other. Print cards with the names of objects in the classroom, and tape them to the objects. Print a matching set of cards. Give the child a card and ask him to find the matching word and go to it (door, desk, table, window). Offer help when necessary. Print cards with the names of objects in the classroom, and tape them onto the objects. Point them out to the child, for example, "This is the door, the word says door." Make individual word cards on which you have printed a word and glued a picture (desk, apple, key, door, truck). Introduce the word cards one at a time. Once the child identifies the word on one card, introduce another card.	Chart paper Magic markers Magazines Scissors Construction paper Oaktag (for word cards) Masking tape

Curriculum Area: Reading

Behavioral Objective: The child develops a basic sight vocabulary.

Activity	Adaptations/Modifications	Materials
Make name cards for the objects found in the classroom (for example, table, desk, chair, sink, door, window, shelf, toys, floor, etc.). Tape these cards to the objects they name. As part of the daily classroom routine, review the printed names of the objects. Print a second set of cards. Ask the child to match the duplicate cards to the cards on the objects. Repeat the activity until the child identifies the words on the cards without the cue of the object.	Make a chart of local supermarkets and department stores. On envelopes, print the names of the stores or paste newspaper ads for the store. Give the child newspaper and scissors, and go through the newspaper and cut out ads for the stores on the chart and the envelopes. Give the child the envelopes. Ask the child to put the ads he cut out into the corresponding envelope. As you walk with the child in the community, point out traffic signs. Return to the classroom, make signs of WALK, DON'T WALK, STOP, ONE WAY, DO NOT ENTER. Review the signs with the child. Set up a play pedestrian city; include traffic lights, STOP signs, WALK, DON'T WALK, and DO NOT ENTER. Encourage the child to obey the signs. Play the game often, introducing new signs. Take a walk in the community, pointing out signs in public buildings (for example, PUSH, PULL, IN, OUT, EXIT, ENTRANCE). Return to the classroom. Print cards of these words. Review them with the child until he recognizes the words when he sees them. Take a field trip to a shopping center, and encourage the child to point out and identify familiar signs. Make a family chart. On chart paper, print the names of the child's family members. Next to the name, glue a picture of the family member. Review the chart with the child. As the child becomes familiar with the printed names of family members, cover the pictures and see if the child can identify the printed word without the picture cue. Praise his efforts; correct any mistakes.	Oaktag cards Magic markers Chart paper Pictures of family members Newspaper Scissors Envelopes Paste or glue

degree of difficulty ← increase   decrease →

191

Curriculum Area: Reading

Behavioral Objective: The child recites the alphabet.

Activity	Adaptations/Modifications	Materials
Introduce "The Alphabet Song." Sing the song each day, slowly, so the child can hear each word. Sing a line at a time, and ask the child to repeat each line after you sing it. Do this until the child can sing the alphabet. Praise his efforts. Sing the song each day.	*degree of difficulty* ← decrease increase → Once the child is able to sing "The Alphabet Song," recite the alphabet, using the same rhythm as the song, but not the tune, and encourage the child to do the same. Once the child is able to sing "The Alphabet Song," let him stand by the alphabet cards, sing the alphabet, and point to the letters as he sings them. Make alphabet cards, one letter to a card, and tape them to a blackboard or bulletin board in alphabetical order. Sing "The Alphabet Song," pointing to each letter as you sing it. Sing the song again, encouraging the child to sing along, and point to each letter as you say it. Sing the first line of "The Alphabet Song." Ask the child to sing along with you. Once the child can sing the first line, introduce the second, third, and so on, until the child can sing the entire song with you.	Alphabet cards Bulletin board or blackboard "The Alphabet Song"

Curriculum Area: Reading		
Behavioral Objective: The child identifies the letters of the alphabet (uppercase).		
Activity	Adaptations/Modifications	Materials

Materials:

Blackboard
Chalk
Alphabet cards
Thumbtacks
Tape
Bulletin board
Oaktag cards
Magic markers

Adaptations/Modifications:

Print simple words on the board or cards. Ask the child to find letters within the word; for example, "This says DOOR. Can you find the R in DOOR?"

As the child recognizes more alphabet letters, repeat the activity and the adaptations, using more letters until all the alphabet letters are being used in the activities.

Tack or tape alphabet cards on a bulletin board, blackboard, or wall. Give each child a letter card. Ask him to match it to one of the alphabet cards, and to tell you the name of the letter. Praise his efforts; correct any errors. Practice often.

Make a letter card for each uppercase letter. Tack a number of cards (6–8) on the bulletin board in alphabetical order: A, B, C, D, E, F, G, H. Ask each child to identify each letter. Add series of 6–8 letters until the child identifies the letters in the alphabet.

Using alphabet cards, review the order of the letters: A, B, C, D, etc. Ask the child to recite the alphabet. As he does, point to each letter.

degree of difficulty
← decrease   increase →

Activity:

On the blackboard, print many capital As. Print them in a variety of sizes and positions (upside down, sideways). Point to an A. Say, "This is the letter A. What is this letter?" Ask other questions about the letter; for example, "Is it upside down?" Repeat the activity for each letter, introducing letters one at a time.

Curriculum Area: Reading	

Behavioral Objective: The child identifies the letters of the alphabet (lowercase).

Activity	Adaptations/Modifications	Materials
Place the alphabet cards of the upper-case letters on a blackboard of bulletin board. Recite the alphabet with the child. Introduce new alphabet cards with lowercase letters. Place each letter under the corresponding uppercase letter card. As you do so, recite the letters: a, b, c, d, e, f, g, and so on. Beginning with a, ask the child to go through the lowercase letter, repeating the letters as you say them. Repeat until the child recognizes the lowercase letters.	Using simple books, encourage the child to locate specific lowercase letters; for example, "Can you find a lower case "a" on this page?" Print simple words on cards, using lowercase letters; for example, "door." Ask the child, "This word says "door." Can you find the lowercase r in door?" Correct any mistakes and praise the child's efforts. Print lowercase letters on the board in alphabetical order. Print uppercase letters on the board in alphabetical order. Ask the child to draw a line from the A to the a, B to the b, etc., naming each letter as he draws the lines. Using the format of the activity, introduce a, b, c. Once the child recognizes lowercase a, b, c, introduce d, e, f, and so on, until the entire alphabet has been introduced.	Blackboard Bulletin board Chalk Alphabet cards (lowercase) Alphabet cards (uppercase) Oaktag cards Magic markers Simple books

degree of difficulty

← increase   decrease →

Curriculum Area: Reading

Behavioral Objective: The child identifies the days of the week when he sees them printed.

Activity	Adaptations/Modifications	Materials
Make a large calendar for each month. Print in the names of the days of the week (do *not* use abbreviations). As part of the daily classroom routine, use the calendar. Say, "Today is Tuesday, January 3rd, 1979." Ask the child to repeat the statement. Remind the child that, if today is Tuesday, yesterday was Monday, and tomorrow will be Wednesday.	Make activity boxes, using old shoe boxes. Print the child's name and the name of a day of the week on each one, and put games, toys, or puzzles inside each box. On Monday, give the child boxes labeled Monday through Friday. During activity time, instruct the child to choose his box, saying, "Today is Monday. Andrew, choose the activity box that has your name and Monday printed on it." Offer assistance when necessary. Print the days of the week on flash cards. Review them with the child until he can identify each one. Make an activities chart. Have a column for each day of the week. Under each day, draw simple rebus pictures of activities the child does on that specific day (for example, church on Sunday, and bowling on Tuesday). Review the chart, pointing out the printed words that represent the days of the week. Sing songs that include the days of the week (for example, "This Is the Way We Wash Our Clothes") to familiarize the child with the names and order of the days of the week.	Large sheets of oaktag Magic markers Song, "This Is the Way We Wash Our Clothes" Flash cards Shoe boxes Small games and toys Puzzles

degree of difficulty
increase ← → decrease

195

Curriculum Area: Reading

Behavioral Objective: The child identifies his address when he sees it written.

Activity	Adaptations/Modifications	Materials
On an envelope, print the child's address. Show it to the child, read the address, and tell the child it is his address. Ask him to repeat the address after you say it. Each day, review the address with the child until he recognizes his address when he sees it written.	degree of difficulty decrease → ← increase Put an activity in an envelope on which the child's address has been printed. Tell the child to find the envelope that has his address printed on it and to do the activity inside the envelope (for example, coloring paper, doing a sewing card). Give the child cards with addresses printed on them. As he looks through them, encourage the child to pick out his address. Develop a bulletin board. Take a picture of the child's house and put it on the bulletin board. Under the picture, put a card or sentence strip on which his address is printed. Ask the child to find his house and read his address. Using a sentence strip, print the child's address. Each day show the child his address. Do this on a daily basis.	Envelopes Sentence strips Magic markers Bulletin board Pictures of the child's house Oaktag (for cards) Coloring papers Sewing cards

Curriculum Area: Reading

Behavioral Objective: The child identifies the contents of containers from their labels.

Activity	Adaptations/Modifications	Materials
Set up a store or kitchen area within the classroom. Bring in empty containers, cans, plastic containers, and boxes, and set them up on shelves. Pretend to go grocery shopping. As you choose each item, encourage the child to look at the label, read the words, and name the product. If the child does not recognize the product, point out the word (for example, "sugar," "flour," "tea," "soup"). Play grocery shopping often, helping the child to identify the words on labels.	Ask the children to bring in empty food containers and labels they can read. Develop a collage-type bulletin board, using the labels and containers. "Read" the labels with the children each day, adding new ones as the children bring them in. As the child recognizes the labels on foods, go through magazines and cut out pictures of food containers, or use labels from food containers the child can read. Paste the pictures on construction paper and make a food scrapbook. Add new pictures or labels as the child recognizes them. Plan a special snack. Make a simple shopping list, and go to the grocery store. Show the child the list. Encourage him to match the words on the list to the words on food packages. Purchase the needed items. Return to school and prepare the snack. Make flash cards of the foods the child says he likes. Practice with the child until he recognizes the words. ← increase decrease → degree of difficulty ← decrease increase →	Empty food containers Flash cards Grocery list Grocery store Construction paper Glue or paste Magazines Scissors Food labels Bulletin board

197

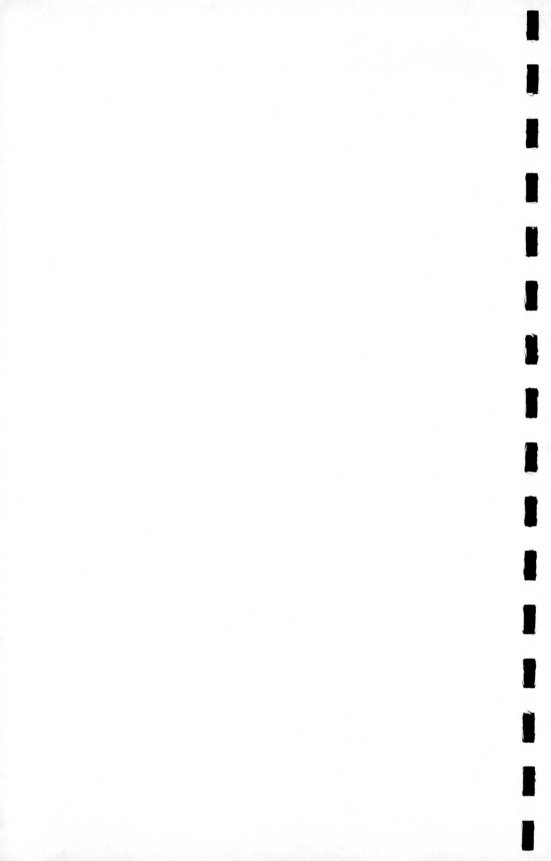

Section IV
INTERVENTION STRATEGIES

Chapter 15
Models for Intervention

The proliferation of intervention programs that are currently in use for all types of children can trace its beginnings to the compensatory educational programs that were initiated during the early and mid 1960s. The majority of these programs were initiated on the basis of early research findings from demonstration projects, which indicated that there could be dramatic *initial* gains in the intelligence of deprived children if they participated in well designed preschool intervention programs.

Many early and present intervention programs were based upon applied research in the area of child development. Keogh and Kopp (1978) have reported that the growth of early intervention programs over the last 10 years is extraordinary. The majority of these programs reflect broad variations in focus, emphasis, content, implementation, schemes, and target populations. A review of the programs by Keogh and Kopp yielded the following generalizations: First, in the majority of cases, contemporary programs had an educational rather than a medical focus. Second, the majority of programs were aimed at the preschool years, with the number of infant programs increasing rapidly. Third, despite the presence of a variety of handicapping conditions and a great amount of diagnostic data, programs were frequently nonspecific to a given child. In essence, content in this latter group was aimed at enhancement of cognitive and affective skills that were common to all children. Risley (1972) presented an interesting consideration regarding preschool intervention programs when he stated:

> Most preschool intervention programs have a real or imagined curriculum of lessons, experiences, or activities which purport to teach children skills, concepts, or attitudes which may enable them to achieve in elementary school. The curriculum usually occupies children for three or less hours per day, five or less days a week, and nine or so months per year for one year. Whether this 600-hour "inoculation" can conceivably make the child immune to later educational difficulties, irrespective of his life during the other twenty-one hours of the day, the other days of the week, or the intervening months or years is currently in doubt.

I have found with depressing regularity that skills, attitudes, or concepts last only as long as they are supported. The effect of any specific teaching intervention diminishes as time passes and life goes on. Skills, attitudes, and concepts persist after the teaching has stopped only when there are other identifiable conditions which maintain their continued use and therefore their practice and elaboration.

I suggest that if our objective is primarily one of producing academic success, we should integrate our pre-school programs with our neighborhood schools, teaching specifically the skills, attitudes, and concepts which those schools are prepared to maintain. I think that if we did this, the basic nature of a successful "Head Start" program would become clear: not enriched exposure to farms, zoos, and railway stations; not developing concepts of similarities, size, categorization, or conservation; nor even socialization and citizenship—but simply 600 hours of survival training (pp. 93-94).

(From *Preschool Programs for the Disadvantaged: Five Experimental Approaches to Early Childhood Education,* J. C. Stanley, ed. The Johns Hopkins University Press. Copyright 1972.)

MAJOR INTERVENTION MODELS

There are four major intervention models (described below) that appear to permeate the field of educational programming for the preschool child and have been especially effective when used with the disadvantaged preschooler.

Behavioral Model

The behavioral model was devised on the basis of Skinner's work and has also been associated with applied behavioral analysis or functional analysis of behavior models. Preschool programs based upon this model tend to follow behavioral principles and concentrate on observable events. Diagnostic information is typically collected on a daily basis and progress is measured on individual children, using developmental norms as a basis for assessing instruction. Perhaps the most widely known intervention model employing behavioral techniques is the Bereiter-Engelmann model, which was initially developed to train children at the poverty level.

Other behavioral model programs tended to address those children who were delayed in their developmental progress. Many went under the generic title of behavior modification intervention programs, but all appeared to be aimed at those children with some impairment and, more specifically, those who appeared to demonstrate a need for tight behavioral control for behavior problems.

Normal Developmental Model

While the foundation for the behavioral model can be attributed to the work of Skinner, the normal developmental model bases its genesis in the philosophy advocated by Dewey. This intervention approach was especially popular during the last two decades when there was a proliferation of nursery school programs. The model attempted to provide teachers and parents with suggestions on how to educate their children in a more humane fashion than was currently existent. Positive attitudes toward children were emphasized, with praise, warmth, and reasoning paralleling strong limits and structure. Achievement was predicated upon the child's readiness to achieve and drew highly upon Gesell norms for determination of this state of readiness.

The normal developmental model is probably the major model used today in public instruction. It continues to measure success according to a grade-by-grade mean level achievement in all areas. It has been criticized for its inability to include reforms in individualized instruction and cross-grade groupings. Anastasiow (1978) has suggested that:

> The strength of the Normal Developmental Model is the utilization of normal guidelines in development; but its strength is also its major weakness, for practitioners of the model rarely ameliorate or otherwise try to deal with the child other than according to an average pace of development. The unusual child is usually referred out of the classroom for diagnosis and treatment, after which, in many cases, nothing is done (p. 102).

Cognitive Developmental Model

The cognitive developmental model is fundamentally based upon the principles of Piaget. These principles postulate that development is sequential, hierarchical in organization, universal, and irreversible (Anastasiow, 1978). Piaget's theory suggests that the student is an active learner who constructs his own intelligence. He learns how the world works by going through six specific stages in the sensorimotor period, hypothetically culminating with the child's having the capacity for insight. It is at the end of this sensorimotor period that the child constructs what he views as reality through procedures that involve deferred imitation, drawing, symbolic play, internalized imitation or mental images, and verbalization of events. As the child grows older, his knowledge of the physical world and logicomathematical world increases and his social knowledge begins to escalate.

It requires a variety of programming and teaching strategies to implement a model such as this one which addresses the different stages of development suggested by Piagetian theory. For example, physical knowledge is enhanced by teaching the child about objects and how his actions on objects, such as tasting, feeling, or throwing, affect them. Knowledge is increased in the logicomathematical world by encouraging the child's native curiosity of how things work or go together and providing the child with experiences to undertake these types of explorations. Social knowledge, which comprises manmade rules as well as the names given things in the language the child speaks, is encouraged by providing the child with objects to experience and with which to experiment.

One major component of this model that has inspired some controversy is the requirement that the experiences the teacher provides to the student be appropriate to the age of cognitive development of the child or near the age, so that he will be able to make cognitive transitions. Unfortunately, there is still difficulty in determining a child's cognitive age, especially for those disadvantaged children who may be delayed or present a special handicapping condition which creates the dilemma of judging when a child is ready to receive a new repertoire of experiences.

Cognitive Learning Model

A more recent model (Bricker and Bricker, 1974), which integrates the utilization of operant procedures for lesson strategies and remediation, is called the cognitive learning model. It draws heavily upon cognitive, psycholinguistic, and perceptual theories to help diagnose the child's present level of functioning and to plan intervention programs. This model attempts to look at behavior without necessarily trying to find the basis for explaining it. Like the cognitive developmental model, the cognitive learning model utilizes the theories of Piaget as well as those of Bruner for the conception of the child. It is a model that relies heavily upon the child's participation as an active explorer of his environment and his ability to make discoveries as well as synthesize information. This model would suggest that the child who cannot actively explore his environment or the school's environment would be taught how to perform this activity. For example, the preschool disadvantaged child, who may be deficient in his ability to explore, would be encouraged through a variety of instructional strategies to explore; consequently, his learning would be accelerated. In essence, the cognitive learning model is, at least in part, an outgrowth of the behavioral model or application of behavioral analysis as a technology for teaching, evaluating, and diagnosing children.

ASSESSMENT OF EARLY INTERVENTION

In summary, the normal developmental model appears to lack strength in many areas. The behavioral model, while able to serve a wide variety of children, appears to be unable to accurately demonstrate that it can focus on complex skill development or on intensive remediation. The cognitive developmental model offers the advantage of encouraging creativity as well as problem-solving techniques as it focuses upon the child's individual needs. The cognitive learning model also appears to meet a wide variety of student needs and may be especially useful with the preschool child who presents learning problems.

Early intervention programs, and especially those that have been offered to the child during the first three years of life, fully support the efficacy of early approaches to intervention (Tjossem, 1976). It appears that the majority of good early intervention programs, which include mother-child-teacher interaction systems, are the prime agents responsible for producing long term developmental gains. While many preschool programs have been developed during the past few years, those specifically designed for disadvantaged preschool children, although initially successful, have generated questions as to whether or not the early gains in cognitive skills produced by these programs are sustained. It appears clear that when intervention has been discontinued the cognitive skill gains tend to be reduced. Therefore, the search for early intervention programs that will produce long term benefits must continue.

It is somewhat disappointing to report that evaluations of intervention programs specifically aimed at combating the effects of poverty on children indicate that these programs have not always been effective or successful. The failure of these early programs to provide lasting compensatory education for the disadvantaged child has resulted in an attempt to closely examine the family and the earliest years of development for possible answers as to why these interventions have been unsuccessful.

Tjossem (1976) has stated that evidence of developmental delay or disorder has for years been taken as the basis for early intervention. It must follow that the programs developed to provide these interventions have largely been of a compensatory nature. Many compensatory programs have been predicated on the belief that children are capable of learning alternative means of handling situations and, for the most part, do learn these alternative strategies. Unfortunately, what has occurred in many situations is that the compensatory programs have developed alternative ways of teaching children and in teaching them those ways of coping with situations, have neglected teaching the basic prerequisite academic or preacademic skills, which will be required of the child as he participates in the first- and second-grade school years. The end result is a child with a compensatory technique that enables him to progress through kindergarten and possibly first grade but then takes its toll as the child moves into second grade, where many of the prerequisite skills his peers have developed are not a part of the preschool disadvantaged child's repertoire.

Furthermore, Tjossem (1976) has suggested that the move toward early initiation of intervention for disadvantaged children can conflict with established patterns of diagnosis and identification. It is therefore imperative that new approaches to the identification of children who will need intervention programs be encouraged.

It quickly becomes evident that the preschool disadvantaged child is in need of an intervention program as early in his life as possible. It is somewhat ironic that those professionals charged with identifying, screening, diagnosing, and ultimately referring these children to schools or related intervention programs are the very people who often do not know what services are available or the mechanism for referring the child. As an example, the physician, who often is the first to see the child, has access to medical records, family history, and is able to observe the child's performance developmentally, is often slow in making referrals to community intervention resources (Tjossem, 1976). The reason suggested for this lack of action is that the disadvantaged child does not present an obvious "disabling" condition, as a handicapped child might, and most physicians are neither aware of what type of intervention programs would be appropriate nor of whom to contact for this information. Many physicians view pursuing a placement for a child as a matter out of the medical realm and often suggest the parent investigate the possibilities that might exist for their child. While the authors are not advocating that the physician or other professionals actively assume a major role in finding intervention programs for the children they evaluate, they are advocating that someone work with the parent to find an appropriate program for the child.

Chapter 16
Preschool Demonstration Projects

Most of the demonstration projects presented in this chapter were initially developed to enrich the lives of disadvantaged children by providing services of a compensatory nature. The rationale for many of these programs was that effective school and home learning under optimal conditions could overcome the barriers to learning that environmental factors often impose. A further basis for developing model programs was the belief that patterns of learning and personality development are fairly well solidified by the end of the child's early years and early intervention was a necessity in order to change negative attitudes, habits, and self-concepts, elements which are so formative a part of a preschool child's daily experiences.

Although preschools for all types of children three to five years of age are now generally available, it has become increasingly clear that the initiation of intervention programs should begin before three years of age. Most professionals (Starr, 1971) are in agreement that the period from birth to thirty-six months is especially crucial and receptive to interventions, because it coincides with the rapid development of language skills as well as other related cognitive abilities. For this reason several of the projects discussed in this chapter may have been developed for younger than preschool-age children, but their content is often appropriate for the disadvantaged preschool-age child.

There continues to be a pressing need to develop appropriate curricula for the disadvantaged preschool child. The project descriptions that follow have been selected as only a *sample* of the information currently available, which either directly addresses the disadvantaged preschool population or has been modified or adapted for suitability for use with children of this age. The next chapter has been devoted to programs that address a handicapped population because much of this material and project information is currently being adapted for use in contemporary preschool programs for the disadvantaged.

Almost all of the projects described here and in the following chapter emphasize parent involvement and, in addition, have components that address four major dimensions traditionally associated with early childhood deprivation. These include:

1. Language development: Preschool disadvantaged children continue to demonstrate underdeveloped expressive and receptive language skills. Often speech patterns will conflict with the dominant language norms of white middle class teachers.
2. Self-concept: Often an inadequate self-image characterizes these children. They consistently exhibit self-doubt and an inferiority about themselves and their skills, which lead to a lessened feeling of personal worth.
3. Social skills: Social amenities associated with middle class standards are often not part of the preschool disadvantaged child's repertoire. He often has difficulty relating to his peers and to authority figures, which can lead to not being accepted as part of his school group.
4. Cultural differences: Most often disadvantaged children will come from a very low socioeconomic stratum. They more than likely will be members of a minority group whose culture and mores may be radically different than those of their classmates.

Throughout this book, constant reference is made to the work of Bereiter and Engelmann (1966), whose book, *Teaching Disadvantaged Children in the Preschool,* remains as a major source of information for teachers working with this population of children. The program presented by Bereiter and Engelmann has long been modified by educators and has since been superseded by the DISTAR program of Engelmann and others, the Conceptual Skills Program of Bereiter and others, and the Open Court Kindergarten Program of Bereiter and Hughs. It is strongly suggested that the readers of this book become familiar with the program suggested by Bereiter and Engelmann, because they will recognize many concepts, slightly or largely modified, that these two authors have presented within the following demonstration projects.

THE CAROLINA ABECEDARIAN PROJECT

The Carolina Abecedarian Project was a longitudinal and multidisciplinary approach to the prevention of developmental retardation. It was based on the premise that to be born poor should not subject a person to a lifetime of substandard achievement. It emphasized Hunt's (1961) and Bloom's (1964) views that the low quality of environmental inputs to the poverty level child may be an important factor in the etiology of retardation. This project incorporated the rationale that children from homes of extreme poverty may be deprived of the various learning experiences and that the environmentally disabled child is often part of a disadvantaged family. These families are characterized as having multiple and interacting social, cultural, economic, and physical problems that affect the preschool child. This project, which was originated in 1972, began as an attempt to bring together a multidisciplinary team of researchers that would address itself both to demonstrating that developmental retardation could be prevented and to explaining how certain psychological and biological processes were affected by such preventative attempts.

An extensive amount of information is collected on each child during the year. This includes medical information, nutritional information, social institutions with which the child's family has contact, and other biological, social, and intellectual information that may have had a debilitating effect on the child.

Those parents involved in the program receive the services of family support through social work agencies, nutritional supplements, medical care, transportation, some payment for participation in the project, and, when appropriate, a diaper service. The original curriculum component of the project developed a series of learning activities for infants ranging in age from birth to three years. As the activities were developed, they became part of the intervention treatment for the child. These activities were compiled and constitute the Carolina Infant Curriculum.

PROJECT HEAD START

The term *Head Start* was not specifically written into the language of the Economic Opportunity Act of 1964 (Beitler, 1967). Rather, the term was created in 1965, and, through the Director of the President's War on Poverty, Sargent Shriver, the project was to be initiated as soon as possible.

Head Start was conceived as one preventive measure to help "eradicate poverty in the United States" (Riley and Epps, 1967). It was to be a total preschool program, dealing with children whose families had a low or limited income.

Head Start (Office of Economic Opportunity, 1968) was designed to be a vital part of a community action program to break the cycle of poverty. It was viewed as being the foundation for a child's full-time education and employment potential, and as an asset to social well-being. The objective stated for the educational program of Project Head Start was to "bring young children in an environmentally disadvantaged background a rich program of pre-school activities." This was to be effected through the interdisciplinary cooperation of health, social services, and educational resources (Office of Economic Opportunity, 1968).

Head Start contained five major components, which are outlined below:

1. Health: Head Start centers provided a complete medical examination, including a hearing test, as well as the other standardized medical proce-

dures designated as necessities for all children and especially those children who might be in need of health care.

2. Nutrition: Head Start centers provided at least one hot meal and one snack each day.
3. Education: Teaching methods were developed to meet the particular and individual needs of each child and group of children.
4. Parent involvement: The Head Start program was required to invite the participation of parents in all phases of its planning and operation. Often classes were held for parents in home economics, the purchase and preparation of surplus foods, and child care within the home environment.
5. Social and psychological services: The Head Start staff was required to work closely with all appropriate community agencies and to use its expertise to reinforce that of the agency on behalf of the child and his family.

There have been many controversies associated with the Head Start program. Cull and Hardy (1975) reported that "Head Start has not appeared to have produced any lasting change in children's understanding of language skills or in their ability to learn." They go on to state that by the age of five or six, children living in poverty are still far behind their middle class counterparts and, from an educational point of view, they are already a part of the group of children requiring remedial services. An extremely critical point is the view presented that the improvement of the behavior of children enrolled in Head Start through socialization experiences and activities is not enough. What is now being advocated is the need for intensive systematic training to bring these children closer to the verbal and abstract level required for success in school. In essence, teaching academics may now become a priority area for many such programs.

The failure of the early Head Start programs to include active participation from the mothers of the children, although it was stated as one of their main goals, has also contributed to the failure of Head Start children in achieving success in future grades. Lacking the input from parents, the children were slow to learn and their retention was low. New federally funded pilot programs on Long Island, New York, in which instructions were given to mothers of culturally disadvantaged two-year-olds in how to teach their children at home, have resulted in children learning more quickly, with their retention capacity significantly higher than that of children in traditional Head Start programs.

In spite of much criticism of Project Head Start, recent research has indicated that low income children with preschool education are better able to keep up in regular school than their counterparts who did not attend preschool (Newsnotes, 1977). In this study, a consortium of 12 early education scientists reviewed Head Start and other preschool children and found the majority were less likely to require special education or be kept back a grade when compared to other children of the same backgrounds.

Inclusion of the Handicapped

The 1972 Amendments to the Economic Opportunity Act mandated that not less than 10% of the Head Start enrollment nationwide be reserved for handicapped children. Research, which has evaluated the effect of this mandate (Ensher et al., 1977), indicates that subsequently reasonable progress has been made in meeting the needs of the handicapped in these programs. However, labeling appears to have increased and there are questions regarding whether or not Head Start is accommodating young children with severe disabilities.

THE MONTESSORI METHOD

There are many pros and cons concerning the method developed by Dr. Maria Montessori, which has been extensively used throughout the United States since the 1960s and is presently undergoing a rebirth of popularity. One of the major advantages of the Montessori method is that it is based on the assumption that many of the children coming into the program exhibit a high degree of unlearned skills. The Montessori method was initially developed for handicapped children and was then applied to children from the most deprived backgrounds.

It does not take any previous learned knowledge into consideration and incorporates into its program the simplest of life's experiences, such as how to wash, dress, move about, and carry things, and how to feel, touch, and see things. Each of the skills is presented at its most primitive level or form. Motor exercises are developed, again from the very basic prerequisite level, and a careful structural path is laid from the concrete to the abstract (see Lillard, 1972). The Montessori emphasis on the development of positive self-image through work and real accomplishment has special meaning for the deprived child and provides this type of individual opportunities to determine whether or not he can achieve in his own environment. This is accomplished by allowing the child to achieve success on his own with the materials in the classroom and, through this activity, to understand and value his own talents. It has been suggested that the most meaningful component of the Montessori method is the relationship that Montessori develops with the parents. This is extremely critical because the environment within the home and the attitude and aspirations of the parent have proved to have more impact on the child than any other single influence.

Lillard (1972) has suggested that:

> [An] area in which the Montessori approach is particularly meaningful today concerns family life. Montessori emphasized the family as the natural

unit for the nurture and protection of the child, and stressed particularly the uniqueness of the mother's relationship to the child, beginning at birth. In our society, where family life is being rapidly diminished, and undermined, this support of the family is much needed. Montessori's inclusion of the parents in the life of the classroom and the guidance they are given in carrying out their role at home appears to be especially meaningful (p. 142).

The Montessori program and the Montessori method have often been called a "structured environment" approach to working with preschool children (Bissel, 1970). It has become increasingly clear that there are two major components of the Montessori method. One is the environment, which would include the educational materials and exercises, and the other is the teacher, who prepares this environment. Lillard (1972) has stated that if young people are to meet the challenge of survival that faces them today, it is imperative that their education allow independence, initiative, creativity, inner discipline, and self-confidence. This has often been considered the major focus of Montessori education.

In 1965, a Cincinatti Montessori Project was funded through which a research team developed tests for use in evaluating the results of the educational experiences of the children. The tests that were developed became known as the Cincinatti Autonomy Test Battery. In combination with the Cincinatti Board of Education and the Carnegie Corporation of New York, which funded the research component and a good portion of the classroom expenses, the Cincinatti Montessori Project test results concluded that the children taught in a Montessori program were most ready for first grade instruction, as defined by instruments such as the Metropolitan Readiness Test, when compared to control classes without the preschool experience. Additional results yielded conclusions that children from the Montessori program appeared to be more extroverted, verbal, and personable than other groups of children in the research study. They appeared to have more to say, could express it better, and had fewer articulation problems than the other children.

As with any method, however, the Montessori approach may not be applicable to all children. In fact, it has been openly criticized for addressing populations of high middle and middle class students, rather than the deprived population for which it was originally developed. In using the Montessori method, the criticism that it too often emphasizes social and emotional adjustment at the expense of cognitive development, must be considered.

A new concern which has recently surfaced is that many programs which designate themselves as "Montessori-type" programs may indeed bear a very faint resemblance to what constitutes a traditional and true Montessori program. Parents who are eager and anxious to provide the best educational opportunity for their young child may very well place a child in such a program only to find out that the teachers are not Montessori trained and the philosophy is not commensurate with what is recognized as the Montessori philosophy. In essence, many programs use Montessori-type materials but not necessarily the Montessori philosophy.

Bereiter (1972) has stated:

> One source of difficulty in describing the Montessori program is that it is sequential, the infant program containing activities appropriate for children from three to five years or older. It is the higher-level activities, involving work with letters, numbers, and science concepts, that have drawn attention to the Montessori method as a possible vehicle for cognitive enrichment and acceleration, but it is entirely possible that disadvantaged preschool children, brought in for one year of Montessori schooling, never work their way up to these activities. The lower-level activities, which center upon housekeeping skills and sensory training, are not ones that would be expected to produce noteworthy cognitive gains. As for the higher-level activities, they differ from those in most instructional programs in being strictly tied to a few concrete representations of concepts. As Mussen, Conger, and Kagan (1969) point out, such a method tends to produce failure to abstract in young children (p. 9).

(From *Preschool Programs for the Disadvantaged: Five Experimental Approaches to Early Childhood Education*, J. C. Stanley, ed. The Johns Hopkins University Press. Copyright 1972.)

While the authors have elected to briefly describe the Montessori method as one of the sample projects to be included in this section, the readers are advised that a wealth of material can be found in the numerous Montessori books and handbooks currently available, which describe in depth this particular method. A listing of these books is included in the reference section. Sample activities, which can be used with the disadvantaged preschool child, especially in terms of presenting skills in their most basic form, are also included in many of these readings.

MOTHER-CHILD HOME PROGRAM

The Mother-Child Home Program is a parent-centered program that uses curriculum materials appropriate for the child two to four years of age. The project is based upon the concept that children need to be taught how to play with toys and other materials, which, in turn, fosters development in the cognitive area and other skill areas. The program employs what is called a home visitor, who takes on the function of a toy demonstrator. This individual typically visits the home of the preschool child for 1½-hour sessions, twice a week, over a two-year period. During these visits the demonstrator talks with the mother and introduces a new toy or book that would be appropriate for her child. The visitor demonstrates how the toy is to be played with and emphasizes how it can be used to develop, for example, the child's language skills.

When and if family problems enter into the session, the visitor refers the mother to the appropriate support services. Often family problems are so overwhelming that a strong home visitor is necessary to ensure that the session maintains its focus on how to use toys, books, and other materials with the child, rather than becoming a counseling session for the mother.

This program does not require any direct teaching of the mother since it employs a modeling technique through which the visitor demonstrates how to work and play with materials and then asks the mother to imitate the demonstration she has just seen. Through these observations and the modeling of play techniques, the mother is slowly taught how to interact with her child and eventually becomes the principal facilitator of play once the visitor has left, between visits, and after the program has been completed.

The Mother-Child Home Program has been successful to the degree that the children in the program have made educational gains that seem to be carried into the primary grades. In addition, many mothers who have completed the program have become demonstrators themselves and worked with other parents who required this type of intervention and support.

OMNIBUS PROGRAMS

The Omnibus Programs are those that provide comprehensive services to parents and children. The initial Omnibus Program was started at Syracuse University Children's Center in 1964. Active parent education groups encourage parent involvement with the educational activities of the children through a daily 6–9 hour program, starting from six months of age and older. Nutritional education is provided, and babies as well as toddlers benefit from this program. Obviously, as with any program, the degree of benefit varies with the quality of the home environment.

"Home Start," a federal effort by the Office of Child Development and the Department of Health, Education, and Welfare, is an example of an Omnibus Program. Home start has been a demonstration project for local Head Start programs, is home based, and includes early childhood education, health care, social services, and parent involvement as its major components.

The June, 1974 *Guide for Planning and Operating Home-Based Childhood Development Programs* (see references) provides the details for implementing such programs when agency support is available.

THE SONOMA PROJECTS

Three programs, collectively named the Sonoma Projects, were developed by the Sonoma County Office of Education, in collaboration with Santa Rose Junior College and California State College. The Sonoma Projects systematically investigated intervention strategies that produced positive educational outcomes for infants, toddlers, and preschool-age children. The three projects were empirically based intervention programs that provided comprehensive education experiences to both handicapped and nonhandicapped children from six months to six years of age.

The curriculum content of the programs emphasized the areas of language, motor, perceptual-cognitive, self-help, and social-emotional development. Criterion-referenced assessments were administered to each child to determine baseline behaviors in the above domains. Following assessment, each child received daily comprehensive instruction in a range of curricular areas, based upon a behaviorally oriented format. Teaching approaches included individual attention (adult and one child) as well as small-group instruction by a teacher. Peer tutoring, with teacher supervision, was also arranged, with a nonhandicapped child often serving as the peer model for the handicapped child. In addition to an ideal teacher to student ratio, close supervision and a systematic means of record keeping were employed. Children's behavior was charted daily and each child's behavioral pattern was graphed for further study at staffings. The Sonoma Projects resulted in a continuous effort to identify effective teaching strategies. Interventions or strategies that appeared not to be working were modified or changed and then reanalyzed. This approach to identifying effective instructional techniques and strategies on a continuing basis has enabled the Sonoma Projects to go under the rubric of a "research-service" model, which typically provides a strong measure of quality control and accountability (Guralnick, 1973).

In these specific programs, there were usually two to four nonhandicapped children integrated with a group of six to eight handicapped students. The rationale for pairing specific handicapped children with nonhandicapped children was developed on the basis of the activity or curricular area being taught.

The Sonoma Projects placed a heavy emphasis on parental involvement, with the parents being trained and integrated into the entire educational process. The parents were initially provided training in basic behavioral principles and rudimentary teaching procedures as well as in developmental sequencing. After the training program, the parents were given the opportunity to teach in their child's class and were encouraged to continue, in their own homes, the educational interventions they used in class. The ability of the projects to provide this transition-type of school-home programming has allowed parents to try out ways of effectively working with their children in a therapeutic class setting and then to replicate this programming in the child's natural environment. The problems or questions that surfaced were addressed when the parents met with the project directors or consultants, who were made available as part of the program.

In summary, the Sonoma Projects function within a developmental view of child behavior and an applied behavior analytic teaching model. The projects' goals focus upon replicating educationally effective instructional strategies for the child and his family. The inclusion of the parents as partners in the teaching process, both at home and at school, increases the probability that successful intervention will be achieved.

Chapter 17
Preschool Programs
for the Handicapped

Recent legislation (i.e., Public Law 94-142), has mandated the integration of handicapped children into programs for the nonhandicapped whenever possible. As a result of this legislation, many educators have advocated integrating handicapped children into regular preschool programs as soon as possible. The inclusion of a handicapped population in a nonhandicapped preschool has been recommended for many reasons, but particularly because the non-retarded may operate as good behavioral models and may ultimately enhance the handicapped child's development. It has also been suggested that nonhandicapped children can function extremely well as reinforcing agents to their retarded classmates within the context of child-child interaction (Wynne, Ulfelder, and Dakof, 1975).

Numerous model preschool programs for the handicapped serve as the foundation for many of the preschool programs operating today. Historically, there were two major social movements that resulted in the proliferation of preschool programs. First, was the initiation of the major intervention programs for poverty-level children, such as Head Start in 1965, and foundation-supported programs, such as those established by The Ford Foundation Education Improvement Projects in 1962. Second, was the establishment of the Early Childhood Assistance Act of the Bureau of Education for the Handicapped in 1968. Bricker (1978) has offered an excellent summary of what is happening to contemporary preschool education programs:

> Over the course of our history, the prevailing social philosophy of this country has been shifting from providing educational programs for a select group of children to the gradual inclusion of all the nation's young-rich and poor-normal and handicapped. Recent state and federal legislative enactments have been providing impetus for the inclusion of the even more severely impaired by mandating the establishment of educational services for all school-age children. Furthermore, the development of programs for the preschool handicapped child has been gaining momentum since the early 1970s (p. 302).

It is interesting to note that poverty and handicapped preschool programs were funded with the concept that they could borrow curriculum materials, methodologies, strategies, and theories of learning that were currently successful and being implemented in traditional nonhandicapped preschool programs. Ironically, after many of these projects were funded, it was realized that few, if any, curricular innovations existed within the regular education area and those that did exist were either based on antiquated teaching methodology or had no basic core of curricular information upon which to draw. Additionally, the majority of programs lacked an evaluation component or an assessment procedure to measure whether the program's curricular content was meeting the needs of its students.

Many studies, such as those by Allen, Benning, and Drummond (1972), Devoney, Guralnick, and Rubin (1974), and Ray (1974), have looked at studies of programs which integrate handicapped children with nonhandicapped peers as well as disadvantaged children with nondisadvantaged children. The results of many of these studies appear to be consistent in their findings that retarded or atypical children are still less accepted and more rejected by their nonhandicapped classmates than are nonhandicapped children.

In summary, studies with handicapped and disadvantaged preschool children have indicated that integrated settings do not necessarily result in increased social interaction or acceptance among all groups of children. These results indicate that there apparently needs to be additional emphasis placed upon teaching procedures that will foster positive socialization and interaction among students within the program. "The creation of educational programs to accommodate previously excluded handicapped children has presented the educator with complex problems that have produced significant challenges" (Bricker, 1978).

Cooke, Apolloni, and Cooke (1977) did a thorough review of the literature concerning the use of normal preschool children as behavioral models for handicapped peers. In their specific examples, the handicapped children were retarded and their conclusions were based upon their three years of involvement as program consultants to numerous integrated preschool programs. The experiences of Cooke and his colleagues led them to the following conclusions:

1. Simply placing retarded and nonretarded children together in the same environment will not usually result in cross-group peer imitation or interaction. Special teaching procedures are required to facilitate such outcomes (Snyder, Apolloni, and Cooke, 1977).
2. Children seem to prefer to socially interact with children who are functioning at a similar developmental level (Ray, 1974; Cooke, Apolloni, and Cooke, 1977; Porter et al., 1978).
3. Directly teaching retarded toddlers and preschoolers to imitate non-

retarded age mates seems to be a promising instructional procedure for increasing cross-group social interaction (Devoney, Guralnick, and Rubin, 1974; Peck et al., 1976; Guralnick, 1978) and generalized imitation (Peck et al., 1976; Apolloni, Cooke and Cooke, 1977).

4. Reciprocal peer imitation may be a necessary condition for the development of positive social relationships between retarded and nonretarded children.
5. Nonretarded children's imitation of retarded children does not seem to occur unless it is directly reinforced as part of a training procedure and also unless the behavior emitted by the retarded children is appropriate.
6. Increased reciprocal peer imitation can be produced when peer imitation training is directed at both retarded and nonretarded children rather than just at retarded children.

The rationale for including brief descriptions of preschool programs for the handicapped in this chapter is to demonstrate their curricular impact on what is now being called the contemporary preschool movement. While each program discussed has specific merits, the reader is advised that content and methodology may not always be appropriate when working with nonhandicapped populations.

Another reason for including information concerning preschool programs for the handicapped child is that traditionally many disadvantaged children, especially those who were culturally different and whose native language was not English, were placed in programs for the handicapped and ultimately spent most of their school career in special education classes. For example, in the geographic region of the southwest, which has a sizeable population of Spanish surname children, many culturally different children were classified as handicapped because of a language or communication barrier and ultimately were placed in a special education program.

PROJECT MEMPHIS

Project Memphis was initiated and funded in 1970 as a research and demonstration project through the Memphis State University Department of Special Education and Rehabilitation. During the three-year period of 1970–1973, Project Memphis developed programming material, which included instruments for individual program planning and evaluation and a textbook entitled *Project Memphis*.

The project goal was to enhance developmental progress in preschool exceptional children. The lesson plan manual for Project Memphis consisted of 260 structured lesson plans and 260 lesson plan formats, divided into five areas of personal, social, gross motor–fine motor, language, and perceptual-cognitive skills. The lesson plans are sequentially ordered developmentally and range from birth to five years. They include the title of the skills to be developed, the developmental level at which the skill should occur, and an explanation of why the lesson plan should be taught. The purpose of the lesson plan tells why each skill is important and discusses specific equipment that may be necessary to teach the skills developed in that lesson.

The lesson plan allows the teacher to plan individualized programs and daily activities for each child. All of the plans correspond to the tasks to be taught and enable the teacher to use parents or volunteers to help with the teaching, according to a predesigned format.

Criterion levels of performance are also suggested, and are especially important today, when considering the implementation of Public Law 94-142. The basic philosophy outlining Project Memphis is that an environment for either developmentally delayed or deprived students that is conducive to learning is not enough. It is essential that a program be flexible enough to meet the needs of the individual children it serves. Project Memphis attempts to provide this specific type of learning experience.

PARENT PROGRAMS FOR DEVELOPMENTAL MANAGEMENT (PPDM)

Parent Programs for Developmental Management (PPDM) originated at the Meeting Street School Children's Rehabilitation Center of Rhode Island's Easter Seal Society. The Meeting Street School PPDM has provided services to handicapped infants for more than fifteen years. Originally designed as a home intervention program for cerebral palsied infants, it has gradually expanded to include services to all infants with a handicapping or probable handicapping condition. Adaptations to help young handicapped children, as well as children living in poverty conditions, have also been made.

Opportunities are provided to help all infants maximize their potential through parent-modeling and parent-teaching approaches. It is important to note that the suggestions of PPDM, which comprise a comprehensive therapeutic-educational program originally designed for children ranging in age from birth to three years of age, have been incorporated into many preschool programs working with similar populations.

PPDM, in addition to serving as a community resource, also provides a service to parents which enables them to understand their child's development and encourages them to participate in the teaching of their child. The parent involvement component, which consists of weekly meetings and incorporates audiovisual equipment, allows the fathers of the children to see on tape the progress of their children, has been continually modeled by similar programs. Child advocacy is also a major component of this program, and many of the basic underlying principles were adopted by projects for preschool disadvantaged children.

To summarize, the goals of the program include the following:

1. To act as a community resource to evaluate and treat high risk children
2. To provide a comprehensive developmental management program for the children identified as needing help
3. To act as a resource for parents in understanding their child's problems
4. To assume a role of child advocacy

Typical members of the direct service team have included a pediatrician with neurodevelopmental training, a physical therapist, an occupational therapist, a speech-language therapist, a social worker, and an early childhood special educator. In addition, an adult educator, a psychologist, and other consulting services were available to the PPDM team.

THE PORTAGE PROJECT

The Portage Project is an educational model for early childhood intervention, which was originally funded in 1969 by the Education of the Handicapped Act Public Law 91-230, Title VI, Part C. It was originally developed as an intervention program for handicapped (mentally retarded) and very young children living in rural areas. Funding was given to develop, implement, and demonstrate how a program of early educational intervention, which was in contrast to existing medical model approaches, could be effective. In this respect, the project extended educational outreach services to preschool children whose parents felt they needed additional help in this area. No medical referral was elicited and parent concern was used as the major criterion for including a child for evaluation by the project.

Of major importance was the fact that large numbers of parents reported the need for help and support services for their children. The extent of parental concern for early intervention and identification services marked a new level of parent awareness and involvement which the project attempted to convert into positive action.

The Portage Project Model, in essence, provided screening, educational diagnosis, and planning that directly linked the parent to a program of educational services that were individualized according to each child's need. When a child was found to be in need of project help, a comprehensive array of support services was instituted. These services often were available in the child's community, but many parents did not know how to gain access to them or felt that the child needed to have a medical referral in order to meet eligibility requirements.

The project was administratively organized through a regional education agency, which served a specific number of school districts. The age range of the population served was birth to six years and/or until the child demonstrated readiness skills for his educational program. In the initial project, the children were identified as having some degree of handicapping condition, and all the instruction took place in the child's home. The teaching was done by the parents or a parent surrogate, and a home teacher was assigned to each child and his family. The educators assigned to the project visited each of fifteen families one day per week for 1½ hours and the parents were provided with an individualized curriculum.

The behaviors targeted for instruction were chosen according to a criterion that suggests there must be some assurance of success or else the parents and child will become frustrated. Thus, only three behaviors were taught each week and were usually attainable with a modicum of effort. Baseline information was also recorded by the home teacher on each new task before it was taught. During the following week the parents taught the skills that had been outlined to them. They were also instructed on the reinforcement of desired behavior as well as the handling of inappropriate behavior. The home teacher returned one week later, recorded data on the child's progress, and charted what behaviors the child learned.

Tjossem (1976), in describing home-based precision teaching models, has listed a series of educational advantages, which can directly pertain to the Portage Project. They are as follows:

1. Learning occurs within the natural environment of the parent and the child. This alleviates many of the problems that often surface when skills taught in a classroom setting cannot be easily replicated in the home environment.
2. Direct and continuous access to behavior as it occurs spontaneously and naturally is afforded. This is especially important as one works with the disadvantaged preschool child because differences in the culture and value systems of the family are incorporated directly into the curriculum planning stage. It is the parent who finally determines what it is their child will be taught. In itself, this provides a safeguard against providing a curriculum that is totally oriented to a different class of society than the one in which the student must live.
3. It is suggested that learned behaviors will be better generalized and maintained longer if they are originally learned in the child's natural environment and taught by the child's immediate family or parents.
4. There is greater opportunity for full family participation in the teaching process when instruction occurs in the home.
5. There is the ability to work with a full range of behavior that often does not present itself in a classroom setting. Actions and responses, otherwise not observed, may be the very ones that restrict the preschool child from successfully interacting with his peers or his environment.
6. It has been suggested that the parents who are trained as a result of projects that incorporate the parent as the teacher will learn to handle a variety of new situations and be able to deal with new problem behaviors as they arise.

7. The ability for the home teacher to work on a one-to-one basis with the parent and child in projects that incorporate such a system allows for the maximum amount of individualization of instructional goals.

In summary, the Portage Project is a home-teaching program that directly involves the parents in the education of their children. This is accomplished by asking input from the parents on what to teach and then supporting their information with the critical educational instruction their children need to survive in the school world and, ultimately, society. It also provides the opportunity for parents to learn how to teach, when to reinforce, and how to observe and chart behaviors.

Chapter 18
Parent Involvement

It is well documented that parent involvement in any educational program, particularly in early childhood programs, is highly desirable (van Doorninck, 1977). Home visits, as well as inviting parents into the preschool program have proved to be not only educationally sound but also economically advantageous in terms of cost and time well spent. While there has traditionally been a strong interest in developing home visitation programs for the purposes of enriching the programs of young children, such as those presented by Krajicek and others (1973), it has only been most recently that the emphasis on parent involvement in preschool programs for the disadvantaged has been suggested. While the initial Head Start programs encouraged parental input whenever possible, it rarely materialized into a comprehensive part of the educational program.

Tjossem (1976) has advocated support rather than intervention for parents of young high risk children. This approach has emerged from a review of the literature in the area of preschool disadvantaged children and is felt to be the most promising approach for producing developmental gain. It is important to emphasize that, given appropriate support, parents may effectively act as teachers of high risk children. Without this support, they may reinforce inappropriate behavior as well as become involved in educational areas that may not necessarily be the prerequisite or necessary skills that the young child requires at a specific time in his development.

As with any type of support service or input from professionals, success will depend largely upon how motivated, involved, and acceptive of responsibility the parent is. It is especially important to review the role of the parent or surrogate parent in teaching the preschool disadvantaged child. Evidence presented in the literature offers the clear implication that family involvement is paramount if there is to be success in any intervention program designed for young children.

RESPONSIBILITIES OF PARENT AND TEACHER

It is critical, in reviewing the role of the parent, that certain responsibilities be analyzed and assigned to the parent, not just by the teacher, but as a result of conferencing and a discussion of the child's needs. Tjossem (1976) has suggested that teachers and other professionals have tended to displace parental responsibility and involvement in programs designed for young children, especially in the preschool. It has been suggested that a take-over responsibility by professionals, including parental input, has resulted in many unidimensional programs that often cannot be generalized or translated once a child leaves the school environment. Often the child who has developed certain skills in the preschool program may not be able to practice these skills and at times may be criticized for demonstrating certain skills that may be contrary to the young child's parent's culture or native background. Inevitably, the child becomes confused and frustrated and begins to question whether or not he should be demonstrating the information he has been taught.

Tjossem (1976) offers one of many models that community members might develop if they are to provide service for preschool disadvantaged children or, more specifically, any high risk child. He discusses specific principles that are critical if the parent approach is to be integrated into existing programs. These principles, succinctly stated, include the following:

1. Initiate early all support services
2. Support services should be offered on the basis of perceived risk and need, and not necessarily diagnosis
3. The services that are provided should be family oriented
4. The mother-child interaction system should be enhanced and supported whenever possible
5. All services that are provided should be continuing services and sustained throughout the school year and as long as possible

The requirements of a basic program, such as outlined above, are quite modest, and, under Public Law 94-142, should be made available to any preschool child, whether or not the child is handicapped. The typical support services mentioned for the preschool disadvantaged child include those involving the medical, nursing, and early educational services which are provided in most communities. As with any support service plan, its success will depend upon the availability of trained professionals whose understanding of early childhood principles as well as all phases of childhood development in family life are commensurate with the needs of the population with which they are working. While the literature clearly states that it is the responsibility of the parents to recognize their own power and how they can advance their child with the support and guidance of community resources, it is also recommended that surrogate parents or advocate groups may very well have to support those children who do not have parents or whose parents appear to be unaware of their responsibilities.

One of the sad commentaries that primarily concerns minority disadvantaged children is the absence of the father as a member of the family unit. Traditional role models are frequently absent and the mother often assumes dual roles as caregiver and provider of all the necessities the child needs.

TEACHER-PARENT INTERACTION

Teacher-parent roles are most important in developing a parent program. For example, a parent conference may result in the teacher offering suggestions to the parents on how to reinforce those skills being taught in the educational program or encouraging the parent to develop prerequisite skills or behaviors that will eventually be taught during the educational year.

Hayden (1978) has presented an excellent synopsis of parent involvement over the years when she states:

> . . . [T]he amount and types of [parent] involvement have increased dramatically in recent years. . . .Teachers have learned how much parents can contribute to the effectiveness and efficiency of preschool programs. Parents have learned how much their involvement in these programs can help them in child management and learning in the home setting. The secret of good parent/school relationships is the acceptance of parents as partners, sharing information about the child's progress at home or at school, attending to the perceived needs and concerns of parents, and scheduling opportunities for parent involvement at times that are possible and convenient for parents. Fathers, as well as mothers, and other members of the family should be included in activities that are meaningful and helpful to them as well as to the preschool staff (p. 42).

A major function of the parent-teacher conference should be the teacher's acting as a resource to the parents and her presentation to them of a variety of ways in which their children can learn away from school and *during nonschool hours.*

SUGGESTIONS FOR PARENTS

The publications *Caring For Children* (Murphy, 1974) offer suggestions on the way children learn and can often be used as prerequisite information for those parents who are unaware of how to initiate working with their own children. Included in these publications is the following information, which has proved to be helpful in developing the parent conferences and early phase of parent education programs. The suggestions include:

1. Gain the child's confidence by a) having a warm relationship with the child, giving a friendly smile, making time to listen to the child, offering

praise, and so forth, and b) providing experiences which enable the child to know that he can trust you.

2. Create and provide an atmosphere that is conducive to learning by: a) making learning a happy and relaxed experience, b) providing the child with experiences that allow him to explore and learn to use all his senses, c) providing the child with a variety of materials and toys with which to interact and play with, d) encouraging the child whenever possible through smiling, touch, or verbal praise, and e) spending as much time as possible with the child. This would include reading, playing games, talking, and most importantly *listening* to the child when he has something to say.

3. Provide a good model. Always offer yourself as a good example, as children learn through imitation.

4. Talk and listen. It is suggested that every learning experience be utilized as a chance to talk to the child or to have the child talk to you. Providing an opportunity for a child to sit, play, or take a walk with you as he explains what his feelings are concerning what is going on in his day is a most basic and fundamental component for developing trust and honesty.

5. Help the child to learn to control his behavior. Children who are consistently angry or upset have difficulty learning because their energies are directed toward the anger rather than toward the learning situation. The parent should let the child know that, although he or she loves and cares for him, he or she may not always approve of his behavior. The relationship between parent and child (or teacher and child) will help the child and adult to resolve the situation and eventually control the behavior. While much has also been said concerning the importance of immediately providing the consequences for inappropriate behavior, it is critical that the parent be aware of the fact that most young children often do not know why they are being punished or criticized for some of their acts. It is therefore imperative that the parent, whenever a consequence must be presented to a child for behavior that may be considered inappropriate, explain to the child the exact behavior that created the need for the consequence. This will help the child understand that the resulting consequence or punishment is for the behavior and not because the parent does not like him. Obviously, consequences should immediately follow inappropriate behavior.

6. Provide a warm and loving environment for the child. Much literature supports the view that children who are nurtured in environments that provide love and care grow up feeling that their environment is good and worth learning about. It is important to remember that love and positive attitudes can foster in the child the feeling that people care about him and what he does, which in turn can enhance the child's cognitive development and growth in other skill areas.

IMPORTANCE OF THE HOME UNIT

In summary, a wealth of information suggests that parental support, reinforcement, maternal warmth, and parental verbal intervention affect how the disadvantaged child will function in his preschool setting (Cull and Hardy, 1975). More specifically, the ability for these children to do well on standardized tests and in academic settings appears to be related to the degree of parental involvement the child receives.

In past and present literature, considerable blame for the nonachievement of the disadvantaged preschooler is placed upon the home, which is frequently characterized as an unfavorable environment for learning. Additionally, the attitudes of the parents, especially in relation to their feelings about school, are cited as reasons why preschool children are often unmotivated and, ultimately, fail. Countless projects have been developed to counter the debilitating effects the home may have upon the child. It is wise to remember that it is family members to whom the child typically communicates and goes for safety. In essence, the home unit, whether it be a one-parent family or a system employing a surrogate parent, is the most important influence on the child, and involvement should be incorporated into the school program whenever possible.

Section V
EDUCATIONAL ENVIRONMENT

Chapter 19
Interviewing, Scheduling, and Developing Teaching Strategies

The need to develop appropriate educational programs for the disadvantaged preschool child becomes paramount when one considers the typical disadvantaged preschooler. By the age of four, the preschool disadvantaged child is probably seriously behind his nondisadvantaged peers in the skills necessary for success in school. Thus, there is an urgent need for him to quickly learn what he has missed or has not been exposed to. Through this learning, the likelihood of failure will be significantly increased. Yet a preschool, developed under normal educational practices that cater to those who learn at a normal rate, may not be sufficient. Opportunities for learning at above normal rates must be available for the special needs of the disadvantaged preschool child to be met. A short term preschool exposure, even with intensified teaching, cannot be expected to produce above normal gains in all areas of development. Well rounded programs, while traditionally highly valued as being able to teach the whole child, may not be as advantageous for the disadvantaged child who needs selective instruction to develop the skills that will enable him to survive in the academically oriented school world.

The material that follows in this chapter provides the reader with critical information for the development of an *appropriate* educational environment for the disadvantaged preschool child. In particular, three major aspects are emphasized: preenrollment assessment, scheduling considerations, and teaching strategies.

PREENROLLMENT ASSESSMENT

As each child enters the preschool situation, the teacher may wish to know specific information about him. This information can be divided into several major domains, namely, the physical, intellectual, social, and psychological. While a great amount of this type of information can be obtained through initial interviews, the teacher often does not have this information when she begins to plan her program. The responses to many of the questions commonly asked as part of an initial interview between the parents and the teacher help to formulate the foundations of the student's educational environment.

Parent Questionnaire

A brief synopsis of relevant questions, which may comprise a questionnaire and which the authors have modified from the work of Miller (1970), is as follows:

I. PHYSICAL
1. Does the child's general health appear good?
2. Does he have allergies that may interfere with normal school activities?
3. Is there a sight difficulty?
4. Is there a hearing difficulty?
5. Is the child physically handicapped?
6. Does he tire easily?
7. Is he lethargic or poorly coordinated?
8. Does he appear to get enough rest?
9. Does the child appear to have adequate shelter, clothing, food, and medical attention?
II. PSYCHOLOGICAL
1. What type of home does the child come from?
2. What are his relationships with one or both parents?
3. Has he overwhelming fears? Is he afraid of pets?
4. Is the child withdrawn?
5. Does he daydream?
6. Does he engage in excessive fantasies?
7. Can he play well alone?
8. Has he inner resources or must he be constantly directed?
9. Is his attention span short or sustained?
10. How does the child react to frustration and disappointments?
11. How does the child think of himself?
12. Does he relate things in terms of self, or can he generalize?
13. Does he accept himself and his achievements or is he constantly frustrated and angry at his own inabilities?
14. Does he have an easy, happy acceptance of people and things, or does he rebel against his world?
15. Is he in constant motion?
16. Is he easily angered?
17. Does he cry often?

18. Does he retreat into uncommunicative silence when his wishes are thwarted?

III. INTELLECTUAL

1. Has he a good vocabulary?
2. Does he understand many words that he does not use?
3. Can he express himself verbally?
4. Can he express himself creatively?
5. Does he demonstrate sound judgment and good reasoning powers?
6. Does he have an active imagination?

IV. SOCIAL

1. Is the child overaggressive?
2. Is the child overconfident?
3. Is he boastful?
4. Do children "report" about his roughness, his selfishness?
5. Does he constantly demand attention?
6. Does he appear immature or shy?
7. Is he accepted by his peers?
8. Will other children work with him?
9. Has he one close friend, many friends, no friends?
10. Is he chosen in games? Do children avoid sitting by him?
11. Does he want to make friends but lack the knowledge of how to be friendly?
12. Does he prefer individual or group tasks? Does he avoid doing school-related work?

While many of these questions may be easy to answer because the behaviors in question are readily observable, many will require ongoing observation and monitoring to ensure a valid response. It is suggested that the teacher take into consideration the responses she elicits from these questions and use them to modify or help develop the educational environment.

SCHEDULING CONSIDERATIONS

The teacher should be sensitive to the needs of each child, although there will be times when this may not always be possible. While the authors strongly advocate developing individual programs for each student, according to their needs, there must also be time allotted for all children to work together in groups and as team members. The artful teacher provides individual help to a student, even while he is working as a member of a group, by providing it in an unobtrusive manner. In this way, the child learns to respect the teacher for her skill in not singling him out and embarrassing him among his peers. The teacher should allow the child to work at his own rate while continually encouraging him to be ready to accept new ideas and experiences. In essence, the child must feel a sense of achievement from accomplishing even the most rudimentary of tasks.

The preschool teacher of the disadvantaged should allow the students time to play as well as work. There is a critical need to structure some of these play activities in order to encourage exploration and risk taking.

Of extreme importance is the realization that the preschool teacher of the disadvantaged child may not be able to incorporate all the activities she feels are necessary into a day or into an entire school year. A system of priorities needs to be established that will enable the teacher to instruct the child in those critical skills he needs to develop if he is to succeed later in his school years and to relegate other activities to a time-available status. The functional academics activities in the curriculum section of this source book (Section III) are good examples of mandatory skills the disadvantaged child will need while other curricular areas can be taught as part of other activities.

Daily Schedule

There are numerous ways a daily schedule can be arranged for a preschool program. Once it has been established that the program is for either a half day or a full day, the teacher should map out those activities and objectives she feels will be important to teach. Traditionally, the sequence of activities has taken the following form.

School begins: Children select quiet activities as they enter the room. They may work in small groups, review room displays, do puzzles, draw pictures, or care for room pets.

Take attendance: A daily leader is designated who can check the weather. There may be a flag salute followed by the pledge of allegiance. During the taking of attendance, the children can count out how many boys and girls are in class that day. Questions can be asked, such as "Are there more boys or girls in class today?" If attendance is 100%, there may be a special ceremony, such as putting a star up on the board next to that day.

Song activity time: This may be a time for the children to change their activity and go from a passive activity to a more active one. Children can be arranged in a circle, and old or new songs can be introduced that incorporate rhythm and instruments or singing along with a record. It is important to remember that songs lend themselves to adaptation as games with physical participation and can be used as a lead in for a number of other prereadiness activities. Seasonal songs and fingerplays can be especially effective during this segment of the schedule and create a happy atmosphere in which to present more formidable work.

Preacademic time: This is the time when the teacher presents those objectives and activities designated as readiness or prereadiness. Grouping of children can be undertaken so each student works according to his educational level. Round tables or large desks can be used to help arrange the preschool groups.

Planning time: This can be a time when the teacher and children plan some of their activities together. It may be a time for stories and dramatizations, role playing, art projects, or construction (industrial arts) activities.

Game time: Aside from traditional physical education–type games, reading readiness and number games can be taught during this time along with games that help to develop the child's sensory perceptions.

Snack time: A nutritious snack should be served. This period provides an excellent opportunity for the students to identify food groups or engage in simple conversation.

Rest time: Depending upon whether or not the school program is a half day or a full day, rest time should be built into the program. Some of the children will need to learn that there is a time to talk and a time not to talk; rest time is a time not to talk. Using individual cots or mats will enable the student to practice identifying a piece of equipment that is either his or assigned to him.

Loose end time: This can be an unassigned time that can be used to follow up on activities or to do things for which time was unavailable during the day. Several days during the week it could be used as "structured free-time" or time for a story. This part of the day should also be utilized to discuss with the children what a good or poor day they had and set the scene for what will happen tomorrow.

Clean-up time and dismissal: This is the time when the room is cleaned up, and coats, boots, and other wearing apparel are put on. It also can be the time for giving the students notes that have to be signed and brought back or for special instructions concerning a planned trip that may be taking place the following day.

It is imperative that the teacher develop her day and activities around a framework that allows for the most efficient use of available time. It is also advisable that active activities be alternated with passive activities so the children do not get too wound up or become too lethargic. Before beginning activities, directions that are simple, positive, and straightforward should be given. School rules and courtesies should always be stressed, and positive reinforcement should be given for this behavior.

A Class Routine

It is clear that each child comes to the preschool with a different repertoire of knowledge. This necessitates specific strategies for teaching each child. Of major significance is that the students must learn that there is a set class routine that they can expect each day. When children are accustomed to a specific routine, they are better able to wait for the teacher's attention and are more understanding if the teacher has to spend time with another child.

Daily Evaluation

There should also be a daily evaluation of the activities that were successful and the appropriateness of different activities for individual children. Whenever possible, written records should be kept of the major objectives accomplished and the specific behaviors exhibited by different students that may have positively or negatively affected the teaching and learning process. Children are made to feel more secure when they can predict the order of events. It may be advisable to post on the board or wall a copy of the daily schedule with rebus symbols used to denote key activity areas. This will allow the children to foresee what activities are coming next. This sense of order is often missing from the disadvantaged preschool child's home and will have to be taught as though it were another skill area.

Time Limits

How much time should be devoted to teaching an activity? Most schedules for preschool children average periods of twenty minutes except at the very start of the school year when the use of reinforcement may not be as well planned. During this time fifteen-minute intervals are suggested; this time can then be gradually expanded according to the child's individual needs. It is important to realize that there is no set rule governing the length of time needed for an activity or class routine. Some teachers are very successful with longer periods of time while others feel their children cannot sustain attention for longer than fifteen minutes. It is the responsibility of the teacher to assess what is appropriate for her class.

Groupings

It may be advisable to group certain children as a means of presenting more material without having to consistently repeat or demonstrate it. Groupings also allow the teacher to see how her children react to being with their peers and if they enjoy learning from each other. The idea of grouping children, either by skill areas or abilities, should not be viewed as a means of placing the student in a competitive situation.

Regrouping should be encouraged on the basis of performance in class. Children often react positively to a change in grouping, especially if the new group is either one that offers more of a challenge or one in which they can readily succeed. One major disadvantage of ability grouping is that the teacher may inadvertently set a lower standard of achievement for the lower group. It is the teacher's responsibility to guard against this and carefully monitor each child's progress in accordance with his individual abilities and needs.

TEACHING STRATEGIES

Bereiter and Engelmann, in their book *Teaching Disadvantaged Children in the Preschool* (1966), suggested teaching strategies for the teacher of the disadvantaged preschooler. Some of these suggestions, appropriate for use in today's preschool programs, are listed below:

1. Adhere to a rigid repetitive presentation pattern
2. Employ unison responses when possible
3. Phrase statements rhythmically
4. Require the children to speak in loud, clear voices
5. Do not hurry children or encourage them to talk fast
6. Clap to accent basic language patterns and conventions
7. Use questions liberally
8. Use repetition
9. Be aware of the cues the child is receiving
10. Use short explanations
11. Tailor the explanation and rules to what the child knows
12. Use lots of examples
13. Prevent incorrect responses whenever possible
14. Be completely unambiguous in letting the child know when his response is correct and when it is incorrect
15. Encourage thinking behavior (pp. 111–119)

(Reprinted by permission of Prentice-Hall, Inc., Englewood Cliffs, N. J.)

A wealth of teaching strategies have been developed for those working with the moderately and severely handicapped. The teaching strategies listed below represent those that preschool teachers of the disadvantaged have regarded as especially appropriate for use with their population of students.

1. Discover the student's reinforcement preferences. What might be reinforcing to other students might not be reinforcing to a specific student. A particular reinforcer may need to be found.
2. Be reinforcing at appropriate times, but do not overreinforce and thereby weaken its effectiveness. For example, praise the student for being quiet during quiet time by saying, "I'm glad you're being quiet." However, repetitious use of this phrase may generate the feeling in the student that it is an automatic response and he may no longer accept it as reinforcement.
3. If a student is behaving or performing inappropriately or incorrectly, correct him in a positive manner (for example, "This is the way to play the game"). Simultaneously demonstrate the desired behavior.
4. Program, at all times, to reduce undesirable and disturbing behaviors. If these behaviors persist, they will interfere with attempts to successfully place the student in society.
5. Ignore inappropriate behavior whenever possible. For example, the stu-

dent who continually talks out, if ignored, will not be reinforced for this behavior. As with other strategies, ignoring should not be overûsed, or it will lose its effectiveness.

6. Provide the student with immediate feedback of results; that is praise him as soon as possible after he has attempted, approximated, or achieved a task. If a student is performing a task inappropriately or incorrectly, stop him from continuing the task and indicate your disapproval in any way that he will understand. Demonstrate the acceptable behavior.

7. Even after you are convinced that the student has mastered a particular skill, practice and reinforce the task periodically. Vary the activities as much as possible to maintain student interest. Practice sessions should be scheduled.

8. Show enthusiasm when a student progresses or attempts to comply with your requests. Remember that what may seem to you like very little progress may be a giant step for the student.

9. Use reprimands whenever necessary. Reprimands are not punishment and can be effectively used in the structuring of behaviors. A simple "No" can effectively discourage a student from taking someone else's materials.

10. Serve as a model of behavior in your dress, talk, and daily behaviors. Discuss models of behavior frequently (for example, "Other people like to be near a person who eats politely").

11. Be realistic in planning goals. Objectives developed at too high a level only lead to frustration for you and the student. Review your objectives and modify them as necessary.

12. Organize your lessons to take advantage of the benefits of peer tutoring and buddy systems. The student may learn a skill more readily when it is demonstrated by a peer.

13. Make your learning area as attractive and pleasant as possible. However, the dangers of overstimulation must not be disregarded. Plants, animals, books, toys, and games that are motivating can make a room interesting.

14. Display the student's work on bulletin boards, in display cases, and at school activities. The joy and pride of displayed work is reinforcing.

15. Remain calm and poised no matter what happens. A student often will react negatively to a teacher who does not keep control of the situation. A sense of humor can help maintain the right tone.

16. Be explicit in your directions and commands. Be sure the student knows exactly what kind of behavior is expected. Classroom organization, behavioral management, and successful student performance are, to a large degree, dependent on the instructor's explicitness.

17. Be aware of potential safety hazards in all activities. Sharp tools should

not be used with the student who may not be able to control them, and miniature objects should be kept away from the student who puts nonedible objects into his mouth.

18. Serve nutritious snacks instead of junk foods and other non-nutritional foods that may be unhealthy for the student. Candy, cookies, cake, pretzels, potato chips, soda, and similar foods and beverages have little nutritive value. Do not offer these foods to students as rewards, for snacks, at mealtime, or at parties. Nutritious snacks, such as fresh fruit, raisins, nuts, sunflower and pumpkin seeds, milk, and pure fruit juices, are enjoyed by students and are healthy.

19. Quiet activities should be alternated with activities involving gross motor actions. The resulting variety acts as a motivating factor and an aid to classroom management.

20. Use role playing, puppet play, and creative dramatics to stimulate real experiences and to practice skills.

21. Incorporate music into activities whenever possible. For example, play a tune on an autoharp and sing the instructions appropriate to an activity, such as "Johnny, line up, line up, line up."

22. Use familiar games and songs in activities rather than wasting time searching for educational games or special songs. Keep in mind ethnic, cultural, and geographic preferences.

23. Choose materials and activities that will reflect the student's cultural and ethnic background.

24. Remember to respect the student's privacy. Allow him to have some time of his own during which he is not required to be a participant.

25. Become familiar with community facilities, and use them as learning stations. Make the entire community your classroom or learning area. The neighborhood supermarket is the best place to enhance learning about purchasing foods. The office building and the department store offer opportunities in learning how to use elevators, revolving doors, and automatic doors.

26. Seek the help of resource people who can enrich the educational program. Store managers, bus drivers, firemen, policemen, and road repairmen not only can provide interesting demonstrations and lectures but also may allow you the use of their facilities so that the student can have first-hand experiences. For example, the bus driver can provide you with the use of an empty bus to practice getting on and off.

Parental Role

Supplementing the teacher-initiated strategies, there are certain expectations the teacher should try to develop with the parents or parent surrogates of her preschool children. These would include but not be limited to:

1. Attending all parents meetings (PTA)
2. See to it that their children attend school regularly
3. Get their children ready on time for school
4. See to it that their children receive adequate rest and get to bed at a reasonable hour
5. Continually encourage their children, and not shame them by calling them names
6. Avoid comparing them unfavorably with other siblings
7. Not allow their children who can speak to communicate with a nod or a single word, but require them to speak in full sentences

Chapter 20
Classroom Organization and Physical Arrangements

Unfortunately, not every teacher can teach in a modern, spacious, well lighted, and well equipped room. It is possible, however, for each teacher to arrange and decorate her classroom so that it is pleasant and attractive to her students. The teacher can also be creative in the use of available materials and the maximizing of resources. Probably the strongest asset a teacher can bring to the classroom environment is the warmth of her personality and the friendliness and firmness needed to deal with individual situations. As one can quickly surmise, the key to teaching effectively is not the environment, although this can certainly support a positive teaching atmosphere, but the teacher. It is the teacher who can make the most inadequately equipped classroom seem beautiful and provide the student with an atmosphere that encourages him to want to be there and to express a reluctance to leave.

While this is the era of elaborate equipment, most successful preschool programs for the disadvantaged rely on traditional pieces of furniture and equipment. The room should convey an air of happiness, for it is this quality that will encourage creativity and challenge the students to learn.

To provide the reader with ideas concerning physical arrangements of a preschool room, the authors have solicited from professionals who work with preschool children examples of how their preschool classrooms are physically arranged. The following floor plans are included only as models that have been used effectively with a wide variety of populations of preschool children. It is the responsibility of the teacher to modify one of these plans or develop her own plan as she begins to build her preschool program. It is important to remember that the classroom arrangement that might finally be decided upon will, in all probability, need to be modified during the school year.

243

SUGGESTED FLOORPLAN A

Designed by: Ms. Elizabeth Smith, Teacher, Severely and Profoundly Handicapped

Rationale

Work area:
- High shelves for storing activities out of children's reach
- Tray cabinet with individual trays for classifying art supplies or other materials
- Locking storage cabinet to keep potentially dangerous materials away from children
- Three tables placed together for group activities and separated for small-group work
- Several desks for individual work
- Pegboard screens to separate room and screen off work groups. Can be used to display language activities and for stimulation by using pictures and words on one side of screen. Can be used to hang musical instruments, puppets, or dress-up clothing for make-believe activities on rug side of room
- Refrigerator for storage of snacks and other food

Story, play, and special activities side:
- Personalized coat racks with hooks and shelves for storing clothing
- Mirror near area for self-identification work. Dressing skills can be worked on with students sitting on the rug.
- Low bulletin board and chalk board on wall by rug to assist in displaying storytime visual aids or displaying students work, calendar, or weather board.
- Toy storage by same area to encourage play skills and social interaction during free time
- Folding mats can be placed on rug area for protection when working on gross motor skills
- Climbing equipment, pedal toys, balls, and other large equipment could be stored on this side of the room, safely out of path of activities

Bathroom:
- Shelves to hold personalized self-care items
- Accessible toilets and sinks of appropriate size
- Stools

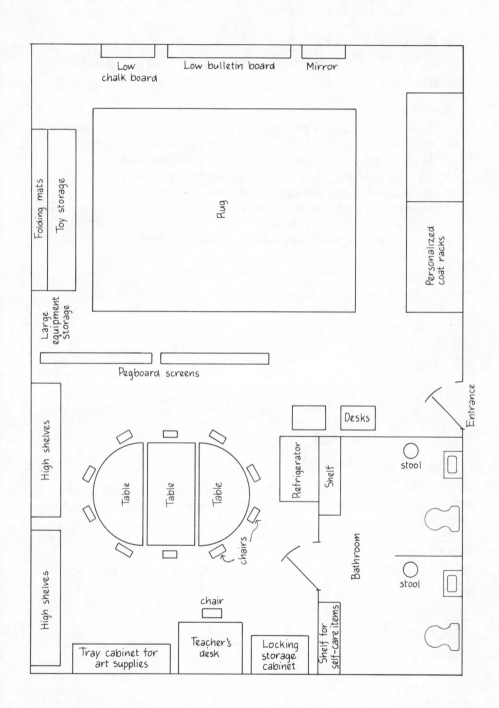

Low chalk board

Low bulletin board

Mirror

Folding mats

Toy storage

Rug

Personalized coat racks

Large equipment storage

Pegboard screens

High shelves

Table

Table

Table

chairs

Desks

Entrance

Refrigerator

Shelf

stool

Bathroom

stool

High shelves

chair

Teacher's desk

Locking storage cabinet

Shelf for self-care items

Tray cabinet for art supplies

SUGGESTED FLOOR PLAN B

Designed by: Ms. Candice Suggars, Teacher, Primary Level, Developmentally Disabled

Rationale
- Color-coded spaces to differentiate learning areas (work, play, quiet)
- Quiet areas separated from more active (higher noise level) areas
- Materials classified (organized) according to different areas
- To avoid confusing children, all materials not within view
- Materials accessible and part of each individual area
- Utilization of real materials for store activities. Real refrigerator and sink for washing dishes (in imagination area) and preparing foods (lunch)
- Areas allow for individualization of children's needs or can be group oriented
- Areas allow for exploration of different feelings

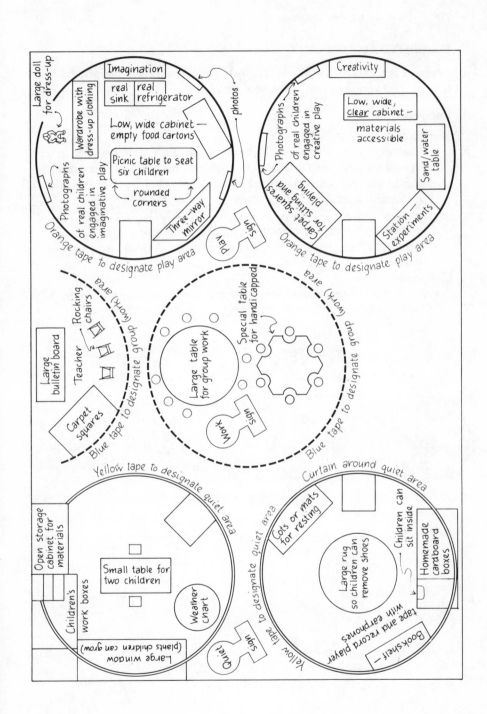

SUGGESTED FLOOR PLAN C

Designed by: Ms. Susan Wade, Teacher, Preschool Level, and Ms. Edith Garrett, Teaching Assistant, Preschool Level

Rationale

Storage cabinets:
- Shelves can be used to contain children's blocks. Children will be able to independently remove blocks from shelves for play and return them. Equipment for other independent activities such as those in the preacademic area can also be stored in similar way
- Storage available for tricycles, wagons, Big Wheels, and related playground equipment (for example, balls and jump ropes)
- Shelves in the cabinet can be used to store paper, crayons, and paint and brushes

Coat room:
- A chest of drawers can be stored here that would allow for keeping track of extra clothes or change of clothing

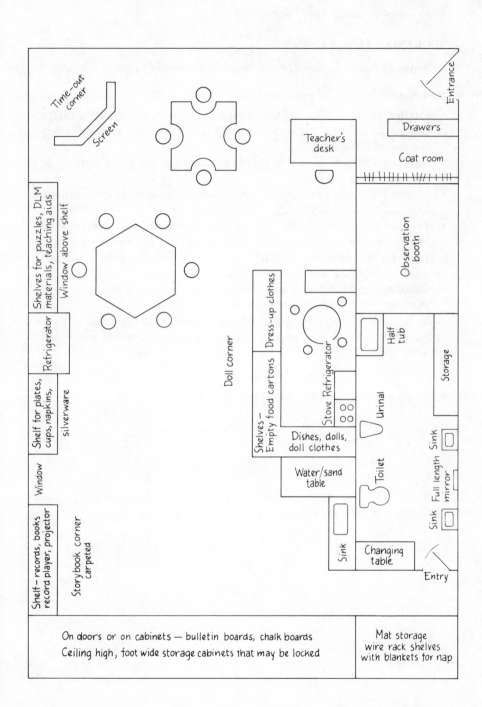

Time-out corner

Screen

Shelves for puzzles, DLM materials, teaching aids

Window above shelf

Refrigerator

Shelf for plates, cups, napkins, silverware

Window

Shelf — records, books record player, projector

Storybook corner carpeted

Doll corner

Shelves — Empty food cartons

Dress-up clothes

Dishes, dolls, doll clothes

Water/sand table

Stove

Refrigerator

Sink

Changing table

Toilet

Urinal

Half tub

Sink

Full length mirror

Sink

Storage

Teacher's desk

Drawers

Coat room

Observation booth

Entrance

Entry

On doors or on cabinets — bulletin boards, chalk boards
Ceiling high, foot wide storage cabinets that may be locked

Mat storage
wire rack shelves
with blankets for nap

SUGGESTED FLOOR PLAN D

Designed by: Ms. Paulette Duda, Teacher, Preschool Level

Rationale
- Puzzles, games, blocks, and toys are stored on low shelves to encourage the children to choose activities and develop play and socialization skills during free-play time
- Two-sided shelves allow storage of materials specific to the learning or paly area each side faces
- Double classroom can serve as natural separation between quiet activity area and more active (louder) activity area
- Personalized cubbyhole for each child to hang coat and store personal belongings (for example, rest mat, change of clothing, boots)
- Housekeeping area has "pretend" sink, stove, and refrigerator, and real dishes, silverware, and cooking utensils
- Dress-up area has "grown-up" clothing to encourage dressing up and role playing
- Music area has record player, records, rhythm instruments, and a large, clear floor area to encourage active participation in musical games and activities

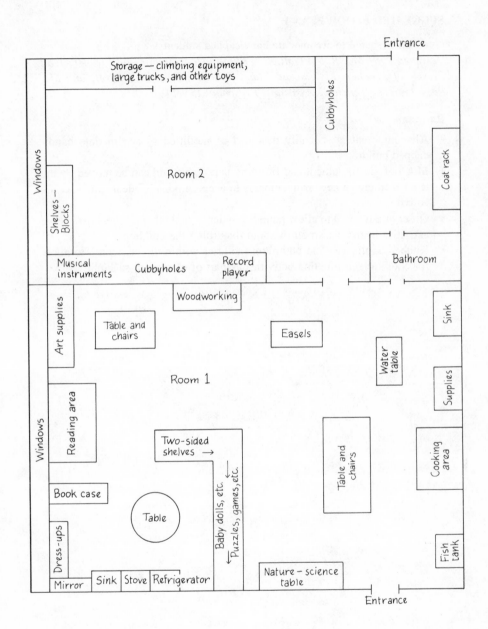

251

SUGGESTED FLOOR PLAN E

(Specially designed to accomodate handicapped students)
Designed by: Ms. Robin Gallico, Training Coordinator and Former Head Preschool Teacher, Ms. Susan Wade, Teacher, Preschool Level, and Ms. Edith Garrett, Teaching Assistant, Preschool Level

Rationale

- All equipment is specially designed or modified to accomodate handicapped children
- Much of the equipment and furniture is portable and can be moved by the teacher to create new arrangements to accommodate students and specific activities
- Observation booth to allow parents, students, and other teachers to observe activities in the classroom without disturbing the children
- Kitchen appliances and bathroom facilities within the classroom to allow for cooking and toileting activities as part of classroom schedule

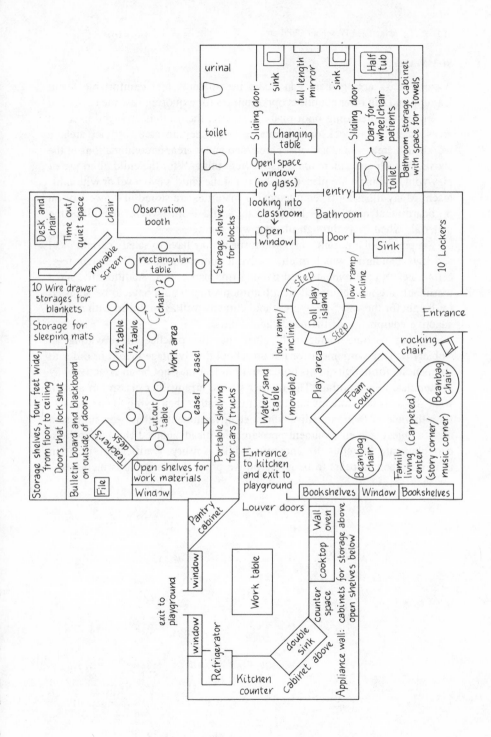

urinal

toilet

Sliding door

sink

full length mirror

sink

Sliding door

Half tub

bars for wheelchair patients

Bathroom storage cabinet with space for towels

Changing table

Open space window (no glass) looking into classroom

entry

Bathroom

toilet

Observation booth

chair

Desk and chair

Time out/ quiet space

movable screen

rectangular table

Storage shelves for blocks

Open window

Door

Sink

10 Lockers

Entrance

(chair?)

½ table

½ table

Work area

10 Wire drawer storages for blankets

Storage for sleeping mats

easel

easel

low ramp/ incline

1 step

Doll play island

1 step

low ramp/ incline

rocking chair

Storage shelves, four feet wide, from floor to ceiling. Doors that lock shut

Bulletin board and blackboard on outside of doors

Cutout table

easel

teacher's desk

Portable shelving for cars/trucks

Play area

Water/sand table (movable)

Foam couch

Beanbag chair

File

Open shelves for work materials

Window

Entrance to kitchen and exit to playground

Beanbag chair

Family living (carpeted) center (story corner/ music corner)

Bookshelves

Window

Bookshelves

Louver doors

Pantry cabinet

window

Work table

Wall oven

cooktop

counter space

cabinets for storage above open shelves below

exit to playground

window

Refrigerator

double sink

cabinet above

Appliance wall:

Kitchen counter

253

SUMMARY

A good class arrangement can make the students feel comfortable about learning and can offer countless opportunities for exploring new ideas. As can be seen in the preceding floor plans, typically, the room is arranged in select areas, such as: a block or toy area, a housekeeping area, a quiet area, a workbench area, a sand and water area, and an art area, or combinations of the above. In each area, there are usually "real things" for the children to use or play with, and most are placed on shelves at the child's eye level or within his reach. Many times tools, equipment, or materials are stored in drawers or on pegboards that have rebus labels so the child learns where to replace the materials when he is through playing with them.

A preschool program's classroom space may have to satisfy certain local and state standards, which often involve a minimum number of square feet, certain health requirements, and passing fire inspections. Additionally, most preschools are now equipped with bathrooms that would have to be adjusted for height for the very young preschool child as well as equipped with rails or adaptive equipment for the handicapped child.

It has become increasingly clear that the practice of providing an "object-rich" environment for the preschool disadvantaged child in order to compensate for deficits in his home environment may not be an effective way to stimulate new learning. The teacher should arrange her classroom around what she feels her students need at that time rather than trying to compensate for a lifetime of living in a disadvantaged environment. It has been suggested that an object-rich environment pressures the disadvantaged child to go from one elaborate stimulus to another. While sensory gratification is often achieved, there appears to be no definitive proof that learning is increased.

Chapter 21
Curriculum Materials and Resources

One of the pressing problems facing teachers of the disadvantaged preschool child, as well as those who teach all levels of students, is what instructional materials to select as they develop their educational programs. While the authors firmly believe that "teacher made" materials are still preferable to many of the commercially made materials, a blend of both types of resources is often advantageous.

It is difficult to recommend specific materials and resources without adding the warning that many commercially prepared items have not been thoroughly field tested or have been pilot tested using a limited population of students. It will be the responsibility of the teacher to investigate which materials appear appropriate for use with her students and to carefully monitor whether or not specific materials fulfill the purpose for which they were selected.

It would be impossible to list all, or even the majority, of educational materials that have been developed over the last few years. Instead, the authors have selected those materials most often reported as being used with a preschool population of disadvantaged students; the teacher is encouraged to review various educational catalogs and brochures, which describe a variety of instructional resources. A few of the materials that are listed may be considered by some teachers as academically high for implementation with a preschool population. These specific resources have been purposely included because many preschool children come to school with scattered academic skills that they have accumulated while playing with peers or have learned from their home environment. For those students, instructional materials should present high goals as a challenging learning experience.

Prices of the resources listed in this chapter are not included because of their ever-changing status. The teacher should refer to current price lists (available from the individual companies) or look up the cost of the product in the current year's educational catalog. Current catalogs can be obtained by writing to the addresses of the companies listed in this section. These catalogs often picture and describe the resources in detail.

The sample resources reported in this chapter have been selected from the areas of reading, arithmetic, language, motor skills, music, and art. For each material, the type of resource, its name or title, its author(s) (when known), its suggested grade level, and its publishing source are listed. The teacher may wish to consult with other teachers who have used these materials or resources before she decides to purchase any of them.

Curriculum Resources and Materials

Reading Resources

Type of resource	Title	Author	Suggested grade level	Publisher or source
Book	Play and Learn Books		Pre-primary–1	Golden Press, Inc. Educational Division 850 Third Ave. New York, N. Y. 10022
Book	Reading Laboratory Books	Witty	Pre-primary–4	Children's Press, Inc. 1224 W. Van Buren St. Chicago, Ill. 60607
Books, records	Time Machine Series	Darby	Pre-primary–3	Harr Wagner Publishing Co. Field Educational Publishing Inc. 609 Mission St. San Francisco, Ca. 94105
Books	Let's Start Book Box		Pre-primary	Scholastic Book Services Scholastic Magazines, Inc. 902 Sylvan Ave. Englewood Cliffs, N. J. 07632
Workbooks	Simplified Reading Readiness Program (Revised)	Goldstein and Levitt	Pre-primary	R. W. Parkinson, Division Follett Publishing Co. 1010 W. Washington Blvd. Chicago, Ill. 60607
Book	Readiness for Reading	Dolch	Pre-primary–1	Garrard Publishing Co. 1607 North Market St. Champaign, Ill. 61820

(continued)

Curriculum Resources and Materials (*continued*)

Reading Resources (*continued*)

Type of resource	Title	Author	Suggested grade level	Publisher or source
Workbooks	Puzzle Series	Dietrick and Greenlee	Pre-primary–2	McCormick Matheas Publishing Co., Inc. P. O. Box 2212 Wichita, Kan. 67201
Book	The Happy Bears	Dolch	Pre-primary–1	Garrard Publishing Co. 1607 North Market St. Champaign, Ill. 61820
Books, manuals, charts	Learning to Think Series	Thurstone	Pre-primary–1	Science Research Assoc., Inc. 259 East Erie St. Chicago, Ill. 60611
Books, workbooks, aids	City Schools Reading Program	Whipple et al.	Pre-primary–1	Follett Publishing Co. 1010 W. Washington Blvd. Chicago, Ill. 60607
Workbooks	Frostig Program for the Development of Visual Perception	Frostig and Horne	Pre-primary–2	Follett Publishing Co. 1010 W. Washington Blvd. Chicago, Ill. 60607
Book	The Big Parade	Knudsen	Pre-primary	McGraw-Hill Book Co., Inc. 330 West 42nd St. New York, N. Y. 10036
Workbooks, aids	Peabody Rebus Reading Program	Woodcock	Pre-primary–1	American Guidance Service, Inc. Publishers Building Circle Pines, Minn. 55014
Books, manual, cards	Laradon—Basic Reading Kit	McGlone et al.	Pre-primary–1	LADOCA Project and Publishing Co. East 51st Ave. at Lincoln St. Denver, Col. 80216

Type	Title	Author/Editor	Level	Publisher
Books	Experimental Developmental Program	Stanck and Munsen	Pre-primary	Benefic Press, 1900 North Narrgansett St., Chicago, Ill. 60639
Textbooks	Developmental Reading Text Workbook Series	Burton, Kemp, et al.	Pre-primary-6	Bobbs-Merrill Co., 4300 W. 62nd St., Indianapolis, Ind. 46206
Books, aids	Dandy Doe's Early Learning Program	Roberts, McNeil, Whitman	Pre-primary-1	American Book Company, 55 Fifth Ave., New York, N. Y. 10003
Student newspaper	My Weekly Reader—Surprise	Editor	Pre-primary	American Education Publications, 55 High St., Middletown, Conn. 16457
Units	Visual-Motor Perception Materials	Cheeves	Pre-primary-3	Teaching Resources, 334 Boylston St., Boston, Mass. 02116
Units	Development of Readiness to Read (Unit 4)		Pre-primary-1	Milton Bradley Company, 74 Park St., Springfield, Mass. 01101
Aids (manual for building reading and number aids)	Teaching Aids and Toys for Handicapped Children	Dorward	Pre-primary-3	Council for Exception Children, MR Division, Reston, Va.
Aids, posters	Let's Start Poster and Story Box		Pre-primary	Scholastic Book Services, Scholastic Magazine, Inc., 902 Sylvan Ave., Englewood Cliffs, N. J. 07632
Aid	Kinesthetic Alphabet		Pre-primary-1	Milton Bradley Company, 74 Park St., Springfield, Mass. 01101

(continued)

Curriculum Resources and Materials (*continued*)

Reading Resources (*continued*)

Type of resource	Title	Author	Suggested grade level	Publisher or source
Kits	Weekly Reader's Pre-School Program		Pre-primary	American Education Publications 55 High St. Middletown, Conn. 06457
Kit	Mark Away, Unit I—Reading	Calway	Pre-primary-3	Paul S. Amidon and Assoc., Inc. 1035-EC Plymouth Bldg. Minneapolis, Minn. 55402
Kit	Reading Readiness Program for the Mentally Retarded	Goldstein and Levitt	Pre-primary	R. W. Parkinson, Division Follett Publishing Co. 1010 W. Washington Blvd. Chicago, Ill. 60607
Records	Take a Bath (Plus Other Pre-School Records)	Hap Palmer		Educational Activities, Inc. Box 392 Freeport, N. Y. 11520
Cards, records	Creative Involvement Cards		Pre-primary-2	Benefic Press 1900 North Narragansett St. Chicago, Ill. 60639
Card game	Picture Readiness Game	Dolch	Pre-primary-1	Garrard Publishing Co. 1607 North Market St. Champaign, Ill. 61820
Card games	Match Games—Sets One and Two	Dolch	Pre-primary-1	Garrard Publishing Co. 1607 North Market St. Champaign, Ill. 61820
Ditto masters	Visual Readiness Skills—Visual Motor Skills—Visual Discrimination	Maney	Pre-primary-1	Continental Press, Inc. Elizabethtown, Pa. 17022

Type	Title	Author	Level	Publisher
Ditto masters	Independent Activities—Seeing Likenesses and Differences—Thinking Skills	Maney	Pre-primary-1	Continental Press, Inc. Elizabethtown, Pa. 17022
Ditto masters	Reading Readiness		Pre-primary	Continental Press, Inc. Elizabethtown, Pa. 17022
Puzzles	Sifo Puzzles		Pre-primary-2	Constructive Playthings 1040 East 85th St. Kansas City, Mo. 64131
Gummed stickers	Word Making Productions		Pre-primary-3	Word Making Productions P. O. Box 305 Salt Lake City, Utah 84110
Filmstrips	Visual Perception Skills	Siegel, Gisonti, and Pasnack	Pre-primary-1	Educational Activities, Inc. Box 392 Freeport, N. Y. 11520
Filmstrips	Reading Readiness Filmstrip Set	Groffman	Pre-primary	Rhime Associates P. O. Box 252 Paramus, N. J. 07652

Arithmetic Resources

Type	Title	Author	Level	Publisher
Book	Touch and Learn Book of Shapes	Sobel	Pre-primary-1	McGraw-Hill Book Co., Inc. 330 West 42nd St. New York, N. Y. 10036
Book	Touch and Learn Book of Numbers	Fletcher	Pre-primary-1	McGraw-Hill Book Co., Inc. 330 West 42nd St. New York, N. Y. 10036
Books, kit	Pre-Number Picture Cards	D'Augustine	Pre-primary-1	Harper and Row Publishing Company, Inc. Keystone Industrial Park Scranton, Pa. 18512

(continued)

Curriculum Resources and Materials (*continued*)

Arithmetic Resources (*continued*)

Type of resource	Title	Author	Suggested grade level	Publisher or source
Workbook	How Many	Von Hilsheimer	Pre-primary–3	Green Valley School P. O. Box 606 EC Orange City, Fla. 32763
Workbook	Happy Ways to Numbers	Ambrose	Pre-primary–1	Holt, Rinehart, and Winston, Inc. 383 Madison Ave. New York, N. Y. 10017
Printed originals and worktext	Alphy's Number Kit	Hebeem	Pre-primary	Visual Products Division 3M Company 2501 Hudson Rd. St. Paul, Minn. 55101
Programmed worktext	Addition and Subtraction Facts		1	Grolier Eductional Corp. 575 Lexington Ave. New York, N. Y. 10022
Worktexts	Arithmetic Foundation Series	Alexander et al.	Pre-primary–2	Harr Wagner Publishing Co. Field Educational Publications, Inc. 609 Mission St. San Francisco, Cal. 94105
Units	Development of Number Readiness (Unit 3)		Pre-primary–1	Milton Bradley Company 74 Park St. Springfield, Mass. 01101
Ditto masters	Complete Arithmetic Series	Schlegel, Eberly, and Stiles	Pre-primary–3	Continental Press, Inc. Elizabethtown, Pa. 17022
Kit	More Or Less	Siegel	Pre-primary–1	Mafex Associates, Inc. Box 519 Johnstown, Pa. 15707

Kit	Cuisenaire Rods	Gattegno and Trivett	Pre-primary–4	Cuisenaire Company of America 9 Elm Ave. Mt. Vernon, N. Y. 10550
Charts, worksheets	Open Door to Mathematics Charts Open Door to Mathematics Worksheets	Deans, Kane, and Oesterle	Pre-primary–1	American Book Company 55 Fifth Ave. New York, N. Y. 10003
Charts	Kindermath	Erickson and Vodacek	Pre-primary	Ginn and Company 72 Fifth Ave. New York, N. Y. 10011
Magnetic aids	Magnetic Visual Aids		Pre-primary–6	Constructive Playthings 1040 East 85th St. Kansas City, Mo. 64131
Aid	Arithme-Sticks		Pre-primary–3	Milton Bradley Company 74 Park St. Springfield, Mass. 01101
Aid	Cubical Counting Blocks		Pre-primary–3	Milton Bradley Company 74 Park St. Springfield, Mass. 01101
Aid	Classroom Counting Frame		Pre-primary–3	Milton Bradley Company 74 Park St. Springfield, Mass. 01101
Aids	Aids for Number Perception	McGlone	Pre-primary–2	LADOCA Project and Publishing Foundation East 51st Ave. at Lincoln St. Denver, Colo. 80216
Film	More and Less	Boundey	Pre-primary–3	Film Associates 11559 Santa Monica Blvd. Los Angeles, Cal. 90025
Film	Comparing: Getting Ready for Measuring Film	Boundey	Pre-primary–4	Film Associates 11559 Santa Monica Blvd. Los Angeles, Cal. 90025

(continued)

Curriculum Resources and Materials (*continued*)

Arithmetic Resources (*continued*)

Type of resource	Title	Author	Suggested grade level	Publisher or source
Game	Shapes Lotto		Pre-primary	Milton Bradley Company 74 Park St. Springfield, Mass. 01101
Game	First Arithmetic Game	Dolch	Pre-primary–1	Garrard Publishing Co. 1607 North Market St. Champaign, Ill. 61820

Language Resources

Books	Hayes Games Books	Hoosier, Wagner, et al.	Pre-primary–8	Hayes School Publishing Co., Inc. 321 Pennwood Ave. Wilkinsburg, Pa. 15221
Book	Informal Dramatics	McIntyre	Pre-primary–4	Stanwix House, Inc. 3020 Chartiers Ave. Pittsburgh, Pa. 15204
Book	Rhymes for Fingers and Flannelboards	Scott and Thompson	Pre-primary	Webster Division McGraw-Hill Book Co. 1154 Reco Ave. St. Louis, Mo. 63126
Workbooks	Best Speech Series	Matthews, Birch, et al.	Pre-primary–3	Stanwix House, Inc. 3020 Chartiers Ave. Pittsburgh, Pa. 15204
Workbook	The Clown Family Speech Book	Pollock and Pollock	Pre-primary–3	Charles C Thomas, Publisher 301-327 East Lawrence Ave. Springfield, Ill. 62703

Books, aids	Invitations to Story Time		Pre-primary	Scott, Foresman and Company 433 East Erie St. Chicago, Ill. 60611
Book, aids	Kindergarten Rhymes with Flannel Cutouts		Pre-primary	Teachers Publishing Co. 23 Leroy Ave. Darien, Conn. 06820
Books	Listen–Hear Books	Slepian and Seidler	Pre-primary–2	Follett Publishing Co. 1010 W. Washington Blvd. Chicago, Ill. 60607
Story test	Louie, the Lazy Listener	Smith and Call	Pre-primary–3	Children's Music Center, Inc. 5373 West Pico Blvd. Los Angeles, Cal. 90010
Workbook	Speak Up	Singer	Pre-primary–3	Hearing and Speech Center of Rochester, Inc. 501 Main Street W. Rochester, N. Y. 14508
Book	The Telephone Book	Hubbel	Pre-primary–1	McGraw-Hill Book Co., Inc. 330 West 42nd St. New York, N. Y. 10036
Books, records	The First Talking Storybook Box		Pre-primary–3	Scott, Foresman and Company 433 East Erie St. Chicago, Ill. 60611
Workbooks	Listen, Mark, and Say	Gotkin, Mason, and Richardson	Pre-primary–2	Appleton-Century-Crofts 440 Park Avenue, South New York, N. Y. 10016
Units	Learning to Develop Language Skills (Unit 2)		Pre-primary	Milton Bradley Company 74 Park St. Springfield, Mass. 01101
Masters	Useful Language: Rhyming; Beginning Sounds		Pre-primary–1	Continental Press, Inc. Elizabeth, Pa. 17022

265

Curriculum Resources and Materials (*continued*)

		Language Resources (*continued*)		
Type of resource	Title	Author	Suggested grade level	Publisher or source
Masters	Listen and Speak to Read	Ortiz and Beck	Pre-primary–2	Hayes School Publishing Co., Inc. 321 Pennwood Ave. Wilkinsburg, Pa. 15221
Kit	Follow Through with Sounds	Harmon, Schumacher, and Sommer	Pre-primary–1	Knowledge Aid Division of Radiant Corp. 8220 N. Austin Ave. Morton Groue, Ill. 60053
Kit	Kit A, Language	Clymer, Christenson, and Russel	Pre-primary–2	Ginn and Company 72 Fifth Ave. New York, N. Y. 10011
Kit	Kit B, Consonants	Clymer, Christenson, and Russel	1–5	Ginn and Company 72 Fifth Ave. New York, N. Y. 10011
Kits	Peabody Language Development Kits	Dunn, Smith, and Horton	Pre-primary–3	American Guidance Service, Inc. Publishers Building Circle Pines, Minn. 55014
Kit	Sounds and Patterns of Language	Martin, Weil, and Kohan	Pre-primary	Holt, Rinehart, and Winston, Inc. 383 Madison Ave. New York, N. Y. 10017
Kit	Think, Listen, and Say	Sayre and Mack	Pre-primary	Eye Gate House, Inc. 14601 Macher Ave. Jamaica, N. Y. 11435
Aids	Seasons Flannel Aid		Pre-primary–1	Milton Bradley Company 74 Park St. Springfield, Mass. 01101

Type	Title	Author	Level	Source
Aids	Human Body Parts Flannel Aid		Pre-primary	Milton Bradley Company, 74 Park St., Springfield, Mass. 01101
Aid	Five-Way Teaching Board (Magnetic type, chalk, etc.)		Pre-primary–3	Milton Bradley Company, 74 Park Street, Springfield, Mass. 01101
Audiovisual aid	Phoviewer, Show and Tell		Pre-primary–6	J. C. Penney Co., Inc., Milwaukee, Wis. 53201 (and other department stores)
Aids	Telephones		Pre-primary–6	Go-Mo Products, Inc., 1441 Headford Ave., Waterloo, Iowa 50704
Aids	Miniature Traffic Signs		Preschool	Milton Bradley Company, 74 Park St., Springfield, Mass. 01101
Pictures	Words and Actions	Shaftel	Pre-primary–3	Holt, Rinehart, and Winston, Inc., 383 Madison Ave., New York, N. Y. 10017
Records, aids	The First Talking Alphabet		Pre-primary–1	Scott, Foresman and Company, 433 East Erie St., Chicago, Ill. 60611
Records	Listening with Mr. Bunny Big Ears	Wilcox and McIntyre	Pre-primary–1	Mafex Associates, Inc., Box 519, Johnstown, Pa. 15707
Records	Sounds I Can Hear		Pre-primary	Scott, Foresman and Company, 433 East Erie St., Chicago, Ill. 60611
Records, cards	Who Said It	Siegel, Gisonti, and Posnack	Pre-primary–2	Educational Activities, Inc., Box 392, Freeport, N. Y. 11520

(continued)

Curriculum Resources and Materials (*continued*)

Language Resources (*continued*)

Type of resource	Title	Author	Suggested grade level	Publisher or source
Record	Once Upon a Time		Pre-primary–1	American Book Company 55 Fifth Ave. New York, N. Y. 10003
Record, book	Read and Hear Books	DeLugg, Potter, et al.	Pre-primary	Hudson Products, Inc. A. A. Records 250 West 57th St. New York, N. Y. 10019
Boards	Story Boards	Hill	Pre-primary–1	Houghton Mifflin Company 1900 South Batavia Avenue Geneva, Ill. 60134
Poster cards	Cards		Pre-primary	Milton Bradley Company 74 Park St. Springfield, Mass. 01101
Poster cards	Animals and their Young Poster Cards		Pre-primary	Milton Bradley Company 74 Park St. Springfield, Mass. 01101
Cards	Play and Say	Warkomski and Irwin	Pre-primary–4	Stanwix House, Inc. 3020 Chartiers Ave. Pittsburgh, Pa. 15204
Games	Language Lotto	Gotkin	Pre-primary–2	Appleton-Century-Crofts 440 Park Ave., South New York, N. Y. 10016
Games	Matrix Games	Gotkin	Pre-primary–2	Appleton-Century-Crofts 440 Park Ave., South New York, N. Y. 10016

Type	Name	Author	Level	Address
Game	Speech—O	Arnold	Pre-primary-1	Go-Mo Products, Inc. 1441 Headford Ave. Waterloo, Iowa 50704
Game	Spin-A-Test	Alberts	Pre-primary-3	Spin-A-Test Co. 350 Forest Hill Ave. Auburn, Cal. 95603
Puzzles	Sesame Street Wood Puzzle Plaques	Children's Television Workshop, Inc. Muppets, Inc.	Pre-primary-1	Milton Bradley Company 74 Park St. Springfield, Mass. 01101
Puppets	Hand Puppets		Pre-primary-3	Go-Mo Products, Inc. 1441 Headford Ave. Waterloo, Iowa 50704
Puppets	Mitten Puppets		Pre-primary-3	Go-Mo Products, Inc. 1441 Headford Ave. Waterloo, Iowa 50704
Filmstrips	Spoken Arts Fairytales	Klein	Pre-primary-3	REBCO Audio-Visual Company 1204 E. Wood Street Decatur, Ill. 62521

Motor Skills Resources

Type	Name	Author	Level	Address
Storybook, record	Dance-A-Story	Barlin	Pre-primary-5	Ginn and Company 72 Fifth Ave. New York, N. Y. 10011
Records	Rhythms—Records	Glazer et al.	Pre-primary-3	Children's Music Center, Inc. 5373 West Pico Blvd. Los Angeles, Cal. 90010
Records	Rhythm, Activities, and Physical Fitness Programs for all Grades	LeCrone and LeCrone	Pre-primary-4	Rhythm Record Company 9203 Nichols Rd. Oklahoma City, Okla. 73120

(continued)

Curriculum Resources and Materials (*continued*)

Motor Skills Resources (*continued*)

Type of resource	Title	Author	Suggested grade level	Publisher or source
Records	Physical Fitness Records		Pre-primary–4	F. A. Owen Publishing Co. Dansville, N. Y. 14437
Records	Honor Your Partner Albums	Carr and Jervey	Pre-primary–3	Educational Activities, Inc. Box 392 Freeport, N. Y. 11520
Record	The Development of Body Awareness and Position in Space	Carr	Pre-primary–1	Educational Activities, Inc. Box 392 Freeport, N. Y. 11520
Record	Basic Concepts Through Dance—Position in Space	Carr and Jervey	Pre-primary–1	Educational Activities, Inc. Box 392 Freeport, N. Y. 11520
Record	Basic Concepts Through Dance—Body Image	Carr and Jervey	Pre-primary–1	Educational Activities, Inc. Box 392 Freeport, N. Y. 11520
Record	Concept Records	Mann, Ralske, et al.	Pre-primary–1	Mafex Associates, Inc. Box 519 Johnstown, Pa. 15707
Record	Body Image—Listening and Moving	Carr and Cratty	Pre-primary–1	Mafex Associates, Inc. Box 519 Johnstown, Pa. 15707
Equipment	Equipment for Movement Skills		Pre-primary–3	Creative Playthings, Inc. Princeton, N. J. 08540

Music Resources

Book	Sing and Learn	Antey	Pre-primary-1	John Day Company, Inc. Box 342D 200 Madison Ave. New York, N. Y. 10016
Song books	Ella Jenkins Records and Books	Jenkins	Pre-primary-1	Children's Music Center, Inc. 5373 West Pico Blvd. Los Angeles, Cal. 90010
Record/pictures	Music Round About Us Program	Wolfe, Krone, et al.	Pre-primary-3	Follett Publishing Co. 1010 W. Washington Blvd. Chicago, Ill. 61607
Records	Let's Start Record Box		Pre-primary	Scholastic Book Services Scholastic Magazines, Inc. 902 Sylvan Ave. Englewood Cliffs, N. J. 07632
Records	Fun While Learning to Sing		Pre-primary-1	F. A. Owen Publishing Co. Dansville, N. Y. 14437
Records	Songs for Children with Special Needs	Purdy et al.	Pre-primary	Constructive Playthings 1040 East 85th St. Kansas City, Mo. 64131
Records	Phoebe James Records	James	Pre-primary-1	Children's Music Center, Inc. 5373 West Pico Blvd. Los Angeles, Cal. 90019
Records	Records to Use with Rhythm Instruments	Pitts, Tipton, et al.	Pre-primary-2	Children's Music Center, Inc. 5373 West Pico Blvd. Los Angeles, Cal. 90019
Records	Resting Time Records	Horne, Robinson, et al.	Pre-primary-2	Children's Music Center, Inc. 5373 West Pico Blvd. Los Angeles, Cal. 90019

(continued)

Curriculum Resources and Materials (*continued*)

Music Resources (*continued*)

Type of resource	Title	Author	Suggested grade level	Publisher or source
Record	Original Children's Activity Songs	Manning	Pre-primary–1	Ardelle Manning Productions P. O. Box 125 Palo Alto, Cal. 94302
Aids, records	Song Flannel Board Packets		Pre-primary–1	David C. Cook Publishing Co. 850 North Grove Ave. Elgin, Ill. 60120
Instruments	Rhythm Instruments		Pre-primary–6	Children's Music Center, Inc. 5373 West Pico Blvd. Los Angeles, Cal. 90019
Film	What Is Rhythm		Pre-primary–4	Film Associates 115599 Santa Monica Blvd. Los Angeles, Cal. 90025

Art Resources

Books	Art Activity Book		1	Dick Blick P. O. Box 1267 Galesburg, Ill. 61401
Aids	Monthly Art Aids		1–2	Continental Press, Inc. Elizabethtown, Pa. 17022

Section VI
CONCLUSION

Chapter 22
Perspectives:
Past and Future

There appears to be general agreement that disadvantaged preschool children are behind other children in many developmental areas when they start school and that the disparity between what is expected of them in school, academically, and the skills they effectively demonstrate when they leave school continues to widen. Logically, it would seem that preschool disadvantaged children must educationally progress at a faster than average rate if they are to compensate for their initial educational deficiencies. It is axiomatic that their program must therefore include content and teaching strategies for promoting growth at as rapid a rate as possible. It is no longer acceptable to provide marginal programs that purport to teach and enrich the lives of disadvantaged children when, in reality, they do little more than perpetuate the child's differences. Sadly, the authors realize that marginal programs may very well continue to exist for this population of children under the rubric of excuses related to the lack of funds or fiscal accountability.

This source book has attempted to emphasize that we should not try to inculcate our beliefs or regulate the societal values of children who come from culturally different backgrounds. It is more appropriate to help these children understand the values that motivate the school's philosophy and that often reflect society's demand for achievement and accomplishment. In essence, the preschool experience can act as a bridge between two cultures: the culture in which the child lives and the one to which he will need to adapt if he is to be successful in contemporary society.

An additional consideration repeatedly brought to light concerns incorporating the parents and the home environment into the content of the student's educational plan. This provision must continue to be mandatory if the preschool curriculum is to be truly responsive to the individual needs of the child.

It is also critical that a strong balance of social and cognitive skills as well as those skills taught in the emotional domain be achieved in the curriculum of the preschool disadvantaged child. In the final analysis, however, the preacademic skills that the child has mastered will ultimately dictate the degree of success he will have as he progresses through the primary grades.

With all of today's carefully designed "model preschool projects," technological advances, and innovative instructional media, we must reiterate the importance of the competent teacher in preparing students for the future; the ultimate responsibility for success or failure of the preschool child lies with her.

This is a source book developed for persons interested in working with disadvantaged preschool children. It does not purport to be a panacea for teachers who are faced with overwhelming numbers of students, unresponsive support systems, or inflexible administrations. It is intended for use as a source of information, upon which the teacher can build and expand, and as a guide to her own artful teaching.

References

Aiken, Lewis R., Jr. 1971. *Psychological and Educational Testing.* Allyn & Bacon, Inc., Boston.

Ainsworth, M. D., and Bell, S. M. 1974. Mother-infant Interaction and the Development of Competence. In K. Connolly and J. Bruner (eds.), *The Growth of Competence.* Academic Press, New York.

Allen, K. E., Benning, P. M., and Drummond, T. W. 1972. Integration of Normal and Handicapped Children in a Behavior Modification Preschool: A Case Study. In G. Semb (ed.), *Behavior Analysis and Education.* University of Kansas Press, Lawrence.

Allen, K. E., Holm, V. A., and Schiefelbusch, R. L. 1978. *Early Intervention—A Team Approach.* University Park Press, Baltimore.

Alpern, G. D., and Boll, T. J. 1972 *Developmental Profile* (manual). Psychological Developmental Publications, Aspen, Col.

Anastasiow, N. J. 1978. Strategies and Models for Early Childhood Intervention Programs in Integrated Settings. In M. J. Guralnick (ed.), *Early Intervention and the Integration of Handicapped and Non-handicapped Children,* pp. 85–111. University Park Press, Baltimore.

Anderson, R. M., Greer, J. G., and Odle, S. J. (eds.). 1978. *Individualizing Educational Materials for Special Children in the Mainstream.* University Park Press. Baltimore.

Anderson, R. M., Greer, J. G., Odle, S. J., and Springfield, H. L. 1978. Prototype Materials for Effective Mainstreaming. In R. M. Anderson, J. G. Greer, and S. J. Odle (eds.), *Individualizing Educational Materials for Special Children in the Mainstream,* pp. 341–386. University Park Press, Baltimore.

Anderson, R. M., Greer, J. G., and Zia, B. 1978. Perspectives and Overview. In R. M. Anderson, J. G. Greer, and S. J. Odle (eds.), *Individualizing Educational Materials for Special Children in the Mainstream,* pp. 5–28. University Park Press, Baltimore.

Anderson, R. M., Hemenway, R. E., and Anderson, J. W. 1969. *Instructional Resources for Teachers of the Culturally Disadvantaged and Exceptional.* Charles C Thomas, Springfield, Ill.

Appleton, T., Clifton, R., and Goldberg, S. 1975. The Development of Behavioral Competence in Infancy. In F. D. Horowitz (ed.), *Review of Child Development Research.* University of Chicago Press, Chicago.

Apolloni, T., and Cooke, T. P. 1978. Integrated Programming at the Infant, Toddler, and Preschool Levels. In M. J. Guralnick (ed.), *Early Intervention and the Integration of Handicapped and Non-handicapped Children.* University Park Press, Balitmore.

Atchley, R. C. 1971. Can Programs for the Poor Survive in Middle Class Institutions? *Phi Delta Kappan.* LIII(4):243–244.

Baer D. M., Wolf, M. M., and Risley, T. R. 1968. Some Current Dimensions of Applied Behavior Analysis. *Journal of Applied Behavior Analysis* 1:91–97.

Beitler, R. 1967 (April 13). *Project Head Start.* Education and Public Welfare Divisions, Washington, D. C.

Bender, M., and Valletutti, P. J. 1976. *Teaching the Moderately and Severely Handicapped.* Vol. I: *Behavior, Self-Care, and Motor Skills.* University Park Press, Baltimore.

Bender, M., Valletutti, P. J., and Bender, R. 1976a. *Teaching the Moderately and Severely Handicapped.* Vol. II: *Communication, Socialization, Safety, and Leisure Time Skills.* University Park Press, Baltimore.

Bender, M., Valletutti, P. J., and Bender, R. 1976b. *Teaching the Moderately and Severely Handicapped.* Vol. III: *Functional Academics for the Mildly and Moderately Handicapped.* University Park Press, Baltimore.

Bereiter, C. 1972. An Academic Preschool for Disadvantaged Children: Conclusions from Evaluation Studies. In J. C. Stanley (ed.), *Preschool Programs for the Disadvantaged: Five Experimental Approaches to Early Childhood Education,* pp. 1–21. The Johns Hopkins Press, Baltimore.

Bereiter, C., and Engelmann, S. 1966. *Teaching Disadvantaged Children in Preschool.* Prentice-Hall, Inc., Englewood Cliffs, N.J.

Bernstein, B. 1961. Social Class and Linquistic Development: A Theory of Social Learning. In A. H. Halsey, J. Floud, and C. A. Anderson (eds.), *Economy, Education and Society* The Free Press of Glencoe, New York.

Bissell, J. S. 1970. *The Cognitive Effects of Pre-School Programs for Disadvantaged Children.* (mimeographed). National Institute of Child Health and Human Development, Bethesda, Md.

Bloom, B. S. 1964. *Stability and Change in Human Characteristics.* John Wiley & Sons, New York.

Bloom, B. S., Davis, A., and Hess, R. 1965. *Compensatory Education for Cultural Deprivation.* Holt, Rinehart, and Winston, Inc., New York.

Bloom L. 1975. Language Development. In F. D. Horowitz (ed.), *Review of Child Development Research,* Vol. 4, pp. 245–304. University of Chicago Press, Chicago.

Bluma, S., Shearer, M., Frohman, A., and Hilliard, J. 1976. *Portage Guide to Early Education* (manual). Copyright, Cooperative Educational Service Agency #12. The Portage Project. Portage, Wis.

Bricker, D. D. 1978. A Rationale for the Integration of Handicapped and Non-handicapped Preschool Children. In M. J. Guralnick (ed.), *Early Intervention and the Integration of Handicapped and Non-handicapped Children,* pp. 3–26. University Park Press, Baltimore.

Bricker, W. A., and Bricker, D. D. 1974. An Early Language Training Strategy. In R. L. Schiefelbusch, and L. L. Lloyd (eds.), *Language Perspectives—Acquisition, Retardation, and Intervention,* pp. 431–468.University Park Press, Baltimore.

Buros, O. 1972. *Mental Measurement Yearbook. 1972.* Gryphon Press, Highland Park, N.J.

Caldwell, B. M. 1967. What Is the Optimal Learning Environment for the Young Child? *American Journal of Orthopsychiatry* 37:8–21.

Cheyney, A. B. 1966. Teachers of the Culturally Disadvantaged. *Exceptional Children* 33:83–88.

Chinn, P. C., Drew, C. J., and Logan, D. R. 1975. *Mental Retardation.* The C. V. Mosby Company, Saint Louis, Mo.

Connolly, K., and Bruner, J. (eds.). 1974. *The Growth of Competence*. Academic Press, New York.

Cooke, T. P., Apolloni, T., and Cooke, S. 1977. Normal Preschool Children as Behavioral Models for Retarded Peers. *Exceptional Children* 43:531-532.

Cull, J. G., and Hardy, R. E. (eds.). 1975. *Problems of Disadvantaged and Deprived Youth*. Charles C Thomas. Springfield, Ill.

Daniels, C. B. 1978. Special Education Market Report. Linc Services, Inc., Westerville, Ohio.

Deutsch, M. 1965. The Role of Social Class in Language Development. American Journal of Orthopsychiatry 25:78-88.

Deutsch, M. 1966. Nursery Education: The Influence of Social Programming on Early Development. In J. L. Frost and G. R. Hawkes (eds.), *The Disadvantaged Child— Issues and Innovations,* pp. 145-152. Houghton Mifflin Company, Boston.

Devoney, C., Guralnick, M. J., and Rubin, H. 1974. Integrating Handicapped and Non-handicapped Preschool Children: Effects on Social Play. *Childhood Education* 50:360-364.

Dusewicz, R. A. 1975. Early Intervention for the Disadvantaged. In J. G. Cull and R. E. Hardy (eds.), *Problems of Disadvantaged and Deprived Youth,* pp. 137-139. Charles C Thomas, Springfield, Ill.

Elardo, R., Bradley, R., and Caldwell, B. 1975. The Relation of Infants' Home Environments to Mental Test Performance From Six to Thirty-six Months: A Longitudinal Analysis. *Child Development* 46:71-76.

Engel, M. And Keane, W. M. 1975. Black Mothers and their Infant Sons: Antecedents, Correlates, and Predictors of Cognitive Development in the Second and Sixth Year of Life. Paper presented at the Biennial Meeting of the Society for Research in Child Development, April, Denver.

Ensher, G. L., Blatt, B. and Winschel, J. F. 1977. Head Start for the Handicapped: Congressional Mandate Audit. *Exceptional Children* 43:202-209.

Erdman, R. L., and Olson, J. L. 1966. Relationships between Educational Programs for the Mentally Retarded and the Culturally Deprived. Mental Retardation Abstract 3:311-318.

Federal Legislation and Programs for Underpriveleged Young People. 1964. *ALA Bulletin* 58:705-711.

Frost, J. L., and Hawkes, G. R. (eds.). 1966. *The Disadvantaged Child—Issues and Innovations*. Houghton Mifflin Company, Boston.

Gallington, R. O. (ed.). 1970. *Industrial Arts for Disadvantaged Youth*. McKnight and McKnight Publishing Co., Bloomington, Ill.

Ginglend, D. R., and Stiles, W. E. 1965. *Music Activities for Retarded Children*. Abingdon Press, Nashville, Tenn.

Goodenough, F. L., and Harris, D. B. 1963. *Goodenough-Harris Drawing Test*. Harcourt, Brace and World, New York

Guide for Planning and Operating Home-Based Child Development Programs. 1974 (June). Office of Child Development, Department of Health, Education, and Welfare, Home Start, P. O. Box 1182, Washington, D. C. 20013.

Guralnick, M. J. 1973. A Research Service Model for Support of Handicapped Children. *Exceptional Children* 39:277-282.

Guralnick, M. J. (ed.). 1978. *Early Intervention and the Integration of Handicapped and Non-handicapped Children*. University Park Press, Baltimore.

Havighurst, R. J. 1966. Who are the Socially Disadvantaged? In J. L. Frost and G. R. Hawkes (eds.), *The Disadvantaged Child—Issues and Innovations,* pp. 15-22. Houghton Mifflin Company, Boston.

Hayden, A. H. 1978. Early Childhood Education. In K. E. Allen, V. A. Holm, and R.

L. Schiefelbusch (eds.), *Early Intervention—A Team Approach,* pp. 27–56. University Park Press, Baltimore.

Hayden, A. H., and Haring, N. G. 1976. Early Intervention for High Risk Infants and Young Children. In T. D. Tjossem (ed.), *Intervention Strategies for High Risk Infants and Young Children,* pp. 573–607. University Park Press, Baltimore.

Heggen, J. R. 1970. Industrial Arts Teachers for Disadvantaged Youth. In R. O. Gallington (ed.), *Industrial Arts for Disadvantaged Youth,* pp. 75–94. McKnight and McKnight Publishing Company, Bloomington, Ill.

Hirshoren, A., and Umansky, W. 1977. Certification for Teachers of Preschool Handicapped Children. *Exceptional Children* 44:191–193.

Horowitz, F. D. 1978. Normal and Abnormal Child Development. In K. E. Allen, V. A. Holm, and R. L. Schiefelbusch (eds.), *Early Intervention—A Team Approach,* pp. 3–26. University Park Press, Baltimore.

Horowitz, F. D., and Dunn, M. Infant Intelligence Testing. In F. D. Minifie and L. L. Lloyd (eds.), *Communicative and Cognitive Abilities—Early Behavioral Assessment,* pp. 21–36. University Park Press, Baltimore.

Hunt, J. McV. 1961. *Intelligence and Experience.* Ronald Press, New York.

Ispa, J., and Matz, R. D. 1978. Integrating Handicapped Preschool Children within a Cognitively Oriented Program. In M. J. Guralnick (ed.), *Early Intervention and the Integration of Handicapped and Non-handicapped Children,* pp. 167–190. University Park Press, Baltimore.

Israel, B. L. 1966. An Approach to Teaching Children Handicapped by Limited Experience. In J. L. Frost and G. R. Hawkes (eds.), *The Disadvantaged Child—Issues and Innovations,* pp. 324–328. Houghton Mifflin Company, Boston.

Johnson, O., and Bommarito, J. 1976. *Tests and Measurement in Child Development—A Handbook.* Jossey-Bass Publishers, San Francisco, Cal.

Kallen, C. A. 1975. Privation or Deprivation: A Discussion on the "Culturally Deprived" Child. In J. G. Cull and R. E. Hardy (eds.), *Problems of Disadvantaged and Deprived Youth,* pp. 11–16.Charles C Thomas, Springfield, Ill.

Kaplan, B. A. 1966. Issues in Educating the Culturally Disadvantaged. In J. L. Frost and G. R. Hawkes (eds.), *The Disadvantaged Child—Issues and Innovations.* Houghton Mifflin Company, Boston.

Karnes, M. B., and Badger, E. E. 1969. Training Mothers to Instruct their Infants at Home. In M. B. Karnes (ed.), *Research and Development Program on Preschool Disadvantaged Children: Final Report,* pp. 249–263. U.S.O.E., Washington, D.C.

Keogh, B. K., and Kopp, C. B. 1978. From Assessment to Intervention: An Elusive Bridge. In F. D. Minifie and L. L. Lloyd (eds.), *Communicative and Cognitive Abilities—Early Behavioral Assessment,* pp. 523–548. University Park Press, Baltimore.

Krajicek, M. J., and Tearney, A. I. (eds.). 1977. *Detection of Developmental Problems in Children—A Reference Guide for Community Nurses and Other Health Care Professionals.* University Park Press, Baltimore.

Krajicek, M. J., Turner, C., Barnes, P., and Borthick, W. 1973. *Stimulation Activities Guide for Children from Birth to Five Years.* John F. Kennedy Child Development Center, University of Colorado Medical Center, Denver.

Lansford, A. 1977. The High Risk Infant. In M. J. Krajicek and A. I. Tearney (eds.), *Detection of Developmental Problems in Children—A Reference Guide for Community Nurses and Other Health Care Professionals,* pp. 79–87. University Park Press, Baltimore.

Lavatelli, C. S. (ed.). 1971. *Language Training in Early Childhood Education.* University of Illinois Press, Urbana.

LaVeck, B. V. 1978. The Developmental Psychologist. In K. E. Allen, V. A. Holm, and R. L. Schiefelbusch (eds.), *Early Intervention—A Team Approach,* pp. 219-244. University Park Press, Baltimore.

Lavin, D. E. 1965. *The Prediction of Academic Performance: A Theoretical Analysis and Review of Research.* Russell Sage Foundation, New York.

Laycock, V. K. 1978. Assessing Learner Characteristics. In R. M. Anderson, J. G. Greer, and S. J. Odle (eds.), *Individualizing Educational Materials for Special Children in the Mainstream,* pp. 29-56. University Park Press, Baltimore.

Levenstein, P. 1970. Cognitive Growth in Preschoolers through Verbal Interaction with Mothers. *American Journal of Orthopsychiatry* 40:426-432.

Lillard, P. P. 1972. *Montessori—A Modern Approach* Schocken Books, New York.

Litton, F. W. 1978. *Education of the Trainable Mentally Retarded—Curriculum, Methods, Materials.* The C. V. Mosby Company, St. Louis, Mo.

McAfee, O. 1972. An Integrated Approach to Early Childhood Education. In J. C. Stanley (ed.), *Preschool Programs for the Disadvantaged: Five Experimental Approaches to Early Childhood Education,* pp. 67-91. The Johns Hopkins Press, Baltimore.

Meier, J. H. 1976. Screening, Assessment, and Intervention for Young Children at Developmental Risk. In T. D. Tjossem (ed.), *Intervention Strategies for High Risk Infants and Young Children,* pp. 251-287. University Park Press, Baltimore.

Miller, H. L. (ed.). 1967. *Education for the Disadvantaged.* The Free Press, New York.

Miller, L. B., and Dyer, J. L. 1975. Four Preschool Programs: Their Dimensions and Effects. Monographs of the Society for Research in Child Development. 40:Nos. 5 and 6 (serial no. 162).

Miller, M. E. 1970. *A Practical Guide for Kindergarten Teachers.* Parker Publishing Company, Inc., New York.

Minifie, F. D., and Lloyd, L. L. (eds.). 1978. *Communicative and Cognitive Abilities—Early Behavioral Assessment.* University Park Press, Baltimore.

Montessori, M. 1964. *The Montessori Method.* Schocken Books, New York.

Montessori, M. 1969. *Dr. Montessori's Own Handbook.* Schocken Books, New York.

Montessori, M. 1970. *Spontaneous Activity in Education.* Schocken Books, New York.

Moore, D. R. 1971. Language Research and Preschool Language Training. In C. S. Lavatelli (ed.), *Language Training in Early Childhood Education,* pp. 3-48. University of Illinois Press, Urbana.

MR 72, Islands of Excellence. 1972. Report of the President's Committee on Mental Retardation. DHEW Publication No. (OS) 73-7. U. S. Department of Health, Education, and Welfare, Washington, D.C.

Murphy, L. B., and Leeper, E. M. 1974. Caring for Children—Number One—The Ways Children Learn. DHEW Publication No (OHD) 75-1026. U. S. Department of Health, Education, and Welfare, Office of Human Development, Office of Child Development, Washington, D.C.

Murphy, L. B., and Leeper, E. M. 1974. Caring for Children—Number Two—More Than a Teacher. DHEW Publication No. (OHD) 75-1027. U. S. Department of Health, Education, and Welfare, Office of Human Development, Office of Child Development, Washington, D.C.

Murray, F. B., and Pikulski, J. J. 1978. *The Acquisition of Reading—Cognitive, Linguistic, and Perceptual Prerequisites.* University Park Press, Baltimore.

Mussen, P. H., Conger, J. J., and Kagan, J. 1969. *Child Development and Personality.* 3rd ed. Harper & Row, New York.

Neill, G. 1974. Washington Report. *Phi Delta Kappan* LVI(1):80-81.

Neill, G. 1977. Washington Report. *Phi Delta Kappan.* 59(1):66–67.

Neill, G. 1977. Washington Report. *Phi Delta Kappan.* 59(4):283–284.

Neill, G. 1978. Washington Report. *Phi Delta Kappan.* 59(8):571–572.

Newsnotes. 1972. *Phi Delta Kappan.* LIV(3):216–221.

Newsnotes. 1974. *Phi Delta Kappan.* LV(8):582–586.

Newsnotes. 1977. *Phi Delta Kappan.* 59(1):69–74.

Newsnotes. 1978. *Phi Delta Kappan.* 59(6):432–437.

Noar, G. 1967, 1972. Teaching the Disadvantaged. National Education Association, Washington, D.C.

Nordquist, M. 1978. A Behavioral Approach to the Analysis of Peer Interactions. In M. J. Guralnick (ed.), *Early Intervention and the Integration of Handicapped and Non-handicapped Children,* pp. 53–84. University Park Press, Baltimore.

Norman, D., and Balyeat, R. 1973. Whither ESEA III? *Phi Delta Kappan.* LV(3):190–192.

Office of Economic Opportunity. 1968. *Head Start—A Community Action Program.* U. S. Government Printing Office, Washington, D.C.

Olson, J. L., and Larson, R. G. 1966. An Experimental Curriculum for Culturally Deprived Kindergarten Children. In J. L. Frost and G. R. Hawkes (eds.), *The Disadvantaged Child—Issues and Innvations,* pp. 175–182. Houghton Mifflin Company, Boston.

Painter, G. 1971. A Tutorial Language Program for Disadvantaged Infants. In C. S. Lavatelli (ed.), *Language Training in Early Childhood Education,* pp. 79–100. University of Illinois Press, Urbana.

Pappadakis, N., and Totten, W. F. 1972. Financing the New Dimensions of Community Education. *Phi Delta Kappan* LIV(3):192–194.

Peck et al. 1976. Teaching developmentally delayed toddlers and preschoolers to imitate the free play behavior of nonretarded classmates: Trained and generalized effects. Unpublished manuscript.

Piaget, J., and Inhelder, B. 1969. *The Psychology of the Child.* Basic Books, New York.

Porter, et al. 1978. Social interactions in heterogeneous groups of retarded and normally developing: An observational study. In G. P. Sackett and H. C. Haywood (eds.), *Observing Behavior, Vol. I: Theory and Applications in Mental Retardation.* University Park Press, Baltimore.

Purvis, J., and Samet, S. (eds.). 1976. *Music in Developmental Therapy.* University Park Press, Baltimore.

Quick, A. D., and Campbell, A. A. 1976. *Lesson Plans for Enhancing Preschool Developmental Progress: Project MEMPHIS.* Kendall/Hunt, Dubuque, Iowa.

Quick, A. D., and Campbell, A. A. 1977. A Model for Preschool Curriculum: Project MEMPHIS. *Mental Retardation* 15:42–46.

Quick, A. D., Little, T. L., and Campbell, A. A. 1974. *Instruments for Individual Program Planning and Evaluation.* Fearon Publishers, Belmont, Cal.

Quick, A. D., Little, T. L., and Campbell, A. A. 1974. *Project MEMPHIS: Enhancing Developmental Progress in Preschool Exceptional Children.* Fearon Publishers, Belmont, Cal.

Ramey, C. T., Farran, D. C., Campbell, F. A., and Finkelstein, N. W. 1978. Observations of Mother-Infant Interactions: Implications for Development. In F. D. Minifie and L. L. Lloyd (eds.), *Communicative and Cognitive Abilities—Early Behavioral Assessment,* pp. 397–442. University Park Press, Baltimore.

Ramey, C. T., Mills, P., Campbell, F. A., and O'Brien, C. 1975. Infants' Home Environments: A Comparison of High-Risk Families and Families from the General Population. *American Journal of Mental Deficiency* 80:40–42.

Ray, J. S. 1974. Ethological Studies of Behavior in Delayed and Non-Delayed Toddlers. Paper presented at the annual meeting of the American Association on Mental Deficiency, Toronto.

Rees, H. E. 1968. *Deprivation and Compensatory Education*. Houghton Mifflin Company, Boston.

Rheingold, H. L., and Bayley, N. 1959. The Later Effects of an Experimental Modification of Mothering. *Child Development* 30:363-372.

Riessman, F. 1962. *The Culturally Deprived Child*. Harper & Brothers, New York.

Riley, C. M. D., and Epps, F. M. S. 1967. *Head Start in Action*. Parker Publishing Company, New York.

Risley, T. 1972. Spontaneous Language and the Preschool Environment. In J. C. Stanley (ed.), *Preschool Programs for the Disadvantaged: Five Experimental Approaches to Early Childhood Education,* pp. 92-110. The Johns Hopkins Press, Baltimore.

Roberts, P. 1977. Use of Screening Tools. In M. J. Krajicek, and A. I. Tearney (eds.), *Detection of Developmental Problems in Children,* pp. 31-46. University Park Press, Baltimore.

Rosenham, D. L. 1965. Cultural Deprivation and Learning: An Examination of Method and Theory. Paper presented at the annual meeting of the American Education Research Association, February.

Ross, S. L., Jr., DeYoung, H. G., and Cohen, J. S. 1971. Confrontation: Special Education Placement and the Law. *Exceptional Children* 38:5-12.

Sabatino, D. A., Kelling, K., and Hayden, D. L. 1973. Special Education and the Culturally Different Child: Implications for Assessment and Intervention. *Exceptional Children* 39:563-567.

Schiefelbusch, R. L. (ed.) 1978. *Language Intervention Strategies*. University Park Press, Baltimore.

Schirmer, G. J. (ed.). 1972. Curriculum Cards for Preschool Children, Delta-Schoolcraft Intermediate School District, 810 No. Lincoln Road, Escanaba, Michigan, 49829. Adapt Press, Sioux Falls, S.D.

Schumaker, J. B., and Sherman, J. A. 1978. Parent as Intervention Agent. In R. L. Schiefelbusch (ed.), *Language Intervention Strategies,* pp. 237-316. University Park Press, Baltimore.

Scriven, M. 1976. Some Issues in the Logic and Ethics of Mainstreaming. Proceedings from July, 1975, Dean's Projects Conference. *Minnesota Education* 2:61-68.

Shearer, M., and Shearer, D. 1972. The Portage Project: A Model for Early Childhood Education. *Exceptional Children* 36:210-217.

Sigel, I. 1971. Language of the Disadvantaged: the Distancing Hypothesis. In C. S. Lavatelli, (ed.), *Language Training in Early Childhood Education,* pp. 60-78. University of Illinois Press, Urbana.

Smilansky, S. 1968. *The Effects of Sociodramatic Play on Disadvantaged Preschool Children*. John Wiley & Sons, Inc., New York.

Smith, R. M., and Neisworth, J. T. 1975. *The Exceptional Child—A Functional Approach*. McGraw-Hill Book Company, New York.

Snyder, L., Apolloni, T., and Cooke, T. P. 1977. Integrated Settings at the Early Childhood Level: The Role of Nonretarded Peers. *Exceptional Children* 43:262-266.

Spicker, H. H. 1971. Intellectual Development through Early Childhood Education. *Exceptional Children* 37:629-640.

Spradlin, J. E., Karlan, G. R., and Wetherby, B. 1976. Behavior Analysis, Behavior Modification, and Developmental Disabilities. In L. L. Lloyd (ed.), *Communica-*

tion Assessment and Intervention Strategies, pp. 225–264. University Park Press, Baltimore.

Stanley, J. C. (ed.). 1972. *Preschool Programs for the Disadvantaged: Five Experimental Approaches to Early Childhood Education*. The Johns Hopkins Press, Baltimore.

Starr, R. H., Jr. 1971. Cognitive Development in Infancy: Assessment, Acceleration, and Actualization. *Merrill-Palmer Quarterly* 17:153–186.

Stevens, G. D. 1976. Early Intervention with High Risk Infants and Young Children: Implications for Education. In T. D. Tjossem (ed.), *Intervention Strategies for High Risk Infants and Young Children*, pp. 727–732. University Park Press, Baltimore.

Tjossem, T. D. (ed.). 1976. *Intervention Strategies for High Risk Infants and Young Children*. University Park Press, Baltimore.

van Doorninck, W. J. 1977. Families with Children at Risk for School Problems. In M. J. Krajicek and A. I. Tearney (eds.), *Detection of Developmental Problems in Children—A Reference Guide for Community Nurses and Other Health Care Professionals*, pp. 151–159. University Park Press, Baltimore.

Venezky, R. L. 1978. Reading Acquisition: The Occult and the Obscure. In F. B. Murray and J. J. Pikulski (eds.), *The Acquisition of Reading—Cognitive, Linguistic, and Perceptual Prerequisites*, pp. 1–22. University Park Press, Baltimore.

Walls, R. T., Werner, T. J., and Bacon, A. 1976. *Behavior Checklists*. West Virginia University, Morgantown.

Washington Report. 1971. *Phi Delta Kappan*. LIII(1):75–76.

Weaver, S. J. 1963. Interim Report: Psycholinguistic Abilities of Culturally Deprived Children. (mimeographed). George Peabody College for Teachers, Nashville, Tenn.

Weintraub, F. J. 1972. Recent Influences of Law Regarding the Identification and Educational Placement of Children. *Focus on Exceptional Children* 4:1–11.

Westinghouse Learning Corporation. 1969. *The Impact of Head Start*. Ohio University, Athens.

What the Preschool Programs Learned about the Deprived Child in New Haven, Connecticut, Dade County, Florida, and Baltimore, Maryland. 1965 (September). *Grade Teacher*.

White, B. L. 1975. *The First Three Years of Life*. Prentice-Hall, Englewood Cliffs, N.J.

Wynne, S., Ulfelder, L. S., and Dakof, G. 1975. Mainstreaming and Early Childhood Education for Handicapped Children: Review and Implications of Research. U. S. Department of Health, Education, and Welfare, U. S. Office of Education, Bureau of Education for the Handicapped, Division of Innovation and Development, Washington, D.C.

Yarrow, L. J., Rubenstein, J. L., and Pederson, F. A. 1975. *Infant and Environment: Early Cognitive and Motivational Development*. Hemisphere Publishing Corp., Washington, D.C.

Index